Pragmatism's Freud:
The Moral Disposition of Psychoanalysis

Psychiatry and the Humanities, Volume 9

Assistant Editor
Gloria H. Parloff

Published under the auspices of the
Forum on Psychiatry and the Humanities,
The Washington School of Psychiatry

Pragmatism's Freud
The Moral Disposition
of Psychoanalysis

Edited by
Joseph H. Smith, M.D.
William Kerrigan, Ph.D.

The Johns Hopkins University Press
Baltimore and London

The Johns Hopkins University Press, 701 West 40th Street,
Baltimore, Maryland 21211
The Johns Hopkins Press Ltd., London

⊗The paper used in this publication meets the mini-
mum requirements of American National Standard for
Information Sciences—Permanence of Paper for Printed
Library Materials, ANSI Z39.48-1984.

Library of Congress Cataloging-in-Publication Data

Pragmatism's Freud.

   (Psychiatry and the humanities ; v. 9)
   Includes bibliographies and index.
   1. Psychoanalysis—Addresses, essays, lectures.   2. Ethics—Addresses, essays,
lectures.   3. Freud, Sigmund, 1856–1939—Addresses, essays, lectures.
I. Smith, Joseph H., 1927–   .   II. Kerrigan, William, 1943–
      .   III. Series.
RC321.P943 vol. 9   616.89 s   85-45867
[BF175.F85]   [150.19′52]
ISBN 0-8018-3324-8 (alk. paper)

Contributors

Annette Baier
Professor of Philosophy, University of Pittsburgh

Gordon Braden
Associate Professor of English, University of Virginia

David Damrosch
Assistant Professor of English and Comparative Literature, Columbia University

James W. Earl
Professor, Department of English, Fordham University

William Kerrigan
Professor of English, University of Maryland

Richard King
Faculty, American Studies, University of Nottingham

Richard Rorty
Kenan Professor of Humanities, University of Virginia

Joseph H. Smith
Supervising and Training Analyst, Washington Psychoanalytic Institute; Clinical Professor of Psychiatry, Uniformed Services University of the Health Sciences

Contents

Introduction

Joseph H. Smith and
William Kerrigan

With the publication of *Philosophy and the Mirror of Nature* (1979), a collection of essays entitled *The Consequences of Pragmatism* (1982), and numerous other essays and reviews, Richard Rorty has emerged as one of the most influential philosophers of our day. Although certain of his positions overlap those of Wittgenstein, Heidegger, and Derrida, his voice is notably American—colloquial, unevasive, straightforwardly polemical, and given the severity of the disillusionment he urges upon us, distinctly upbeat. His work gives the impression of a fuller person, more rooted and historically specific than the cramped, pseudoscientific mentalities familiar in so much philosophical writing. It may well be that, after his opinions about language and science have passed into quaintness, Rorty will be remembered for the unintimidated independence of his thought, for having at a crucial juncture in intellectual history shown his countrymen how to place new European ideas inside an American individual, reactivating in modern form the traditions of personhood bequeathed to us by an Emerson or a James.

Like other contemporary intellectuals, Rorty believes himself to be participating in a major paradigm shift in the history of Western thought. You are no longer a rational animal hoping to discover the truth. Criteria of theoretical success once presumed necessary to the life of the mind no longer prevail, and this is hard. If, adapting a convention of philosophical writing, we think of our minds as composers of numbered lists of mutually consistent propositions, these are precious holdings—the only guides we have. Discarding, say, number three or number twenty-five is a sorrowful business, and there is a considerable stock of intellectual defense mechanisms designed to avoid this divestment; for example, many of us sequester our beliefs by limiting our encounters with contemporary thought to a small professional arena. Rorty thinks that our lists are longer than need be. He wants to cut allegiances down to the bone, minimizing our debts to the Enlightenment, in order to fashion minds able to see their way through problems of all kinds, knowing no more than what they need to know because they know, as good pragmatists, what they *really* need. Whereas other leading deconstructive thinkers seem almost mesmerized by the romantic lure of disbelief itself, Rorty always considers the local task of clearing away the traditional goals and distinctions that bedevil this or that issue against a broad sense of intellectual purpose, which might as well be described as rethinking the foundations of America without the spurious philosophical assumptions historically linked to those foundations.

Readers of Rorty's recent work tend to think of him as a particularly lucid exponent of late Heidegger and his follower Derrida. But one acquires a better grasp of the internal drama of Rorty's career by returning to the introduction of his anthology, *The Linguistic Turn*, written in 1967—a fateful year in the history of modern thought, being Derrida's *annus mirabilis,* during which the father of deconstruction disseminated his first three books. To mention only one of the uncanny anticipations, note 75 of Rorty's introduction became *Philosophy and the Mirror of Nature.* Long before he read Derrida, in other words, Rorty was Rorty. Deconstruction has supplied him with a new jargon for encouraging the "linguistic turn" and viewing philosophy "as proposal rather than discovery" (1967, 31), but the positions Rorty has developed in recent years were essentially in place in 1967. There is something reassuringly heroic about this record of tried and reaffirmed conviction, if only because the new paradigm, with its lessened expectation about certainty, has left no small number of its converts floating in harborless seas, vulnerable to the currents of the moment. When Rorty opens up a new topic or engages a major intellectual peripheral to his prior work—and he is admirably fearless in this regard—there are two excitements in the air, for we can hope to witness not only his clarification of fresh questions but also another test of the durability of his new paradigm, its suppleness and its ability to meet the entirety of our intellectual needs. That is precisely the occasion here: the Weigert lecture that opens this book is Rorty's first extended comment on the work of Freud. The two of them get along surprisingly well. Postmodernist pragmatism does indeed have a Freud. He is its ethical model, at least in the personal sphere.

The main lines of Rorty's thought and (other than the lecture herein and his "Freud, Morality, and Hermeneutics" [1980]) the main positions pertinent to Freud and psychoanalysis are to be found in *Philosophy and the Mirror of Nature*. Rorty's purpose there was to deconstruct the idea of mind as mirror of nature that descends from Greek ocular metaphors (associated with "the Greek contrast between contemplation and action, between representing the world and coping with it," 10). Those metaphors were central to Cartesian dualism and to the emergence in the seventeenth century of epistemology as the essence of systematic philosophy.

For Rorty, epistemology as a theory of knowledge was based on confusing "the justification of knowledge-claims and their causal explanation—between, roughly, social practices and postulated psychological processes" (10). Explaining, for instance, how a person came to hold a belief is not to justify the belief. Justification is public. Explanation may be private, if for no other reason than that different persons may have arrived at the same belief by different routes. In fact, considering the variously nuanced multiplicity of determinants, people always do. The difference Rorty draws is between two ways of viewing ourselves—"between men as objects of explanation and men as moral agents, concerned to justify their beliefs and their actions"—and he advocates that we "give up the notion that these two ways . . . need to be 'synthesized'" (256).

This amounts to giving up a great deal. It is to give up philosophy as tribunal of reason, the quest for certainty, and, as in Derrida, a host of dualistic distinctions in which one pole of the dualism is ground or foundation for, or in some way dominant over, the other. It is to arrive at epistemological behaviorism or pragmatism, the essence of which is "explaining rationality and epistemic authority by reference to what society lets us say, rather than the latter by the former" (174). If the study of the nature of human knowledge is the study of certain ways in which human beings interact, rather than some ontologically founded, specifically philosophical way of describing human beings, it involves "a pragmatic view of truth and a therapeutic use of ontology (in which philosophy can straighten out pointless quarrels between common sense and science, but not contribute any arguments of its own for the existence or inexistence of something)" (175). As for knowledge and truth, philosophy would "have no more to offer than common sense (supplemented by biology, history, etc.)" (175).

Of course, the "therapeutic" giving up of pseudoproblems and pseudoknowledge-claims would also be required of psychology. Rorty aims "to disassociate empirical psychology from the remnants of epistemology by defending it against both Wittgensteinian criticisms and

Chomskyan compliments" (210–11). His position is that "when Wittgensteinians criticize psychology it is not really psychology but the confusion of epistemology with psychology which is their target" (254). This means that while it may be permissible to reify or anthropomorphize (235–36) and all right to have "raw feels, a priori concepts, innate ideas, sense-data, propositions, and anything else which a causal explanation of human behavior might find it helpful to postulate . . . we *cannot* . . . take knowledge of these 'inner' or 'abstract' entities as *premises* from which our knowledge of other entities is normally inferred, and without which the latter knowledge would be 'ungrounded'" (177).

Although this is largely directed at Chomsky, it could as well apply to certain of Freud's usages—for example, his tendency toward economic pseudoexplanation, and perhaps to the place of Eros and Thanatos in his thinking. However, when Freud specifically focused on theory as scaffolding or tool, as in the introductory passages to "Instincts and Their Vicissitudes" (*S.E.* 14:109), he seems to have been strictly in compliance with this Rortyan caveat. Could it be that the battle of paradigms initiated by James, Dewey, Wittgenstein, and Heidegger was already within Freud?

Certainly Freud's dominant allegiance was to the then-reigning paradigm that knowledge could be "a matter of rightly ordered inner representations—an unclouded and undistorting Mirror of Nature" (Rorty 1979, 248) and that eventually the findings of a wide variety of disciplines, psychoanalysis prominently among them, would flow together "and spell out one great Universal Language of Nature" (249). It is also certain that he saw psychoanalysis as potentially a general psychology, treatment of the ill being only one of its applications. Even the mystery of sublimation was occasionally submitted to sanguine predictions that "certainly one day" it would be characterized "in metapsychological terms" (*S.E.* 21:79). Finally, his ideas that changed the world were those that applied to illness and health alike—unconscious processes and the role of sexuality and aggression.

However, certain of Freud's statements about ego interests, moral positions, sublimation, and sublimatory processes involved in health could be seen as conveying an attunement to the issue of justification as opposed to explanation unmatched in many of his followers—as if the warrant to intervene with metapsychological explanation is, after all, more there in the case of the ill person than the healthy. His statements about health were apt to be aphoristic—for example, "where id was, there ego shall be," or that what holds the human community together is "work . . . and the power of love" (*S.E.*

21:101). His summary of what men desire—"honour, power, wealth, fame, and the love of women" (*S.E.* 16:376)—is a statement of ego interests that he more or less leaves at that. Sublimation, though he did not exactly lay down his pen about the matter, did give him pause. In regard to morality, throughout much of "Thoughts for the Times on War and Death" (*S.E.* 14), as elsewhere, he mulls over motives for goodness without invoking detailed metapsychological explanation beyond the sad reflection that more persons are good out of dread of the community than out of a true ennoblement of instinct or real transformation of egoistic into altruistic inclinations. It is more a meditation on the question of how people (and nations) *can* justify their behavior or how it is they can live and function *without* justifying their behavior than a quest for explanation.

On the model of Freud's account of love and hate—phenomena that refuse "to be fitted into our scheme of the instincts" (*S.E.* 14:133) and are not "relations of *instincts* to their objects, but . . . relations of the *total ego* to objects" (*S.E.* 14:137)—one could say that these remarks on ego interests, morality, sublimation, and health refer to behavior, attributes, and relations of the whole person.[1] There is no reliable concept of the whole person or the self in psychoanalytic metapsychology, despite the efforts of Hartmann, Kohut, and others, and for that reason metapsychology cannot be a language of moral deliberation or moral judgment, both of which address the entire person. When Freud writes of love, work, and other sublimatory processes, he writes not so much as a psychoanalyst wielding an authoritative technical vocabulary, but as a person.

It is the wager of Baier, Damrosch, Braden, and Kerrigan in their essays here that the level of discourse pertaining to the whole person provides the best way to bring to light the Freudian ethic—the ethic in Freud and his discourse, and the ethic bequeathed by him to subsequent vocabularies of moral deliberation. Freud believed that in fortunate development Eros prevails in the direction of the ethical. Modes of fulfilling basic desires are found that do minimum harm to the self and its objects, to the self and the human order, to the self and the world. Otherwise, in the long run, nothing works. Morale is tied to morality. Virtue is health, and maybe even a kind of pragmatic wisdom.

This is a big jump, to be sure, and backward at that, to a starting point prior to the Aristotelian division between the practical virtues of morality and the intellectual virtues of wisdom and insight.[2] This division between practical morality, always entailing contingency and compromise, and something higher was preserved by medieval writers, and contributed to the Cartesian and Kantian cast of Western thought. It is the sort of dichotomization questioned by Derrida's deconstruction and Rorty's pragmatism.

What if, in the realm of morality and the justification of beliefs, there is nothing but contingency and compromise? Is it still possible that fortunate development might be toward the ethical—and not just in some cultures but in any culture that could hold together and *be* a culture? Such is the main thrust of Freud's *Civilization and Its Discontents*. Although Freud mentioned in passing that "sometimes one seems to perceive that it is not only the pressure of civilization but something in the nature of the [sexual] function itself which denies us full satisfaction and urges us along other paths" (*S.E.* 21:105), the gist of what he wrote was that being ethical does not arise out of human nature but is imposed by (and as) a necessity of civilization. Perhaps this was already a renunciation, like Rorty's, of the idea that we can or ought to have any fixed and grounded vocabulary of moral deliberation.

Emphasizing these elements in Freud's thought is, in any event, one strategy for understanding where he has taken us and is closer than it might first appear to be to that of Smith's essay in this book. Seeing similarity or difference depends on whether one views "custom"—a root meaning common to both "ethical" and "moral"—as that to which the individual conforms on the basis of habit and intellectual assent, or as the achievement by one's own doing of a way of life, wrought in the internalized conflict of an individual in a particular community. The latter view is highlighted here by King, Smith, and Earl. Smith, the psychoanalyst in this group, takes this to be Freud's position and the one most pertinent to day-to-day analytic work. Rorty might seem (but, we think, only seem), by his inattention to the dynamics and affective intensity of such structural development, to endorse the view of custom and morality as adynamic habit. But Rorty is not (and several of the other humanist contributors are not) aiming to elucidate structural change in development or analysis. He is instead describing Freud's influence on how we make and view moral statements and his role in providing a vocabulary of moral deliberation that does not require ethics to be ontologically grounded. This places Freud on the side of those "moral philosophers who think that rights and responsibilities are a matter of what society bestows . . . [rather than] those who think that there is something inside a man which society 'recognizes' when it makes its bestowal" (Rorty 1979, 177).

Rorty is as critical of our current concept of mind, of foundations, of essentialism ("the notion that one could distinguish between what people were talking about and what they were saying about it by discovering the essence of the object being discussed" [1979, 268]), of epistemology, and of metaphysics as Schafer is of what he sees to be the similar problems of metapsychology and the dubious hope that psychoanalysis could become a general psychology. To understand the muddles of their fields (and, for Schafer, his patients) both advocate the genetic approach. Diagnosis is not enough, and Rorty (1979, 33) draws the analogy between his study of the history of ideas and the psychiatrist's study of how the patient came to suffer the particular malady he or she presents.

But neither of them undertakes genetic inquiry with the notion that there is one right track toward clear thinking and health, or that cure comes merely from knowledge of what derailed development in the past. Schafer's point is that in analysis multiple life histories are constructed, the telling of each a present narration understood "as much through its emotional mode, form, and sequelae as through its content . . . [and in which] the elucidation of the present . . . retains top priority. In the process of trying to explain how the analysand got to be 'that way' in the present, one keeps on finding out what 'that way' is" (1983, 209). Schafer further wrote:

> The view customarily taken has been that one learns about the life history from the analysis of transference and resisting, that is, from the analysis of the analytic encounter itself; further, this knowledge of the life history is held to be in itself a final criterion of insight and an essential determinant of analytic results. On the present view, however, things are turned around. It seems now that the analyst goes on learning about the analytic encounter as he or she goes on developing the psychoanalytic life histories. The more freely and completely one knows relevant versions of the past, the richer one's empathic comprehension of what is taking place in the psychoanalytic sessions and the keener one's interpretations of transference and resisting. The convincing emotional experience of analysis, which is so essential to its results, lies in the present, as Freud emphasized long ago in his technical papers. In his role of investigator, however, Freud saw this experience as a means to the ultimate end of reconstructing a single past. (1983, 208)

This view accords not only with Rorty's use of the genetic approach but also with the priority he gives to seeing "human beings as generators of new descriptions rather than beings one hopes to be able to

describe accurately" (1979, 378). There may well be an area of agreement here that overrides those points of disagreement between Schafer and himself that Rorty describes in "Freud, Morality, and Hermeneutics" (1980).

Several of the contributors to this volume seem less troubled by
questions posed by Freud and outlined by Rorty in the article just
mentioned[3] than they are by Rorty's claim in the present volume that
Freud is an apostle of the aesthetic. Rorty expressly reverses the hierarchy of Kierkegaardian categories. In this regard, one might wonder
whether it would be begging the question, or showing Rorty (and
Rieff) to be begging the question, to suggest that expanding the
aesthetic and opening up more options would be especially prominent
in the cure of the tightly bound-up obsessional. Prominent in the cure
of the hysteric, on the other hand, would be a narrowing down of
options, a less anxious, flighty quest for options, and a more centered
awareness of the ethical. Freud believed that the successful analysis of
either would result in a more reliable ethical stance, less rigid and less
corruptible in the obsessional and less spasmodic and vulnerable in
the hysteric.

The concluding three articles of this volume deal with the desire for
fame, not just ordinary, garden-variety, Nobel-prize-winning fame,
but what Kerrigan calls fame-for-being, like that won by Milton,
Shakespeare, or Freud. The articles explore the issue in Petrarch (Braden) and Freud himself (Damrosch and Kerrigan). These essays suggest that the very impetus that might carry a person to fame-for-being
can also be a stumbling block in the achievement of that goal. The
danger seems not so much a matter of being inhibited by guilt, or by
fear of vanquishing or being vanquished by a jealous father, as of
being overwhelmed by ambition itself—a kind of drowning in a vor-
tex of one's own greed. The to-be-great intuitively know they have to
keep an eye on this greed, track it, and resist it. This can perhaps take
the form of silent, covert resistance, as in the case of Freud, or of
lavishly overt and constant reckoning with it, as in the case of
Petrarch. In either instance, it would no doubt be fair to assume that
in some of those to-be-famous the greatest desire for fame is matched
by the greatest resistance, and that it is from the strength of both sides
of this conflict that great sublimations are wrought. In Freud's words,
"whether that struggle ends in health, in neurosis, or in a countervail-
ing superiority of achievement, depends on . . . the relative strength
of the conflicting forces" (S.E. 10:50).

The to-be-famous do not resist fame. They resist letting themselves
be taken over by greed for fame. They resist the regressive pull of the

desire to return to maternal adulation. They require of themselves a work that has a chance, at least, of justifying the adulation of the world as mother substitute, but always with the knowledge that if their ambition lends them to focus on the fame rather than the work, they will have lost their bearings.

Maybe those prone to being taken over by greed for fame—those whose fame flares briefly and dies quickly—are the ones who were short on maternal adulation in the first place. More likely, compensatory moves are such that greatness could derive from either extreme. Freud, in any event, notes that self-reliance ("an unshakeable optimism" [*S.E.* 5:398] and a "confidence in success which not seldom brings actual success along with it" [*S.E.* 17:156]), was born of being one's mother's undisputed favorite, something, he said, that stays with a man for a lifetime. He could make such a statement in a way that still came through as the sober and restrained self-observation that one suspects it was.

Is there a metamoral to this fable of a greedy ambition that bears watching, that can turn from its deployment in work and engulf its erstwhile master? Perhaps in great achievements the wish for fame, what Samuel Johnson termed "the wish to fill the minds of others" (Bate 1977, 491), is not just a matter of a changed aim but involves a transformation of egoism into altruism in accord with the effect of great creations in improving the lot of all. Great achievements may appear to us transcendent and sublime, somehow beyond the disappointing ordinariness of the world. But they may also seem intimate and familiar, for all good work implies sublimation. We may respond to great achievement as a shining instance of the similar though more modest transformations that we ordinary people have achieved and are always called upon to achieve anew, notwithstanding our avowed desire for "honour, power, wealth, fame, and the love of women."[4]

In the first sentence of *Civilization and Its Discontents (S.E.* 21:64) Freud spoke of a similar cluster of desires ("power, success, and wealth") as false standards that "underestimate what is of true value in life." Nonetheless, he conceded, "There are a few men from whom their contemporaries do not withhold admiration, although their greatness rests on attributes and achievements which are completely foreign to the aims and ideals of the multitude," and he cautioned against the inclination "to suppose that it is after all only a minority which appreciates these great men, while the large majority cares nothing for them" (64). The metamoral may be not simply that works of genius present a special challenge to metapsychological explanation but that any person's developed capacities to love and to work are also sublimatory achievements of the whole person and thus pose the same challenge.

Put that way, one might be inclined to interpret Freud's response to art and health as his acknowledgment that a more intense effort was required to explain them. But perhaps his reluctance to expend this effort implied that products of sublimation, developed ego interests, including the capacities of love and work as signs of health, are matters where the importance of explanation fades by comparison with the importance of justification, and that psychoanalysis *might* not have any more to offer than common sense about art and health. It would be compatible with both interpretations that, though undaunted in venturing accounts of superego pathology, he was given pause by any instance of sublimation. In his mind, sublimation was not the finding of one's "true self," not the finding of a center, not the overcoming of the gap between a present and projected self, but one species of particularly perfect functioning within that gap. It was a solution to conflict that was not just a matter of doing minimum harm to self and others, as in ordinary compromise solutions, but of actually enhancing the morale of the self and, in the case of great achievements, improving the lot of all. It was an act wrought by the whole person but one that rendered the "always already" decentered person, nevertheless, more whole. It was in the face of this that Freud was ready to lay down his arms.

If it seems a forced transposition from what Freud said most explicitly in relation to art to suggest that he harbored a similar attitude toward love, work, freedom, and morality, one might bear in mind what he wrote to Putnam on knowledge and the good, commented on herein by Smith, and the passages already cited here on love and work as other instances of his being constrained by a reserve similar to that which he displayed in relation to art. More broadly, it seems likely that the prospects of achieving either a deeper common-sense understanding or a more adequate theory of sublimation are not propitious if it is assumed in advance that its only instances are works of art and other cultural objects. A better start would be to assume that internalization, structure building, making something one's own, achieving a reliable ethical stance, and achieving an ethically constrained freedom that opens the possibility of widened choice among workable options constitute but a partial listing of instances of sublimation or developmental events involving sublimatory processes.

To start in this way makes giving precedence to aesthetics over ethics or ethics over aesthetics inconsequential, more a matter of rhetorical strategy or of personal preference or vision than an ordering of how things are. At the level of its cultural function, the moral disposition of psychoanalysis lies in showing convincingly that having a wider range of options is inconceivable outside structural, including ethical, constraints, just as having a reliable ethical stance is inconceivable outside the freedom to choose. In order for a dynamic and structural account to show "the presentness of the past" (Bloom 1975, 39; see Rorty's comment 1979, 168) in this interrelationship and thus contribute to the self-description of the age, attention to reality (the adaptive approach) and attention to the past (the genetic approach) are required. It is by virtue of its special way of showing the presentness of the past in relation to the ethical that psychoanalysis has its place alongside philosophy and literary criticism in this volume and in this age.

Notes

1. Statements at this level, often unnoted in favor of their metapsychological or sometimes simplistic hydraulic contexts, are scattered throughout Freud's work. Who but a careful reader would remember that he wrote (shades of First Corinthians, chapter 13) that "a person in love is humble" (*S.E.* 14:98) or that "we are never so defenceless against suffering as when we love" (*S.E.* 21:82). One of Rorty's points is that Freud made love itself morally dubious—that is, even though love involves the whole person, Freud has inflicted credence on one's doubts about loving. Could it be reaction formation, denial of hate, denial of one's lack of courage to love, or narcissistic rather than object love? The good news is that what goes on out of awareness can also be one's ally. Rorty's contrast between the unconscious as seething cauldron and the witty, linguistic partner that "feeds us our best lines" coincides with the historical sequence. The early idea of "*The* unconscious" gave way in the structural point of view to unconsciousness as a quality only, precisely because not only id but also ego and superego factors could be unconscious—sometimes, in "specially perfect functioning" (*S.E.* 14:195), all working together.

2. To jump prior to Aristotle is not to land on "virtue is wisdom" or knowledge in the way Socrates meant it. The determinants of virtue for Freud were different than for Socrates. "Knowledge" and "remembering" in Freud are not Socratic recollecting. For Freud and subsequent Freudians, recollecting is not getting back to that which was dimly known in advance, but remembering and working through toward the achievement of a new unity, manifested by a more coherent narrative and a new flexibility and freedom that can allow narratives to develop and change. The emphasis here is not on the Socratic idea that knowledge of the good is all that is required to do the good. The idea of "the good" as some ideal abstraction, the knowledge of which evokes good conduct, is the reverse of any psychoanalytic meaning that could be given to "virtue is wisdom."

Maybe for analysts the token of wisdom is the high morale that goes along with the virtues of being able to love and work. By comparison with that, abstract ideas of "the good" were as superfluous to Freud as they are to Rorty.

3. For example: "If high culture survives, we are in for another few hundred years of getting adjusted to the availability of the psychoanalytic vocabulary" (Rorty 1980, 177); "can we hang on to the idea of 'humanity' . . . ?" (177); "can we live with a vocabulary for predicting and controlling our actions which does not overlap with familiar vocabularies of moral deliberations?" (178); the nineteenth century replaced "the love of God with the love of scientific truth. . . . What Freud did . . . was to make *love, itself,* morally dubious" (178); "neither the religious nor the secular and liberal morality seems possible, and no third alternative has emerged. The problem is that love (and, therefore, courage and cowardice, sacrifice and selfishness) looks different after one has read Freud" (180).

4. In referring to just ordinary endeavor "open to everyone," Freud wrote, "No other technique for the conduct of life attaches the individual so firmly to reality" as work, (which "by means of sublimation . . . makes possible the use of existing inclinations, [and] persisting . . . instinctual impulses" (*S.E.* 21:80 n.1). In addition he wrote: "One gains the most if one can sufficiently heighten the yield of pleasure from the sources of psychical and intellectual work. When that is so, fate can do little against one. A satisfaction of this kind, such as an artist's joy in creating, . . . or a scientist's in solving problems or discovering truths, has a special quality. . . . At present we can only say figuratively that such satisfactions seem 'finer and higher'" (*S.E.* 21:79).

Freud above all knew that artistic or scientific achievement did not change men or women into angels. They might well still be left to struggle with large quotients of egoism. However, an essential dimension in what he meant by sublimation involves an alteration in egoism integral to the moment of both its extraordinary and ordinary instances. He characterized the sublimatory transformation of egoism in the scientist as culminating in "working with all for the good of all" (*S.E.* 21:77–78) and, regarding art, "At the head of . . . satisfactions through phantasy stands the enjoyment of works of art—an enjoyment which, by the agency of the artist, is made accessible even to those who are not themselves creative" (*S.E.* 21:80–81).

References

Bate, Walter. *Samuel Johnson.* New York: Harcourt Brace Jovanovitch, 1977.

Bloom, Harold. *A Map of Misreading.* New York: Oxford University Press, 1975.

Freud, Sigmund. *The Standard Edition of the Complete Psychological Works of Sigmund Freud.* Edited and translated by James Strachey. 24 vols. London: Hogarth, 1953–74.

The Interpretation of Dreams (1900–1901), vols. 4, 5.

"Five Lectures on Psycho-Analysis" (1910), vol. 10.

"On Narcissism: An Introduction" (1914), vol. 14.

"Thoughts for the Times on War and Death" (1915), vol. 14.

"Instincts and Their Vicissitudes" (1915), vol. 14.

"The Unconscious" (1915), vol. 14.

Introductory Lectures on Psycho-Analysis (1917), vol. 15.

"A Childhood Recollection from *Dichtung und Warheit*" (1917), vol. 17.

Civilization and Its Discontents (1930), vol. 21.

Kuhn, Thomas S. *The Structure of Scientific Revolutions.* Chicago: University of Chicago Press, 1970.

Rorty, Richard, ed. *The Linguistic Turn.* Chicago: University of Chicago Press, 1967.

———. *Philosophy and the Mirror of Nature.* Princeton: Princeton University Press, 1979.

———. "Freud, Morality, and Hermeneutics." *New Literary History* 12 (1980): 177–85.

———. *The Consequences of Pragmatism.* Minneapolis: University of Minnesota Press, 1982.

Schafer, Roy. *The Analytic Attitude.* New York: Basic Books, 1983.

Pragmatism's Freud:
The Moral Disposition of Psychoanalysis

1   Freud and Moral Reflection

Richard Rorty

The Mechanical Mind: Hume and Freud

Freud thought of himself as part of the same "decentering" movement of thought to which Copernicus and Darwin belonged. In a
famous passage, he says that psychoanalysis "seeks to prove to the ego
that it is not even master in its own house, but must content itself
with scanty information of what is going on unconsciously in its
mind." He compares this with the realization that "our earth was not
the centre of the universe but only a tiny fragment of a cosmic system
of scarcely imaginable vastness" and with the discovery, by Darwin, of
our "ineradicable animal nature" (*S.E.* 16:284–85).

Copernicus, Darwin, and Freud do have something important in
common, but Freud does not give us a clear idea of what that is. It is
not evident that successive decenterings add up to a history of humili-
ation; Copernicus and Darwin might claim that by making God and
the angels less plausible, they have left human beings on top of the
heap. The suggestion that we have discovered, humiliatingly, that
humanity is less important than we had thought is not perspicuous.
For it is not clear what "importance" can mean in this context. Further, the claim that psychoanalysis has shown that the ego is not
master in its own house is unhelpful, for the relevant sense of "mastery" is unclear. Does our sense of our importance, or our capacity for
self-control, really depend on the belief that we are transparent to
ourselves? Why should the discovery of the unconscious add humilia-
tion to the discovery of the passions?

I think one gets a better idea of the similarity Freud was trying to
describe by contrasting a world of natural kinds with a world of

1

machines—a world of Aristotelian substances with a world of homogenous particles combining and disassociating according to universal laws. Think of the claim that "man is a natural kind" not as saying that human beings are at the center of something, but that they *have* a center, in a way that a machine does not. A substance that exemplifies an Aristotelian natural kind divides into a central essence—one that provides a built-in purpose—and a set of peripheral accidents. But an artifact's formal and final causes may be distinct; the same machine, for example, may be used for many different purposes. A machine's purpose is not built in.[1] If humanity is a natural kind, then perhaps we can find our center and so learn how to live well. But if we are machines, then it is up to us to invent a use for ourselves.

What was decisive about the Copernican Revolution was not that it moved the human being from the center of the universe, but that it began, in Dyksterhuis's phrase, the "mechanization of the world picture."[2] Copernicus and Newton between them made it hard to think of the universe as an edifying spectacle. When an infinite universe of pointless corpuscles replaced a closed world, it became hard to imagine what it would be like to look down upon the Creation and find it good.[3] The universe began to look like a rather simple, boring machine, rambling off beyond the horizon, rather than like a bounded and well-composed tableau. So the idea of a center no longer seemed applicable. Analogously, the result of Darwin's and Mendel's mechanization of biology was to set aside an edifying hierarchy of natural kinds. Viewing the various species of plants and animals as the temporary results of interactions between fortuitous environmental pressures and random mutations made the world of living creatures as pointless as Newtonian mechanics had made cosmology. Mechanization meant that the world in which human beings lived no longer taught them anything about how they should live.

In trying to see how Freud fits into this story of decentering-as-mechanization, one should begin by noting that Freud was not the first to suggest that, having mechanized everything else, we mechanize the mind as well. Hume had already treated ideas and impressions not as properties of a substratal self but as mental atoms whose arrangement *was* the self. This arrangement was determined by laws of association, analogues of the law of gravitation. Hume thought of himself as the Newton of the mind, and the mechanical mind he envisaged was—viewed from above, so to speak—just as morally pointless as Newton's corpuscularian universe.

Hume, however, suggested that the mechanization of neither nature nor the mind mattered for purposes of finding a self-image. With a sort of protopragmatist insouciance, he thought that talk about the atoms of Democritus, Newton's shining lights, and his own "impressions and ideas" offered, at most, a handy way of describing things and people for purposes of predicting and controlling them. For moral purposes, for purposes of seeing life as having a point, such talk might be irrelevant. Like Blake, Hume was prepared to say that the view from above—the view of the Baconian predictor and controller—was irrelevant to our sense of centeredness. His pragmatical reconciliation of freedom and determinism, like his reconciliation of armchair skepticism with theoretical curiosity and practical benevolence, is an invitation to take the mechanization of the mind lightly—as no more than an intriguing intellectual exercise, the sort of thing that a young person might do in order to become famous.

It is tempting to respond to Freud in the same way that Hume responded to his own mechanizing efforts: to say that for purposes of moral reflection a knowledge of Freudian unconscious motivation is as irrelevant as a knowledge of Humean associations or of neurophysiology. But this response is unconvincing. Unlike Hume, Freud *did* change our self-image. Finding out about our unconscious motives is not just an intriguing exercise, but more like a moral obligation. What difference between Hume's and Freud's ways of extending mechanization to the mind accounts for Freud's relevance to our moral consciousness?

If one views Freud's dictum that the ego is not master in its own house as saying merely that we often act in ways that could not have been predicted on the basis of our introspectible beliefs and desires, Freud will be merely reiterating a commonplace of Greek thought. If one views it as the claim that the mind can, for purposes of prediction and control, be treated as a set of associative mechanisms, a realm in which there are no accidents, Freud will be saying little that Hume had not said. So one must find another interpretation. One gets a clue, I think, from the fact that the phrase "not even master in its own house" is to the point only if some other person is behaving as if he or she were in charge. The phrase is an appropriate response to the incursion of an unwanted guest—for example, to the onset of schizophrenia. But it is not an appropriate reaction, for example, to an explanation of the dependence of our mood on our endocrine system. For glands are not, so to speak, quasi people with whom to struggle. Nor are neurons, which is why the possible identity of the mind with the brain is of no moral interest. Physiological discoveries can tell us how to predict and control ourselves—including how to predict and control our beliefs and desires—without threatening or changing our self-image. For such discoveries do not suggest that we are being shouldered aside by somebody else.

Psychological mechanisms will seem more decentering than physiological mechanisms only if one is of a naturally metaphysical turn of mind, insistent on pressing the questions, "But what am I *really?* What is my *true* self? What is *essential* to me?" Descartes and Kant had this sort of mind and so, in our day, do reductionist metaphysicians such as B. F. Skinner and antireductionist champions of "subjectivity" and "phenomenology" such as Thomas Nagel and Richard Wollheim. But the mechanization of nature made protopragmatists of most people, allowing them to shrug off questions of essence. They became accustomed to speaking one sort of language for Baconian purposes of prediction and control and another for purposes of moral reflection. They saw no need to raise the question of which language represented the world or the self as it is "in itself."[4] Yet Freudian discoveries are troubling even for pragmatists. Unlike the atoms of Democritus or Hume, the Freudian unconscious does not look like something that we might usefully, to achieve certain of our purposes, describe ourselves as. It looks like somebody who is stepping into our shoes, somebody who has different purposes than we do. It looks like a person using us rather than a thing we can use.

This clue—the fact that psychological mechanisms look most disturbing and decentering when they stop looking like mechanisms and start looking like persons—has been followed up by Donald Davidson. In a remarkable essay called "Paradoxes of Irrationality," Davidson notes that philosophers have always been upset by Freud's insistence on "partitioning" the self. They have tended to reject Freud's threatening picture of quasi selves lurking beneath the threshold of consciousness as an unnecessarily vivid way of describing the incoherence and confusion that may afflict a single self. They hope thereby to remain faithful to the common-sense assumption that a single human body typically contains a single self. Davidson defends Freudian partitioning by pointing out that there is no reason to say "You unconsciously believe that *p*" rather than "There is something within you which causes you to act as if you believed that *p*," unless one is prepared to round out the characterization of the unconscious quasi self who "believes that *p*" by ascribing a host of other beliefs (mostly true, and mostly consistent with *p*) to that quasi self. One can only attribute a belief to something if one simultaneously attributes lots of other mostly true and mostly consistent beliefs. Beliefs and desires, unlike Humean ideas and impressions, come in packages.[5]

Davidson puts these holistic considerations to work as follows. He identifies (not explicitly, but, if my reading of him is right, tacitly) being a person with being a coherent and plausible set of beliefs and desires. Then he points out that the force of saying that a human being sometimes behaves irrationally is that he or she sometimes exhibits behavior that cannot be explained by reference to a single such set. Finally, he concludes that the point of "partitioning" the self between a consciousness and an unconscious is that the latter can be viewed as an alternative set, inconsistent with the familiar set that we identify with conciousness, yet sufficiently coherent internally to count as a person. This strategy leaves open the possibility that the same human body can play host to two or more persons. These persons enter into causal relations with each other, as well as with the body whose movements are brought about by the beliefs and desires of one or the other of them. But they do not, normally, have conversational relations. That is, one's unconscious beliefs are not *reasons* for a change in one's conscious beliefs, but they may *cause* changes in the latter beliefs, just as may portions of one's body (e.g., the retina, the fingertips, the pituitary gland, the gonads).

To see the force of Davidson's suggestion is to appreciate the crucial difference between Hume and Freud. This is that Hume's mental atoms included only subpropositional components of beliefs—mostly names of perceptible and introspectible qualia. The mechanization of the self that Hume suggested, and that associationist psychology developed, amounted to little more than a transposition into mentalistic terminology of a rather crude physiology of perception and memory. By contrast, Freud populated inner space not with analogues of Boylean corpuscles but with analogues of persons—internally coherent clusters of belief and desire. Each of these quasi persons is, in the Freudian picture, a part of a single unified *causal* network, but not of a single person (since the criterion for individuation of a person is a certain minimal coherence among its beliefs and desires). Knowledge of all these persons is necessary to predict and control a human being's behavior (and in particular his or her "irrational" behavior), but only one of these persons will be available (at any given time) to introspection.

The Rational Unconscious as Conversational Partner

If one accepts this Davidsonian explanation of Freud's basic strategy, then one has taken a long step toward seeing why psychoanalysis can aptly be described as a decentering. For now one can see Freudian mechanisms as having, so to speak, a human interest that no physiological or Humean mechanism could have. One can see why it is hard to dismiss the Freudian unconscious as just one more useful, if paradoxical, redescription of the world that science has invented for purposes of saving the phenomena—the sort of redescription that can be ignored by everyday, practical purposes (as, for example, one ignores heliocentrism). The suggestion that some unknown persons are caus- ing us (or, to stress the alienation produced by this suggestion, causing our bodies) to do things we would rather not do is decentering in a way that an account of heavenly bodies (or of the descent of man) is not. One will be thrown off base by this suggestion even if one has no interest in Aristotelian, metaphysical questions about one's "essence" or one's "true self." One can be entirely pragmatical in one's approach to life and still feel that something needs to be *done* in response to such a suggestion.

To take Freud's suggestion seriously is to wish to become acquainted with these unfamiliar persons, if only as a first step toward killing them off. This wish will take the place, for a pragmatical Freudian, of the religious and metaphysical desire to find one's "true center." It initiates a task that can plausibly be described as a moral obligation—the task whose goal is summed up in the phrase "where id was, there shall ego be." This goal does not require the Aristotelian notion that one's ego is more "natural" or more truly "oneself" than one's id. But adopting this goal does restore a point to the imperative "Know thyself," an imperative that one might have thought inappli- cable to the self-as-machine.

On Freud's account of self-knowledge, what we are morally obli- gated to know about ourselves is not our essence, not a common human nature that is somehow the source and locus of moral responsi- bility. Far from being of what we share with the other members of our species, self-knowledge is precisely of what divides us from them: our accidental idiosyncrasies, the "irrational" components in ourselves, the ones that split us up into incompatible sets of beliefs and desires. The study of "the nature of the mind," construed as the study either of Humean association of ideas or of Freudian metapsychology, is as pointless, for purposes of moral reflection, as the study of the laws of celestial motion. What *is* of interest is the study of the idiosyncratic raw material whose processing Humean and Freudian mechanisms are postulated to predict, and of the idiosyncratic products of this process- ing. For only study of these concrete details will let us enter into conversational relations with our unconscious and, at the ideal limit of such conversation, let us break down the partitions.

The view of Freud that I am proposing will seem plausible only if one makes a clear distinction between two senses of "the uncon- scious": (1) a sense in which it stands for one or more well-articulated systems of beliefs and desires, systems that are just as complex, sophis- ticated, and internally consistent as the normal adult's conscious beliefs and desires; and (2) a sense in which it stands for a seething mass of inarticulate instinctual energies, a "reservoir of libido" to which consistency is irrelevant. In the second sense, the unconscious is just another name for "the passions," the lower part of the soul, the bad, false self. Had this been the only sense Freud gave to the term, his work would have left our strategies of character-development, and our self-image, largely unchanged. What is novel in Freud's view of the unconscious is his claim that our unconscious selves are not dumb, sullen, lurching brutes, but rather the intellectual peers of our conscious selves, possible conversational partners for those selves. As Rieff puts it, "Freud democratized genius by giving everyone a creative unconscious" (1961, 36).[6]

This suggestion that one or more clever, articulate, inventive persons are at work behind the scene—cooking up our jokes, inventing our metaphors, plotting our dreams, arranging our slips, and censoring our memories—is what grips the imagination of the lay reader of Freud. As Freud himself said, if psychoanalysis had stuck to the neuroses, it would never have attracted the attention of the intellectuals.[7] It was the application of psychoanalytical notions to normal life that first suggested that Freud's ideas might call for a revision in our self-image. For this application breaks the connection between the Platonic reason-passion distinction and the conscious-unconscious distinction. It substitutes a picture of sophisticated transactions between two or more "intellects" for the traditional picture of one "intellect" struggling with a mob of "irrational" brutes.

The Platonic tradition had thought of articulate beliefs—or, more generally, propositional attitudes—as the preserve of the higher part of the soul. It thought of the lower parts as "bodily," as animallike, and in particular as prelinguistic. But a witty unconscious is necessarily a linguistic unconscious. Further, if "rational" means "capable of weaving complex, internally consistent, networks of belief" rather than "capable of contemplating reality as it is," then a witty unconscious is also a *rational* unconscious—one that can no more tolerate inconsistency than can consciousness.[8] So we need to distinguish the unconscious as "the deepest strata of our minds, made up of instinctual impulses," strata that know "nothing that is negative, and no negation," in which "contradictories coincide" (*S.E.* 14:296), from the unconscious as the sensitive, whacky, backstage partner who feeds us our best lines. The latter is somebody who has a well-worked-out, internally consistent view of the world—though one that may be hopelessly wrong on certain crucial points. One needs to distinguish Freud's banal claim that "our intellect is a feeble and dependent thing, a plaything and tool of our instincts and affects" (*S.E.* 14:301)—which is just a replay of Hume's claim that "reason is, and ought to be, the slave of the passions"[9]—from his interesting and novel claim that the conscious-unconscious distinction cuts across the human-animal and reason-instinct distinctions.

If one concentrates on the latter claim, then one can see Freud as suggesting that, on those occasions when we are tempted to complain that two souls dwell, alas, in our breast, we think of the two as one more-or-less sane and one more-or-less crazy human soul, rather than as one human soul and one bestial soul. On the latter, Platonic model, self-knowledge will be a matter of self-purification—of identifying our true, human, self and expelling, curbing, or ignoring the animal self. On the former model, self-knowledge will be a matter of getting acquainted with one or more crazy quasi people, listening to their crazy accounts of how things are, seeing why they hold the crazy views they do, and learning something from them. It will be a matter of self-enrichment. To say "Where id was, there will ego be" will not mean "Whereas once I was driven by instinct, I shall become autonomous, motivated solely by reason." Rather, it will mean something like: "Once I could not figure out why I was acting so oddly, and hence wondered if I were, somehow, under the control of a devil or a beast. But now I shall be able to see my actions as rational, as making sense, though perhaps based on mistaken premises. I may even discover that those premises were not mistaken, that my unconscious knew better than I did."[10]

The advantage of this way of thinking of the passions is that it enables one to take a similar view of conscience. For just as this view humanizes what the Platonic tradition took to be the urges of an animal, so it humanizes what that tradition thought of as divine inspiration. It makes conscience, like passion, one more set of human beliefs and desires—another story about how the world is, another Weltanschauung. Most important, it makes it *just* another story—not one that (in the case of the passions) is automatically suspect nor one that (in the case of conscience) is automatically privileged. It treats, so to speak, the three different stories told by the id, the superego, and the ego as alternative extrapolations from common experience—in particular, experience of childhood events. Each story is an attempt to make these events coherent with later events, but the stimuli provided by such events are (usually) so diverse and confusing that no *single* consistent set of beliefs and desires is able to make them all hang together.

To view these three (or more) stories as on a par, as alternative explanations of a confusing situation, is part of what Rieff calls "Freud's egalitarian revision of the traditional idea of an hierarchical human nature" (1966, 56). To adopt a self-image that incorporates this egalitarian revision is to think that there is no single right answer to the question "What *did* happen to me in the past?" It is also to think that there is no such answer to the question "What sort of person am I now?" It is to recognize that the choice of a vocabulary in which to describe either one's childhood or one's character cannot be made by inspecting some collection of "neutral facts" (e.g., a complete videotape of one's life history). It is to give up the urge to purification, to achieve a stripped-down version of the self, and to develop what Rieff calls "tolerance of ambiguities . . . the key to what Freud considered the most difficult of all personal accomplishments: a genuinely stable character in an unstable time" (1966, 57). On the view I am offering, Freud gave us a new technique for achieving a genuinely stable character: the technique of lending a sympathetic ear to our own tendencies to instability, by treating them as alternative ways of making sense of the past, ways that have as good a claim on our attention as do the familiar beliefs and desires that are available to introspection. His mechanistic view of the self gave us a vocabulary that lets us describe all the various parts of the soul, conscious and unconscious alike, in homogenous terms: as equally plausible candidates for "the true self."

But to say that all the parts of the soul are equally plausible candidates is to discredit both the idea of a "true self" and the idea of "the true story about how things are." It is to view the enlightened, liberated self—the self that has finally succeeded in shaping itself—as a self that has given up the need to "see things steadily and see them whole," to penetrate beyond shifting appearances to a constant reality. Maturity will, according to this view, consist rather in an ability to seek out new redescriptions of one's own past—an ability to take a nominalistic, ironic, view of oneself. By turning the Platonic parts of the soul into conversational partners for one another, Freud did for the variety of interpretations of each person's past what the Baconian approach to science and philosophy did for the variety of descriptions of the universe as a whole. He let us see alternative narratives and alternative vocabularies as instruments for change, rather than as candidates for a correct depiction of how things are in themselves.

Much of what I have been saying is summarized in Freud's remark, "If one considers chance to be unworthy of determining our fate, it is simply a relapse into the pious view of the Universe which Leonardo himself was on the way to overcoming when he wrote that the sun does not move" (*S.E.* 11:137).[11] This recommendation that we see chance as "not unworthy of determining our fate" has as a corollary that we see ourselves as having the beliefs and emotions we do, including our (putatively) "specifically moral" beliefs and emotions, because of some very particular, idiosyncratic things that have happened in the history of the race, and to ourselves in the course of growing up. Such a recognition produces the ability to be Baconian about oneself. It lets one see oneself as a Rube Goldberg machine that requires much tinkering, rather than as a substance with a precious essence to be discovered and cherished. It produces what Whitehead called "the virtues which Odysseus shares with the foxes"—rather than, for example, those which Achilles shares with the lions, or those which Plato and Aristotle hoped to share with the gods.

From this Baconian angle, the point of psychoanalysis is the same as that of reflection on the sort of character one would like to have, once one ceases to take a single vocabulary for granted and begins the attempt to revise and enlarge the very vocabulary in which one is at present reflecting. The point of both exercises is to find new self-descriptions whose adoption will enable one to alter one's behavior. Finding out the views of one's unconscious about one's past is a way of getting some additional suggestions about how to describe (and change) oneself in the future. As a way of getting such suggestions, psychoanalysis differs from reading history, novels, or treatises on moral philosophy only in being more painful, in being more likely to produce radical change, and in requiring a partner.

Purification and Self-Enlargement

Because morality is associated both with human solidarity and with tragedy, my claim that attention to personal idiosyncrasy "remoralizes" a mechanistic self may seem paradoxical. One might protest, in the spirit of Kant, that the whole point of morality is self-forgetfulness, not making an exception of oneself, seeing oneself as counting for no more than any other human being, being motivated by what is common to all humanity. To emphasize idiosyncrasy is to emphasize the comic variety of human life rather than the tragedies that morality hopes to avert.

The appearance of paradox results from the fact that "morality" can mean either the attempt to be just in one's treatment of others or the search for perfection in oneself. The former is public morality, codifiable in statutes and maxims. The latter is private morality, the development of character. Like Freud, I am concerned only with the latter. Morality as the search for justice swings free of religion, science, metaphysics, and psychology. It is the relatively simple and obvious side of morality—the part that nowadays, in the wake of Freud, is often referred to as "culture" or "repression." This is the side of morality that instructs us to tell the truth, avoid violence, eschew sex with near relations, keep our promises, and abide by the Golden Rule.

The story of progress in public morality is largely irrelevant to the story of the mechanization of the world view.[12] Galileo, Darwin, and Freud did little to help or hinder such progress. They have nothing to say in answer either to the Athenian question "Does justice pay?" or to the Californian question "How much repression need I endure?" Freud, in particular, has no contribution to make to social theory. His domain is the portion of morality that cannot be identified with "culture"; it is the private life, the search for a character, the attempt of individuals to be reconciled with themselves (and, in the case of some exceptional individuals, to make their lives works of art).[13]

Such an attempt can take one of two antithetical forms: a search for purity or a search for self-enlargement. The ascetic life commended by Plato and criticized by Nietzsche is the paradigm of the former. The "aesthetic" life criticized by Kierkegaard is the paradigm of the latter. The desire to purify oneself is the desire to slim down, to peel away everything that is accidental, to will one thing, to intensify, to become a simpler and more transparent being. The desire to enlarge oneself is the desire to embrace more and more possibilities, to be constantly learning, to give oneself over entirely to curiosity, to end by having envisaged all the possibilities of the past and of the future. It was the goal shared by, for example, de Sade, Byron, and Hegel.[14] On the view I am presenting, Freud is an apostle of this aesthetic life, the life of unending curiosity, the life that seeks to extend its own bound rather than to find its center.

For those who decline the options offered by de Sade and Byron (sexual experimentation, political engagement), the principal technique of self-enlargement will be Hegel's: the enrichment of language. One will see the history of both the race and oneself as the development of richer, fuller ways of formulating one's desires and hopes, and thus making those desires and hopes themselves—and thereby oneself—richer and fuller. I shall call such a development the "acquisition of new vocabularies of moral reflection." By "a vocabulary of moral reflection" I mean a set of terms in which one compares oneself to other human beings. Such vocabularies contain terms like *magnanimous, a true Christian, decent, cowardly, God-fearing, hypocritical, self-deceptive, epicene, self-destructive, cold, an antique Roman, a saint, a Julien Sorel, a Becky Sharpe, a red-blooded American, a shy gazelle, a hyena, depressive, a Bloomsbury type, a man of respect, a grande dame.* Such terms are possible answers to the question "What is he or she like?" and thus possible answers to the question "What am *I* like?" By summing up patterns of behavior, they are tools for criticizing the character of others and for creating one's own. They are the terms one uses when one tries to resolve moral dilemmas by asking "What sort of person would I be if I did this?"

This question is, of course, not the only question one asks when reflecting about what to do. One also asks, for example, "How would I justify myself to so-and-so?" and "Would this action violate the general rule that . . . ?" But answers to these questions will reflect the vocabulary of moral reflection at one's disposal. That vocabulary helps one decide to which sort of people to justify oneself. It puts some flesh on abstract rules like the categorical imperative and "Maximize human happiness!" It is distinctions between such vocabularies, rather than between general principles, that differentiate the moralities of communities, historical epochs, and epochs in the life of the curious intellectual. The availability of a richer vocabulary of moral deliberation is what one chiefly has in mind when one says that we are, morally speaking, more sensitive and sophisticated than our ancestors or than our younger selves.

Much could be said about how the addition of specifically psychoanalytic concepts to religious and philosophical concepts (and to the invocation of historical and literary archetypes) has influenced contemporary patterns of moral deliberation.[15] My theme, however, is different. I want to focus on the way in which Freud, by helping us see ourselves as centerless, as random assemblages of contingent and idiosyncratic needs rather than as more or less adequate exemplifications of a common human essence, opened up new possibilities for the aesthetic life. He helped us become increasingly ironic, playful, free, and inventive in our choice of self-descriptions. This has been an important factor in our ability to slough off the idea that we have a true self, one shared with all other humans, and the related notion that the demands of this true self—the specifically moral demands—take precedence over all others. It has helped us think of moral reflection and sophistication as a matter of self-creation rather than self-knowledge. Freud made the paradigm of self-knowledge the discovery of the fortuitous materials out of which we must construct ourselves rather than the discovery of the principles to which we must conform. He thus made the desire for purification seem more self-deceptive, and the quest for self-enlargement more promising.

By contrast, the history of modern philosophy has centered on attempts to preserve an enclave of nonmechanism, and thus to keep alive the notion of a "true self" and the plausibility of a morality of self-purification. Descartes was willing to follow Galileo in dissolving all the Aristotelian natural kinds into so many vortices of corpuscles, with one exception. He wanted the mind to remain exempt from this dissolution. The mind and its faculties (notably intellect, conceived of as immediate, nondiscursive grasp of truth) were to remain as Platonism and Christianity had conceived of them. This enclave of nonmechanism that Descartes claimed to have descried became the preserve of a subject called "metaphysics."[16] Kant recognized the ad hoc and factitious character of this Cartesian attempt to keep the world safe for nonmechanism, and so he developed a different, more drastic, strategy to achieve the same end. He was willing to put mind and matter on a par, and to follow Hume in dissolving what he called "the empirical self" into predictable associations of mental atoms. But he distinguished that self from the true self, the moral self, the part of the self that was an agent of rather than a subject of scientific inquiry.

This still smaller and more mysterious enclave of nonmechanism became the preserve of a subject called "moral philosophy." Kant tried to make morality a nonempirical matter, something that would never again have anything to fear from religion, science, or the arts, nor have anything to learn from them.[17] For, Kant explained, the reason why the New Science had described a world with no moral lesson, a world without a moral point, was that it described a world of appearance. By contrast, the true world was a world that was, so to speak, nothing but point: nothing but a moral imperative, nothing but a call to moral purity.

One result of Kant's initiative was to impoverish the vocabulary of moral philosophy and to turn the enrichment of our vocabulary of moral reflection over to novelists, poets, and dramatists.[18] The nineteenth-century novel, in particular, filled a vacuum left by the retreat of one-half of moral philosophy into idealist metaphysics and the advance of the other half into politics.[19] Another result was what Alasdair MacIntyre calls the invention of "the individual"—a moral self who existed "prior to and apart from all roles,"[20] who was independent of any social or historical context. To say that the moral self exists apart from all roles means that it will remain the same no matter what situation it finds itself in, no matter what language it uses to create its self-image, no matter what its vocabulary of moral deliberation may be. That, in turn, means that the moral self has no need to work out a sensitive and sophisticated vocabulary as an instrument to create its character. For the only character that matters is the one it already has. Once it began to seem (as it did to Kant) that we had always known a priori all there was to know about the "morally relevant" portion of human beings, the Hegelian urge to enrich our vocabulary of moral reflection began to seem (as it did to Kierkegaard) a merely "aesthetic" demand, something that might amuse a leisured elite but which had no relevance to our moral responsibilities.[21]

This account of modern philosophy can be summarized by saying that when modern science made it hard to think of man as a natural kind, philosophy responded by inventing an unnatural kind. It was perhaps predictable that the sequence of descriptions of this self that begins with Descartes should end with Sartre: the self as a blank space in the middle of a machine—an *être-pour-soi,* a "hole in being." By contrast, Freud stands with Hegel against Kant, in an attitude of Nietzschean exuberance rather than Sartrean embarrassment. He offers us a way to reinvent the search for enlargement, and thereby reinvents the morality of character. I can summarize my account of how he does this in five points:

1. Whereas everybody from Plato to Kant had identified our central self, our conscience, the standard-setting, authoritative part of us, with universal truths, general principles, and a common human nature, Freud made conscience just one more, not particularly central, part of a larger, homogenous machine. He identified the sense of duty with the internalization of a host of idiosyncratic, accidental episodes. On his account our sense of moral obligation is not a matter of general ideas contemplated by the intellect, but rather of traces of encounters between particular people and our bodily organs. He saw the voice of conscience not as the voice of the part of the soul that deals with generalities as opposed to the part that deals with particulars, but rather as the (usually distorted) memory of certain very particular events.

2. This identification did not take the form of a reductive claim that morality was "nothing but . . ." delayed responses to forgotten stimuli. Since Freud was willing to view *every* part of life, every human activity, in the same terms, there was no contrast to be drawn between the "merely" mechanical and reactive character of moral experience and the free and spontaneous character of something else (e.g., science, art, philosophy or psychoanalytic theory).

3. Nor did this identification of conscience with memory of idiosyncratic events take the form of the claim that talk about such events was a ("scientific") substitute for moral deliberation. Freud did not suggest that we would see ourselves more clearly, or choose more wisely, by restricting our vocabulary of moral reflection to psychoanalytic terms. On the contrary, Freud dropped the Platonic metaphor of "seeing ourselves more clearly" in favor of the Baconian idea of theory as a tool for bringing about desirable change.[22] He was far from

thinking that psychoanalytic theory was the *only* tool needed for self-enlargement.

4. This Baconian attitude was the culmination of the mechanizing movement that had begun in the seventeenth century. That movement had replaced the attempt to contemplate the essences of natural kinds with the attempt to tinker with the machines that compose the world. But not until Freud did we get a usable way of thinking of *ourselves* as machines to be tinkered with, a self-image that enabled us to weave terms describing psychic mechanisms into our strategies of character-formation.

5. The increased ability of the syncretic, ironic, nominalist intellectual to move back and forth between, for example, religious, moral, scientific, literary, philosophical, and psychoanalytical vocabularies without asking the question "And which of these shows us how things *really* are?"—the intellectual's ability to treat vocabularies as tools rather than mirrors—is Freud's major legacy. He broke some of the last chains that bind us to the Greek idea that we, or the world, have a nature that, once discovered, will tell us what we should do with ourselves. He made it far more difficult than it was before to ask the question "Which is my true self?" or "What is human nature?" By letting us see that even in the enclave which philosophy had fenced off, there was nothing to be found save traces of accidental encounters, he left us able to tolerate the ambiguities that the religious and philosophical traditions had hoped to eliminate.

"The Rich Aesthete, the Manager, and the Therapist"

My account of Freud as a Baconian has taken for granted that the move from Aristotelian to Baconian views of the nature of knowledge, like that from an ethics of purity to one of self-enrichment, was desirable. My enthusiasm for the mechanization and decentering of the world is dictated by my assumption that the ironic, playful intellectual is a desirable character-type, and that Freud's importance lies in his contribution to the formation of such a character. These assumptions are challenged by those who see the mechanization of nature as a prelude to barbarism. Such critics emphasize, as I have, the link between a pragmatic, tinkering approach to nature and the self, and the aesthetic search for novel experiences and novel language. But they condemn both.

The most thoroughly thought-out, if most abstract, account of the relation between technology and aestheticism is offered by Heidegger.[23] But the more concrete criticisms of modern ways of thinking offered by Alasdair MacIntyre in *After Virtue* are more immediately relevant to the topics I have been discussing. MacIntyre would agree, more or less, with my description of the connections between Baconian ways of thought and Nietzschean values. But he takes the fact that the paradigmatic character-types of modernity are "the Rich Aesthete, the Manager, and the Therapist" (MacIntyre 1981, 29) to show that these ways of thought, and these values, are undesirable. In MacIntyre's view, the abandonment of an Aristotelian "functional concept of man" leads to "emotivism"—"the obliteration of any genuine distinction between manipulative and non-manipulative social relations" (22).

MacIntyre is, I think, right in saying that contemporary moral discourse is a confusing and inconsistent blend of notions that make sense only in an Aristotelian view of the world (e.g., "reason," "human nature," "natural rights") with mechanistic, anti-Aristotelian notions that implicitly repudiate such a view. But whereas MacIntyre thinks we need to bring back Aristotelian ways of thinking to make our moral discourse coherent, I think we should do the opposite and make the discourse coherent by discarding the last vestiges of those ways of thinking.[24] I would welcome a culture dominated by "the Rich Aesthete, the Manager, and the Therapist" so long as *everybody* who wants to gets to be an aesthete (and, if not rich, as comfortably off as most—as rich as the Managers can manage, guided by Rawls's Difference Principle).

Further, I think that we can live with the Freudian thought that everything everybody does to everyone else (even those they love blindly and helplessly) can be described, for therapeutic or other purposes, as manipulation. The postulation of unintrospectible systems of beliefs and desires ensures that there will be a coherent and informative narrative to be told in those terms, one that will interpret all personal and social relations, even the tenderest and most sacred, in terms of "making use of" others. Once those extra persons who explain akrasia and other forms of irrationality are taken into account, there are, so to speak, too many selves for "selflessness" to seem a useful notion. But the increased ability to explain, given by Freud's postulation of additional persons, hardly prevents us from drawing the common-sense distinction between manipulating people (i.e., consciously, and deceptively, employing them as instruments for one's own purposes) and not manipulating them. The availability of a description for explanatory purposes does not entail its use in moral reflection, any more than it precludes it.

MacIntyre construes "emotivism" as the only option left, once one abandons the Aristotelian idea of man, because he retains a pre-

Freudian[25] division of human faculties. In terms of this division, "desire" or "will" or "passion" represents the only alternative to "reason" (construed as a faculty of seeing things as they are in themselves). But dividing people up this way begs the question against other ways of describing them—for example, Freud's way. Freud (at least according to the Davidsonian interpretation I have developed here) drops the whole idea of "faculties," and substitutes the notion of a plurality of sets of beliefs and desires. MacIntyre's definition of "emotivism" ("the doctrine that all evaluative judgments and more specifically all moral judgments are *nothing but* expressions of preference, expressions of attitude or feeling" [11]) makes sense only if there is something else such judgments might have been—for example, expressions of a correct "rational" grasp of the nature of the human being.

Moral psychology, like moral discourse, is at present an incoherent blend of Aristotelian and mechanist ways of speaking. I would urge that if we eradicate the former, "emotivism" will no longer be an intelligible position. More generally, if we take Freud to heart, we shall not have to choose between an Aristotelian "functional" concept of humanity, one that will provide moral guidance, and Sartrean "dreadful freedom." For the Sartrean conception of the self as pure freedom will be seen as merely the last gasp of the Aristotelian tradition—a self-erasing expression of the Cartesian determination to find *something* nonmechanical at the center of the machine, if only a "hole in being."[26] We shall not need a picture of "the human self" in order to have morality—neither of a nonmechanical enclave nor of a meaningless void where such an enclave ought to have been.

It seems a point in my favor that MacIntyre does not answer the question of whether it is "rationally justifiable [*pace* Sartre] to conceive of each human life as a unity" (MacIntyre 1981, 189) by saying (with Aristotle) "yes, because the function of man is. . . ." Rather, he offers us "a concept of a self whose unity resides in the unity of a narrative which links birth to life to death as narrative beginning to middle to end" (191).[27] MacIntyre tacitly drops the Aristotelian demand that the themes of each such narrative be roughly the same for each member of a given species, and that they stay roughly constant throughout the history of the species. He seems content to urge that in order for us to exhibit the virtue of "integrity or constancy" we must see our lives in such narrative terms. To attempt that virtue is just what I have been calling "the search for perfection," and I agree that this search requires the construction of such narratives. But if we do drop the Aristotelian demand, contenting ourselves with narratives tailored ad hoc to the contingencies of individual lives, then we may welcome a Baconian culture dominated by "the Rich Aesthete, the Manager, and the Therapist"—not necessarily as the final goal of human progress, but at least as a considerable improvement on cultures dominated by, for example, the Warrior or the Priest.

On my account of Freud, his work enables us to construct richer and more plausible narratives of this ad hoc sort—more plausible because they will cover *all* the actions one performs in the course of one's life, even the silly, cruel, and self-destructive actions. More generally, Freud helped us see that the attempt to put together such a narrative—one that minimizes neither the contingency nor the decisive importance of the input into the machine that each of us is—must take the place of an attempt to find the function common to all such machines. If one takes Freud's advice, one finds psychological narratives without heroes or heroines. For neither Sartrean freedom, nor the will, nor the instincts, nor an internalization of a culture, nor anything else will play the role of "the true self." Instead, one tells the story of the whole machine *as* machine, without choosing a particular set of springs and wheels as protagonist. Such a story can help us, if anything can, stop the pendulum from swinging between Aristotelian attempts to discover our essence and Sartrean attempts at self-creation *de novo*.

This suggestion that our stories about ourselves must be stories of centerless mechanisms—of the determined processing of contingent input—will seem to strip us of human dignity only if we think we need *reasons* to live romantically, or to treat others decently, or to be treated decently ourselves. Questions like "Why should I hope?" or "Why should I not use others as means?" or "Why should my torturers not use me as a means?" are questions that can *only* be answered by philosophical metanarratives that tell us about a nonmechanical world and a nonmechanical self—about a world and a self that have centers, centers that are sources of authority. Such questions are tailored to fit such answers. So if we renounce such answers, such metanarratives, and fall back on narratives about the actual and possible lives of individuals, we shall have to renounce the needs that metaphysics and moral philosophy attempted to satisfy. We shall have to confine ourselves to questions like, "If I do this rather than that now, what story will I tell myself later?" We shall have to abjure questions like, "Is there something deep inside my torturer—his rationality—to which I can appeal?"

The philosophical tradition suggests that there is, indeed, something of this sort. It tends to take for granted that our dignity depends on the existence of something that can be opposed to "arbitrary will." This thing, usually called "reason," is needed to give "authority" to the first premises of our practical syllogisms. Such a view of human dignity is precisely what Freud called "the pious view of the Universe." He thought that the traditional oppositions between reason, will, and emotion—the oppositions in terms of which MacIntyre constructs his history of ethics—should be discarded in favor of distinctions between various regions of a homogenous mechanism, regions that embody a plurality of persons (that is, of incompatible systems of belief and desire). So the only version of human dignity that Freud lets us preserve is the one MacIntyre himself offers: the ability of each of us to tailor a coherent self-image for ourselves and then use it to tinker with our behavior. This ability replaces the traditional philosophical project of finding a coherent self-image that will fit the entire species to which we belong.

Given this revisionary account of human dignity, what becomes of human solidarity? In my view, Freud does nothing for either liberal or radical politics, except perhaps to supply new terms of opprobrium with which to stigmatize tyrants and torturers.[28] On the contrary, he diminishes our ability to take seriously much of the traditional jargon of both liberalism and radicalism—notions such as "human rights" and "autonomy" and slogans such as "man will prevail" and "trust the instincts of the masses." For these notions and slogans are bound up with Aristotelian attempts to find a center for the self.

On the other hand, Freud does nothing to diminish a sense of human solidarity that, rather than encompassing the entire species, restricts itself to such particular communal movements as modern science, bourgeois liberalism, or the European novel. If we avoid describing these movements in terms of metaphysical notions like "the search for truth," or "the realization of human freedom," or "the attainment of self-consciousness," histories of them will nevertheless remain available as larger narratives within which to place the narratives of our individual lives. Freud banishes philosophical metanarratives,[29] but he has nothing against ordinary historical narratives. Such narratives tell, for example, how we got from Galileo to Gell-Man, or from institutions that defended merchants against feudal overlords to institutions that defend labor against capital, or from Don Quixote to Pale Fire.[30]

Letting us see the narratives of our own lives as episodes within such larger historical narratives is, I think, as much as the intellectuals are able to do in aid of morality.[31] The attempt of religion and metaphysics to do more—to supply a backup for moral intuitions by providing them with ahistorical "authority"—will always be self-defeating. For (given the present rate of social change) another century's worth of history will always make the last century's attempt to be ahistorical look ridiculous. The only result of such attempts is to keep the pendulum swinging between moral dogmatism and moral skepticism.[32] What metaphysics could not do, psychology, even very "deep" psychology, is not going to do either; we pick up Freud by the wrong handle if we try to find an account of "moral motivation" that is more than a reference to the historical contingencies that shaped the process of acculturation in our region and epoch.

Historical narratives about social and intellectual movements are the best tools to use in tinkering with ourselves, for such narratives suggest vocabularies of moral deliberation in which to spin coherent narratives about our individual lives. By contrast, the vocabulary Freud himself used in much of his writing—an individualist, Stoic vocabulary, charged with ironic resignation—does little for the latter purpose. It has too much in common with the vocabulary of the self-erasing narratives of Rameau's nephew, Dostoevsky's "Underground Man," and Sartre's Roquentin: stories about machines chewing themselves to pieces. By contrast, narratives that help one identify oneself with communal movements engender a sense of being a machine geared into a larger machine. This is a sense worth having. For it helps reconcile an existentialist sense of contingency and mortality with a Romantic sense of grandeur. It helps us realize that the best way of tinkering with ourselves is to tinker with something else—a mechanist way of saying that only he who loses his soul will save it.

Notes

This paper is a revised version of the Edith Weigert Lecture, sponsored by the Forum on Psychiatry and the Humanities, Washington School of Psychiatry, October 19, 1984.

In deciding what revisions to make, I profited greatly from the seminar with members of the Forum on Psychiatry and the Humanities, held the day after the lecture, as well as from comments on my original version, which I received from Irvin Ehrenpreis, Alexander Nehamas, and J. B. Schneewind.

1. There can be such a thing as a "purer" Aristotelian substance—one that realizes its essence better because it is less subject to irrelevant accidental changes. (Indeed, Aristotle arranges substances in a hierarchy according to their degree of materiality, their degree of susceptibility to such changes—a hierarchy with "pure actuality" at the top.) But there is no such thing as a purified machine, though there may be another machine that accomplishes the same purpose more efficiently. Machines have no centers to which one can strip them down; stripped-down versions of machines are different machines, machines for doing or producing different things, not more perfect versions of the same machine.

2. The Copernican model of the heavens could not have been accepted with-

out also accepting the corpuscularian mechanics of Galileo and Descartes (see Kuhn, *The Copernican Revolution,* on this point). That mechanics was the entering wedge for a Newtonian paradigm of scientific explanation—one that predicted events on the basis of a universal homogenous microstructure, rather than revealing the different natures of the various natural kinds. The reason why "the new philosophy" cast all in doubt was not that people felt belittled when the sun took the place of the earth but that it had become hard to see what, given Newtonian space, could be meant by the universe having a center. As it became harder to know what a God's-eye view would be like, it became harder to believe in God. As it became harder to think of the common-sense way of breaking up the world into "natural" kinds as more than a practical convenience, it became harder to make sense of the Aristotelian essence-accident distinction. So the very idea of the "nature" of something as setting the standards that things of that sort ought to fulfill began to blur.

3. In particular, it became difficult to see what the point of *man* could be—difficult to preserve anything like Aristotle's "functional" concept of man. See MacIntyre, *After Virtue:*

> Moral arguments within the classical, Aristotelian tradition—whether in its Greek or its medieval versions—involve at least one central functional concept, the concept of *man* understood as having an essential nature and an essential purpose or function. . . . Aristotle takes it as a starting-point for ethical inquiry that the relationship of "man" to "living well" is analogous to that of "harpist" to "playing the harp well." . . . But the use of "man" as a functional concept is far older than Aristotle and it does not initially derive from Aristotle's metaphysical biology. It is rooted in the forms of a social life in which the theorists of the classical tradition give expression. For according to that tradition, to be a man is to fill a set of roles, each of which has its own point and purpose: a member of a family, a citizen, soldier, philosopher, servant of God. It is only when man is thought of as an individual prior to and apart from all roles that "man" ceases to be a functional concept. (56)

I take up MacIntyre's suggestion that we need to recapture such a concept in the final section of this essay.

4. Nonintellectuals' conviction that what the intellectuals talk about does not really matter was greatly strengthened when the new Enlightenment intellectuals informed them that the previous batch of intellectuals—the priests—had been *completely* wrong. One consequence of the mechanization of nature, and of the resulting popularity of a pragmatic, Baconian attitude toward knowledge-claims, was a heightened cynicism and indifference about the questions that intellectuals discuss. This is why metaphysical issues about "the nature of reality" and "the true self" have less resonance and popular appeal than religious heresies once did, and why philosophical questions raised within Comte's "positive," postmetaphysical perspective have even less. People always thought the priests a bit funny, but also a bit awe-inspiring. They thought German idealists, and Anglo-Saxon positivists, *merely* funny. By contrast, they take psychoanalysts seriously enough to attempt to imitate them, as in the development of parlor analysis and of psychobabble.

5. Even if, as Hume thought, there is a possible universe consisting only of one

sense-impression, we cannot make sense of the idea of a universe consisting only of the belief that, for example, Caesar crossed the Rubicon. Further, there is no such thing as an incoherent arrangement of Humean mental atoms. But there is such a thing as a set of beliefs and desires so incoherent that we cannot attribute them to a single self.

6. See also Trilling, *Beyond Culture* (79): "[Freud] showed us that poetry is indigenous to the very constitution of the mind; he saw the mind as being, in the greater part of its tendency, exactly a poetry-making faculty." Bersani makes the same point when he says, "Psychoanalytic theory has made the notion of fantasy so richly programmatic that we should no longer be able to take for granted the distinction between art and life, or to feel that the word 'creative' has any analytic value at all" (1977, 138).

7. "The importance of psycho-analysis for psychiatry would never have drawn the attention of the intellectual world to it or won it a place in *The History of our Times*. This result was brought about by the relation of psycho-analysis to normal, not to pathological, mental life" (Freud, *S.E.* 19:205; see also 18:240). Even if analytic psychiatry should some day be abandoned in favor of chemical and microsurgical forms of treatment, the connections that Freud drew between such emotions as sexual yearning and hostility on the one hand, and between dreams and parapraxes on the other, would remain part of the common sense of our culture.

8. See Davidson, "Paradoxes of Irrationality," especially his discussion of "the paradox of rationality" (303).

9. *Any* associationist psychology will make *that* claim. For it is a corollary of the claim that reason is not a faculty of contemplating essence but only a faculty of inferring beliefs from other beliefs. Since the initial premises of such inferences must then be supplied by something other than reason, and if the only faculty relevantly opposed to faculty that can be opposed to "reason" is "passion," then Hume's claim follows trivially. But it would, of course, be more consistent with the mechanistic vocabulary of associationist psychology to drop talk of faculties and, in particular, to drop the terms "reason" and "passion." Once the mind becomes a machine instead of a quasi person, it no longer has faculties, much less higher and lower ones. Hume is interlacing the old vocabulary of faculties with the results of new associationism for the sake of shock value.

10. This way of stating the aim of psychoanalytic treatment may seem to make everything sound too sweetly reasonable. It suggests that the analyst serves as a sort of moderator at a symposium: he or she introduces, for example, a consciousness which thinks that Mother is a long-suffering object of pity to an unconscious, which thinks of her as a voracious seductress, letting the two hash out the pros and cons. It is of course true that the facts of resistance forbid the analyst to think in conversational terms. He or she must instead think in terms of Freud's various topographico-hydraulic models of libidinal flow, hoping to find in these models suggestions about how to overcome resistance, what meaning to assign to novel symptoms, and so forth.

But it is also true that the patient has no choice but to think in conversational terms. (This is why self-analysis will usually not work, why treatment can often do what reflection cannot.) For purposes of the patient's conscious attempt to reshape his or her character, he or she cannot use a self-description in terms of cathexes, libidinal flow, and the like; topographic-hydraulic models cannot form part of one's self-image, any more than can a description of one's endocrine system. When the patient thinks about competing descriptions of his or her mother, the patient has to think dialectically, to grant that there is much to be said on both sides. To think, as opposed to react to a new stimulus, simply *is* to compare and contrast candidates for admission into one's set of beliefs and desires. So, while the analyst is busy thinking causally, in terms of the patient's reactions to stimuli (and in particular the stimuli that occur while the patient is on the couch), the patient has to think of his or her unconscious as, at least potentially, a conversational partner.

These two ways of thinking seem to me alternative tools, useful for different purposes, rather than contradictory claims. I do not think (despite the arguments of, for example, Paul Ricoeur and Roy Schafer) that there is a tension in Freud's thought between "energetics" and "hermeneutics." Rather, the two seem to me to be as compatible as, for example, microstructural and macrostructural descriptions of the same object (e.g., Eddington's table). But to defend my eirenic attitude properly I should offer an account of "resistance" that chimes with Davidson's interpretation of the unconscious, and I have not yet figured out how to do this. (I am grateful to George Thomas, Seymour Rabinowitz, and Cecil Cullender for pointing out this difficulty to me.)

11. It is interesting that in the passage cited Freud is referring back to a passage (*S.E.* 11:76) where he credits Leonardo not only with anticipating Copernicus but with having "divined the history of the stratification and fossilization in the Arno valley," a suggestion that Leonardo anticipated Darwin as well.

12. The Enlightenment attempt to connect the two by seeing both feudalism and Aristotelian science as instances of "prejudice and superstition" was a self-deceptive neo-Aristotelian attempt to preserve the idea of man as an animal whose essence is rationality, while simultaneously identifying rationality with certain newly created institutions.

13. Here I am agreeing with Rieff against, for example Fromm and Marcuse: "Psychoanalysis is the doctrine of the private man defending himself against public encroachment. He cultivates the private life and its pleasures, and if he does take part in public affairs it is for consciously private motives" (Rieff 1961, 278). Rieff seems to me right in saying that Freud had little to say about how and whether society might be made "less repressive": "Like those who worked for shorter hours but nevertheless feared what men might do with their leisure, Freud would have welcomed more constructive releases from our stale moralities, but did not propose to substitute a new one. Our private ethics were his scientific problem: he had no new public ethics to suggest, no grand design for the puzzle of our common life" (1966, 38).

14. See Hans Blumenberg's discussion of "theoretical curiosity," and especially his contrast between the medieval criticism of curiosity and Bacon's praise of it, in *The Legitimacy of the Modern Age*.

15. See, for example, Adam Morton, "Freudian Commonsense." I think that Morton asks just the right questions, although I have doubts about the character-personality distinction that he draws.

16. Consider Leibniz's novel and influential use of the terms *physics* and *metaphysics* to name the study of mechanism and of nonmechanism, respectively—to distinguish between the area in which Newton was right and the area in which Aristotle and the scholastics had been right.

17. As J. B. Schneewind has pointed out to me, this remark is accurate only for Kant's early thinking on morality. Later in his life the purity and isolation claimed for morality in the *Grundlagen* became compromised in various ways. It was, however, the early writings on morality that became associated with Kant's name, and that his successors were concerned to criticize.

18. See Murdoch, *The Sovereignty of Good* (58): "It is a shortcoming of much contemporary moral philosophy that it eschews discussion of the separate virtues, preferring to proceed directly to some sovereign concept such as sincerity, or authenticity, or freedom, thereby imposing, it seems to me, an unexamined and empty idea of unity, and impoverishing our moral language in an important area." Murdoch's claim that "the most essential and fundamental aspect of our culture is the study of literature, since this is an education in how to picture and understand human situations" (34) would have meant something different two hundred years ago. For then the term *literature* covered Hume's *Enquiries* and his *History* as well as novels, plays, and poems. Our modern contrast between literature and moral philosophy is one result of the development that Murdoch describes:

> Philosophy . . . has been busy dismantling the old substantial picture of the "self," and ethics has not proved itself able to rethink this concept for moral purposes. . . . Moral philosophy, and indeed morals, are thus undefended against an irresponsible and undirected self-assertion which goes easily hand-in-hand with some brand of pseudo-scientific determinism. An unexamined sense of the strength of the machine is combined with an illusion of leaping out of it. The younger Sartre, and many British moral philosophers, represent this last dry distilment of Kant's views of the world. (47–48)

19. The latter phenomenon is exemplified by, for example, Bentham and Marx—philosophers who have been responsible for much good in the public sphere but who are useless as advisers on the development of moral character.

20. See the passage from MacIntyre quoted in note 3.

21. For a contemporary account of the contrast between the Kantian and the Hegelian attitudes, see Alan Donagan, *A Theory of Morality* (chap. 1, especially p. 10), on "Hegel's doctrine of the emptiness of the moral point of view."

22. Rieff makes this contrast between Platonic and Baconian attitudes, saying that the latter, the "second theory of theory," views theory as "arming us with the weapons for transforming reality instead of forcing us to conform to it. . . . Psychoanalytic theory belongs to the second tradition" (1966, 55–56). This view of Freud's aim is central to my account of his achievement, and I am much indebted to Rieff's work.

23. See Heidegger's essays "The Question Concerning Technology" and "The Age of the World View" in *The Question concerning Technology and Other Essays*. I suggest a Deweyan response to Heidegger's view of technology at the end of "Heidegger Wider die Pragmatisten" (Rorty 1984)—a response that is in

harmony with that offered by Blumenberg. MacIntyre would join me in repudiating Heidegger's attack on technology but would retain Heidegger's account of the shift in moral consciousness that followed upon the abandonment of an Aristotelian world view.

24. It is tempting to say that I would accept MacIntyre's claim that the only real choice is between Aristotle and Nietzsche, and then side with Nietzsche. But the choice is too dramatic and too simple. By the time MacIntyre gets rid of the nonsense in Aristotle (e.g., what he calls the "metaphysical biology"), Aristotle does not look much like himself. By the time I would finish discarding the bits of Nietzsche I do not want (e.g., his lapses into metaphysical biology, his distrust of Hegel, his *ressentiment,* etc.) he would not look much like Nietzsche. The opposition between these two ideal types is useful only if one does not press it too hard.

25. Or, more generally, premechanist (and thus pre-Humean; see note 9 on Hume and faculty psychology).

26. Metaphysicians like Sartre would, to paraphrase Nietzsche, rather have a metaphysics of nothingness than no metaphysics. This was a trap around which Heidegger circled in his early work but eventually walked away from, leaving Sartre to take the plunge.

27. There seems to be a tension in MacIntyre's book between the early chapters, in which it is suggested that unless we can identify a telos common to all members of our species we are driven to the "emotivist" view that "all moral judgments are *nothing but* expressions of preference" (11), and chapters 14–15. In the latter chapters, which MacIntyre thinks of as a rehabilitation of Aristotelianism (see 239), nothing is done to defeat the suggestion that all moral judgments are nothing but choices among competing narratives, a suggestion that is compatible with the three paradigmatically Aristotelian doctrines that MacIntyre lists on pp. 183–86 of his book. By dropping what he calls "Aristotle's metaphysical biology" (183), MacIntyre also drops the attempt to evaluate "the claims to objectivity and authority" of "the lost morality of the past" (21). For unless a knowledge of the function of the human species takes us beyond MacIntyre's Socratic claim that "the good life for man is the life spent in seeking for the good life for man" (204), the idea of one narrative being more "objective and authoritative" than another, as opposed to being more detailed and inclusive, goes by the board.

28. But diagnoses of the Freudian mechanisms that produce suitable candidates for the KGB and the Gestapo, of the sort made popular by Adorno and others who talk about "authoritarian personalities," add little to the familiar pre-Freudian suggestion that we might have fewer bully boys to cope with if people had more education, leisure, and money. The Adorno-Horkheimer suggestion that the rise of Nazism within a highly developed and cultivated nation shows that this familiar liberal solution is inadequate seems to me unconvincing. At any rate, it seems safe to say that Freudo-Marxist analyses of "authoritarianism" have offered no better suggestions about how to keep the thugs from taking over.

29. I borrow the term *metanarrative* from Jean-Francois Lyotard's *The Postmodern Condition.* For further discussion of how the narrative of bourgeois liberalism can be separated from metanarratives, see Rorty, "Postmodernist Bourgeois Liberalism."

30. See Milan Kundera, "The Novel and Europe." Kundera ends his essay by asking, "But if the idea of progress arouses my suspicion, what are the values to which I feel attached?" and responds, "My answer is as sincere as it is ridiculous: I am attached to nothing apart from the European novel, that unrecognized inheritance that comes to us from Cervantes."

31. I defend this historicist, ethnocentric point at some length in "Solidarity or Objectivity?" and again in "Le Cosmopolitanisme sans Emancipation."

32. For a discussion of the causes and effects of such pendulum swings, see Annette Baier, "Doing without Moral Theory?"

References

Baier, Annette. "Doing without Moral Theory?" In Baier, *Postures of the Mind: Essays on Mind and Morals.* Minneapolis: University of Minnesota Press, 1985.

Bersani, Leo. *Baudelaire and Freud.* Berkeley and Los Angeles: University of California Press, 1977.

Blumenberg, Hans. *The Legitimacy of the Modern Age.* Cambridge, Mass: MIT Press, 1983.

Davidson, Donald. "Paradoxes of Irrationality." In *Philosophical Essays on Freud,* edited by Richard Wollheim and James Hopkins. Cambridge: Cambridge University Press, 1982.

Donagan, Alan. *A Theory of Morality,* Chicago: University of Chicago Press, 1977.

Freud, Sigmund. *The Standard Edition of the Complete Psychological Works of Sigmund Freud.* Edited and translated by James Strachey. 24 Vols. London: Hogarth, 1953–74.

Leonardo da Vinci and a Memory of His Childhood (1910), vol. 11.

"Thoughts for the Times on War and Death" (1915), vol. 14.

Introductory Lectures on Psycho-Analysis (1916), vol. 16.

"Two Encyclopaedia Articles" (1923), vol. 18.

"A Short Account of Psycho-Analysis" (1924), vol. 19.

Heidegger, Martin. *The Question concerning Technology and Other Essays.* Translated by William Lovitt. New York: Harper & Row, 1977.

Kuhn, Thomas S. *The Copernican Revolution.* Cambridge, Mass. Havard University Press, 1957.

Kundera, Milan. "The Novel and Europe." *New York Review of Books,* July 19, 1984, pp. 15 ff.

Lyotard, Jean-Francois. *The Postmodern Condition.* Minneapolis: University of Minnesota Press, 1984.

MacIntyre, Alasdair. *After Virtue.* Notre Dame, Ind.: University of Notre Dame Press, 1981.

Morton, Adam. "Freudian Commonsense." In *Philosophical Essays on Freud,* edited by Richard Wollheim and James Hopkins. Cambridge: Cambridge University Press, 1982.

Murdoch, Iris. *The Sovereignty of Good.* New York: Schocken Books, 1971.

Rieff, Philip. *Freud: The Mind of the Moralist.* New York: Harper & Row, 1961.
——.*Triumph of the Therapeutic.* New York: Harper & Row, 1966.
Rorty, Richard. "Postmodernist Bourgeois Liberalism." *Journal of Philosophy* 80 (1983): 583–89.
——. "Heidegger Wider die Pragmatisten." *Neue Hefte für Philosophie* 23 (1984): 1–22.
——."Le Cosmopolitanisme sans Emancipation: En Réponse a Jean-Francois Lyotard." *Critique* 41 (1985): 569–80, 584.
——. "Solidarity or Objectivity?" In *Post-Analytic Philosophy,* edited by John Rajchman and Cornel West. New York: Columbia University Press, 1985.
Trilling, Lionel. *Beyond Culture.* New York: Harcourt, Brace, 1965.

2   Self-realization and Solidarity: Rorty and the Judging Self

Richard H. King

T o challenge an answer to a question is one thing: to challenge the question and the assumptions behind it is quite another. Richard Rorty's work takes up the latter sort of challenge. As he is fond of saying, many philosophers are still scratching where others no longer itch. Rorty's breezy dismissiveness leads some to consider him insufficiently serious. But there is no reason why Rorty should pull a long face when confronted with questions he no longer takes seriously. The measure of a question's importance does not depend on how many peopɩe have asked it. Rorty's enterprise is serious, for he is engaged in an exploration of what it means to think, judge, and act in a world where foundational or transcendental warrant for those activities no longer exists—of how to be serious without being certain.

This paper pursues three related lines of inquiry concerning Rorty's work. First, how does Rorty's work comport with two distinct tendencies of contemporary thought that I will call "learning from" and "learning about"? Second, can Rorty develop a convincing account of the "judging" self once the "foundational" self has been jettisoned? To answer this will involve a close look at Rorty's account of Freud's description of the self. And finally, can this judging self be described in a way that will do justice to its public as well as private dimensions? My general claim is that Rorty's central idea of a "conversation" offers interesting analogies with the psychoanalytic and political contexts but that he has failed to develop a convincing account of the social "foundations" of the self or to account for the importance of power and force in the conversations he imagines us engaging in. What follows is an exploration of the difficulty Rorty faces when offering a "full-scale discussion of the possibility of combining private fulfillment, self-realization, with public morality, a concern for justice" (1982a, 158).[1]

28

Learning From and Learning About

Contemporary theories of interpretation pull in two opposing directions. One attitude toward a text, person, or event (what I will term the "object") might be called "learning from." One approaches the object expecting or hoping to be instructed or, as Rorty would have it, "edified." Such edification is not just an intellectual exercise since it may be crucially concerned with ethical issues, with learning how to live with oneself and others. It is a form of *Bildung*. Power is located *in* the object and deployed by the person edified in his or her life situation. The objects of our interpretive concern are all potentially meaningful, ready to teach us something if we will but attend to them.

Another impulse in modern thought takes a strikingly different attitude toward its object of address. Instead of setting out to discover what can be learned from, this stance assumes that the most important thing is to "learn about" the object. "Learning about" leads to such questions as "Whose interests are served by this line of thought?" or "What psychological factors led Freud to reject Jung?" or "Who is speaking in this text, and how are we to understand the conditions of its production?" Max Weber's investigation of the relationship between capitalism and Protestantism would be an example of an attempt to "learn about," for Weber suspends any concern about the truth value of Protestantism or the merits of capitalism. Those thinkers, such as Nietzsche, Marx, and Freud, who have developed a "hermeneutics of suspicion" offer more global theories in this same mode. Finally, contemporary figures such as Jacques Derrida and Michel Foucault offer second-order theories informed by the impulse to "learn about." They are suspicious of the hermeneutics of suspicion, debunkers of the debunkers, and call into question such conceptual dichotomies as conscious/unconscious, surface/depth, or false/true.[2]

It is fair to say that the "learning about" impulse dominates contemporary interpretive discourse. The power of received interpretations of texts, events, and persons is confronted, deflected, and undermined. Such approaches seek to gain power *over* the object rather than discover the latent power or meaning *in* an object. Wisdom or edification is "always already" irrelevant. Meaning offered or meaning discovered resembles the emperor's new clothes: there is no "there" there. "Learning about" adopts instead a kind of inverted Socratic position. Where Socrates claimed that he was wise because he realized his ignorance in light of a higher source of truth, Derrida and Foucault offer a negative wisdom in light of the historicity of all things.

But it would be a mistake to make the dichotomy between "learning from" and "learning about" coincide with the difference between foundationalists and pragmatists, or metaphysicians and deconstructionists, or humanists and posthumanists. Rather, what marks the difference between the two modes of approach is a pre-theoretical assumption about meaning in general.[3] Those who assume that we can be engaged in the business of "learning from" assume a multiplicity of possible meanings at large in the world. Our minds and their creations are almost infinitely rich and create, to change the metaphor, a veritable "forest" of meanings. This assumption seems to me at work, for instance, in the writings of Stanley Cavell who discovers profundities applicable to our moral life in the middle-brow domestic comedies produced in Hollywood in the 1930s and 1940s. As Hilary Putnam observes in this spirit, the trouble with correspondence theories of truth and reference is not that correspondences between thought and object do not exist, but that "too many correspondences exist" (1981, 72).[4]

Those, however, who privilege "learning about" assume that the sources of meaning have dried up, that our resources are depleted. (If Nabokov or Marquez is the novelist of plenitude, the paradigmatic voice of loss is Samuel Beckett.) Derrida captures the difference when he writes that totalization of meaning is impossible for two different reasons: because of a "finite richness which it can never master. There is . . . more than one can say," or because "there is something missing from it: a center" (1978, 289). "Learning about" would see Cavell's comedies of remarriage as products of what Theodor Adorno called the "culture industry." Fiction delivers meaning only to retract it by explicit self-referentiality or implicit self-contradiction. What one "learns from" "learning about" is the futility of closure. We live and interpret right at the crossing point of the double bind. The condition for knowledge is its impossibility. Thus, though neither those who "learn from" nor those who "learn about" need a "center" or final truth, the spirit in which they engage in "free play" is radically different.[5]

The question is, where does Rorty fit in with these (admittedly oversimple) dichotomous ways of characterizing contemporary thought? Much of his writing belongs to the subgenre of metaphilosophy, a kind of "learning about." Yet this metaphilosophical effort is a ground-clearing effort, a gesture toward "learning from." I take him to mean something like this when he writes: "If anyone really believed that the worth of a theory depends upon the worth of its philosophical grounding, then indeed they would be dubious about physics or democracy. . . . Fortunately almost nobody believes anything of the sort" (1982a, 168).[6] Thus no physicist or social theorist will abandon his or her work just because someone claims that it is philosophically incoherent or self-deconstructing. The "learning from" enabled by first-order theories is not undermined by a deeper "knowing about." Rorty is not a deconstructionist. Only when a theory faces a competitor at the same level of abstraction and subtends the same objects does the practitioner have to be concerned.

It is precisely at this point that pragmatism's double questions become relevant: "What difference does it make?" and "How does it fit with our other beliefs?" Pragmatism offers no metaphysics or epistemology; it is a way of deciding among competing theories and positions. Because we can make all kinds of sense of things, the question is "What do we need or want at this time for a specific set of reasons?" not "Is this theory grounded in empirical or conceptual certainty?" Fascism, for instance, cannot be discredited because it is "wrong" but because it is destructive of the beliefs and practices we hold as characteristic of a decent society. Thus Rorty's position clearly allows the possibility of "learning from." Our traditions of thinking, judging, and acting are useful in coping with the world.

Most important, Rorty suggests that the best way to proceed is by "conversation" among ourselves. The point of the conversation is not to arrive at final answers by means of knockdown arguments, but continually to adjust our position in the light of persuasive counter-proposals from others. Indeed, persuasion, not proof, is what is at issue. This conversational mode can also be seen as a general trope for Rorty's ideal political and social order, one he identifies with "postmodernist bourgeois liberalism" and claims is anticipated by John Dewey, who allows us "hope and solidarity" (1982a, 204). Thus the conversation is not just a means but also an end in itself.

Before moving to Rorty's discussion of the self, it is necessary to address a couple of troubling matters in Rorty's general position, since they reemerge in his discussion of Freud. Here I do not have in mind the self-contradictory nature of Rorty's position, which many have pointed out. Rorty, for instance, eschews any allegiance to a general theory or method, yet advances pragmatism's "cost-accounting terms"—that is, the difference principle and community consensus as ways to determine the worth of a theory. This suggests that Rorty does in fact have a general method for evaluating positions. But whether Rorty's position is self-contradictory or lets foundationalism sneak back in is relatively unimportant. If all texts or positions undermine themselves, there is no reason why Rorty should escape that fate. But there is also no reason why one should dismiss his thought because of that (1982a, 158).[7]

A central tension in Rorty's thought traces back to the two apparently contradictory tendencies in pragmatism—James's emphasis upon the experience of the individual versus the weight Peirce and Dewey placed upon the community of inquirers and actors. The problem is that the Jamesian tendency is deaf to claims of context and content. James's *Varieties of Religious Experience* is a classical illustration. There James enters into a sympathetic relationship with and tries to classify the psychological transformations making up a religious experience. But he ignores the historical context, the institutional constraints or the theological description of that experience. What he never quite grasps is that there is no religious experience as such, no such thing as belief in general. A religious experience is a response to certain determinate demands comprehensible only within a particular historical and institutional context. (James recognized this when he wrote of "live options" in "The Will to Believe.") Nor is it likely that the religious experience is acceded to because it is perceived as somehow making a difference. It may and indeed should make a difference, but that is not the condition of its acceptance. Thus the difference principle is virtually useless as a descriptive account of the way we come to describe certain experiences as religious. For all his sympathetic attention to religious experience, James ended by psychologizing that experience. In so doing he registered a shift in the culture from religious to psychological modes of self-understanding. Along with Freud, James was a progenitor of the "triumph of the therapeutic."

I have mentioned James because Rorty, despite his allegiance to Dewey, often sounds more like James. Rorty devotes little or no time to institutional analyses. In addition, the working psychology he deploys rarely does justice to the specific power of the traditional philosophical (much less religious) beliefs he seeks to undermine. In sum, Rorty's historicist position is remarkably thin as regards institutional determinations or personal experience. Finally, as a self-described "late Wittgensteinian," Rorty wants to be a "therapist" of modern thought, purging us of those beliefs and theories we no longer need.

The questions then become, Is this enough? Can Rorty generate a richer description of the self in context than my initial sketch has so far suggested? Are there resources in the tradition that he (and we) can "learn from" to flesh out his position? This is not to demand of him a new metaphysics. Clearly he resists either the possibility or desirability of such a move, metaphysics being for Rorty whatever fallback positions we adopt to "give the perturbed spirit rest" (1984a, 5). But we do need from him a description of the self (or subject) as it finds itself in or hopes for a satisfactory community of "solidarity" with others. It is to these matters that I now turn.

From the Foundational to the Judging Self

A central theme of recent thought has been the destruction of the traditional notion, running from Plato to Husserl, that the self is metaphysically grounded or epistemologically privileged, that it has some essential nature, or is what Daniel Dennett has called a "pure semantic engine" (1984, 38–43). At the same time the full implications of A. J. Polan's assertion that "ethical humanism is not reduced to a vacuity as an automatic result of the revealed vacuity of philosophical humanism" (1984, 210) must be unpacked. This is another way of saying that a detailed description of the ethical and political— that is, judging—self must be developed in light of the destruction of the foundational self. Can we imagine a serious but uncertain self?[8]

To explore Rorty's position I would like to examine briefly his attack on "mind" and then move to his examination of Freud, since it is on the Freudian terrain that we meet the question of the relationship of the self to political, social, and cultural reality. Before that, however, it is necessary to sketch in competing notions of the self in contemporary thought and locate Rorty provisionally within that debate. Indeed, much of the historical importance of Rorty's work derives from its location at the intersection of the Anglo-American and Continental, specifically French, traditions.[9]

An initial problem is that these two traditions have developed disparate notions of the self, particularly of the judging self. The Anglo-American tradition has been and is firmly individualist. The liberal tradition of ethical and political thought sees the self as either a conscious maximizer of pleasure and pursuer of self-interest or as a rights-bearer. In the civic humanist tradition the self is only fully human as a participant in the public realm, but the presupposition for that participation is the independent and autonomous citizen. Contemporary psychological self-descriptions in this tradition point to much the same thing with their emphasis upon identity, ego-autonomy, and self-realization. As William Connolly has asserted, this political tradition must assume "agents capable of autonomous action, self-restraint and coherence, and worthy, because of these capacities, to be treated as responsible agents" (1983a, 213). They are capable, as Charles Taylor has pointed out, of "second-order desires" and "strong evaluations" (1976, 281–99).[10] Not only do we have desires and needs, but we formulate desires to adjudicate between first-order desires. In general, then, the judging self in the Anglo-

American tradition is a "free" agent who has intentions and is responsible for his or her plans and projects.

On the other hand, the Anglo-American account of the judging self has tended to neglect institutional determinations of the self, the unconscious, and the body. This tradition of ethical and political thought has never taken the hermeneutics of suspicion entirely seriously. Mistakes, misreadings, infelicities, acting at cross-purposes with oneself, deep-seated psychological and social conflicts, all are deviations from the norm rather than inherent in the nature of things. As a result, agency and responsibility seem largely "unearned" so long as there is no recognition of those dimensions of the judging self that escape conscious and individual determination.

Conversely, Structuralist and post-Structuralist thought (along with French Freudianism) has waged a relentless battle against the notion of a foundational self characterized by self-presence and self-constituted meanings. Following from this, what I have called the judging self is decentered and historicized. As Foucault writes, "The individual . . . is not the vis-à-vis of power; it is, I believe, one of its prime effects" (1980, 98). The modern subject is the historical product of discursive formations and practices, and according to Connolly, without "moral or epistemic privilege" (219). Derrida presents a similar, if less specific, view of the self. If subjected to a deconstructive analysis, "the category of intention will not disappear," but "it will no longer be able to govern the entire scene and the entire system of utterances" (1982, 326). Foucault presents us with an iron cage of determination, while Derrida offers a looser context, one that is not "exhaustively determinable" (1982, 327). For neither thinker does the self control his or her judgments or actions.

But though Foucault and Derrida are hostile to the humanism that makes the judging self dependent on the foundational self, they do not claim that human beings are to be abolished. Rather, they want to undermine the traditional understanding of what it means to be a self with intentions, plans, and projects. According to Foucault, essentialist views of the self deny the "otherness" that fails to conform to the given "regime of truth" and sequester "others" who fail to conform to the "regime of power."[11] For Foucault, whose themes are knowledge, power, and the subject, the task is to "constitute a new politics of truth" (1980, 133). But as Taylor has pointed out, Foucault's theoretical emphasis upon the omnipresence of power as a kind of universal solvent seems to render moral or political position-taking by responsible agents useless or incoherent (1984). Nor, since they are not Marxists, have Derrida and Foucault exchanged the individual subject for a collective one—that is, the proletariat—as a possible subject of judgment and action. In different ways, then, neither has a way to talk about or engage in politics except on an ad hoc basis. At best the subject is a "function" (Derrida in Macksey and Donato 1972, 271).

At first glance (indeed, at second and third glances) the two positions would seem to be poles apart, the two universes of discourse—the Anglo-American and the French—scarcely on speaking terms. But in recent years, primarily under the influence of the late Wittgenstein, Anglo-American descriptions of the self have been forced to take into account the context (language games, forms of life) within which the self thinks, speaks, judges, and acts. Wittgenstein provides the nonfoundational foundations for rethinking the self that Saussure and Lévi-Strauss did in France; Thomas Kuhn has pursued lines of thought remarkably similar to Foucault's; and Rorty is doing the English-language work of Derrida. This emphasis upon the social and institutional contexts of thought and action points to the main area of convergence between the two traditions—the necessity of situating and historicizing the self. Seen in this light Derrida's assertion that "I don't destroy the subject, I situate it" (in Macksey and Donato 1972, 271) and Foucault's "the subject (and its substitutes) must be stripped of its creative role and analyzed as a complex and variable function of discourse" (1977, 138) seem relatively benign, not drastically at odds with Anglo-American understandings of the self.[12]

Yet a significant difference, one that is pretheoretical, marks the way in which the two traditions describe the situated self. When the French describe an object as situated or historical, they seem to imply "only" or "merely" situated or historical. To point to the historicity of the self, for instance, is not simply to locate it in time but to point to an insufficiency or lack. This penumbral assumption of something missing in turn indicates a desire for a fixed position, a still point of negativity from which to attack positivity. "Learning about" implies a kind of negative "transcendental" that is impossible to realize. Seen in this way, the melodramatic rhetoric of Foucault and Derrida, trading as it does on metaphors of rupture, abysses, and traces, betrays their nostalgia for metaphysics. "Always already there" is the plaintive sigh of historicity.

For recent ethical and political theorists in the Anglo-American world, however, to be situated historically is not "merely" all we have. Rather, it is all and just what we need. We must be somewhere at some time under certain conditions; only in a situation do our attempts to judge and act make any sense at all. Thus, according to

Taylor, "What is common to all the varied notions of situated freedom is that they see free activity as grounded in the acceptance of our defining situation. . . . This cannot be seen as a set of limits to be overcome" (1979, 160).[13] The unsituated self which claims for an abstract freedom is both impossible and dangerous. This basic recognition of our situatedness does not imply moral or political conformity. To be situated constitutes the possibility of judging and acting.

After this detour one can see how Rorty's notion of the judging self fits well with the notion of the situated self. As he writes: "The moral self . . . [is] a network of beliefs, desires and emotions with nothing behind it. . . . For purposes of moral and political deliberation and conversation, a person just is that network" (1983b, 585–86). Further, this moral self implies "no inferential connection between the disappearance of the transcendental subject—of 'man' as something having a nature which society can repress or understand—and the disappearance of human solidarity" (1982a, 207). Thus Rorty retains the concept of a moral or "judging" self but, along with Derrida and Foucault, rejects the foundational self.

What, then, is Rorty's judging self like? In terms developed in the tradition of philosophy of mind, Rorty agrees with the Ryle-Dennett attack on "mind" as an ontological entity separate from the body, the Anglo-American counterpart of the Husserlian subject, which the French aim to undermine. This mind-body dualism, he claims, is parasitic on the attempts to establish human beings as "knowers" and "agents" as opposed to animals or nonagent actors. Moreover, though Rorty agrees that terms such as "mental states" may be used, he objects to the essentialist line of John Searle that posits "real essences" such as intentionality beyond the "reach of language" in order to distinguish humans from computers. Thus, by rejecting prelinguistic powers, not to mention mind, Rorty clears the way for a judging self without foundational underpinnings (1982b).[14]

Further, though Rorty's position coincides with the French attack on humanism, it is not his view that past traditions or practices are useless or inaccessible, however flawed they may be in light of archaeological or deconstructive readings. Our moral and political self-descriptions derive from these traditions. Though we have no essence, we do have a history. For Rorty, incommensurability between discursive formations (paradigms) does not imply untranslatability but rather the lack of a neutral language or theory to assess truth-claims in either discursive formation (1979, 315–33; 1983a). Traditions, in short, can be mined "for some current purposes." Remembering does not imply nostalgia or loss (1984d, 3).

Freud and the Judging Self

Rorty's present engagement with Freud's thought is significant for several reasons. It marks the first time he has gone "inside" the self to describe its virtual functioning. Second, it represents a chance to see how someone from the Anglo-American tradition confronts a description of the self/psyche that is richer and more complex than the one developed in that tradition. Finally, Rorty's analysis of the Freudian description of the self offers a chance to see the way Rorty does (or does not) make the move from the private to the social, from self-realization to solidarity.

For Rorty, Freud most importantly supplies us with new terms of moral redescription. At issue is not whether Freud is right about human nature, since there is no such thing, but whether he enables us to see ourselves in new ways and to contemplate changing our lives. Despite the fashionable proliferation of Freudian and pseudo-Freudian jargon in everyday life, Rorty suspects that we have not yet fully absorbed the implications of Freud's psychoanalytic theory into our available moral vocabularies.[15] The significance, then, of Rorty's "Freud and Moral Reflection," chapter 1 in this volume, lies in its attempt to explore such issues.

Though full of characteristically sharp questions and insights, Rorty's essay can be broken down into five major points (page numbers refer to this volume).

1. Freud viewed the self not as a "natural kind" but as a mechanism without a center, a mechanical self that is of moral interest, composed of quasi-personages, not smaller mechanisms or corpuscles. (The metaphors quickly get mixed in Rorty's account, but, in one sense, that is his point.) Nor is there any hierarchy of functioning, no one privileged quasi-personage within the self.

2. The Freudian self is a thoroughly private entity, concerned with "self-enrichment" (8) and the "development of character"(10) rather than with public morality or justice. Contrary to conventional wisdom, Freud does not enjoin self-knowledge so much as he does self-alteration, and thus departs from both the Socratic and the Kantian conceptions of morality.

3. The unconscious is not a cauldron of seething passions and impulses, but a complex, systemic "rational" personage that has its own logic and language. This is not to say that it is reasonable in the world's terms but that it is highly creative and "feeds us our best lines" (7). In looking at this point in combination with point 1, we can see how Rorty interprets Freud as denying the traditional linkage

between the rational and the conscious, the irrational and the unconscious.

4. A further implication of points 2 and 3 is that the self engages
in, indeed *is,* a "conversation" among its constituent equal parts. The
ideal result is a nominalistic, ironic persona, able to tolerate ambiguities and live in the world without fixed principles or transcendent
values. Freud is a kind of Kierkegaardian "apostle of this aesthetic
life" (11), less a traditionalist or modernist than a postmodernist.

5. Finally, the self continually attempts to construct a narrative
about its place in the world. This personal narrative is not subsumed
in any master narrative; rather, what is available are larger historical
narratives of movements, causes, and institutions, to any number of
which the self may belong.

The first thing to note is that Rorty's Freud derives from the Freud
offered by Philip Rieff and Alasdair MacIntyre, two of Freud's most
distinguished "conservative" readers.[16] However, though Rorty
accepts Rieff's reading of Freud in particular, he does not agree with
the negative implications for the self or culture that Rieff detects in
Freud's work. Put another way, Rorty's reading of Freud is a quintes-
sentially "liberal" one, a "Jamesian" individualistic account, not a
"Deweyan" communal one. The point I want to develop here is that
Rorty's account of the self as informed by Freud contradicts Rorty's
description of the self (as described here) as situated and contextual-
ized, as making judgments and taking actions in light of the relevant
community of inquiry and action.

The first matter to take up concerns Rorty's claim that Freud was
concerned with the individual, not society—with private, not public,
morality. Following Rieff, this is true in the sense that "psychological
man" is one who takes himself as the object of ultimate concern and
keeps the claims of the larger community at arm's length. But true
though this may be of the ethical preferences of psychological man, it
neglects the prior truth that the self in Freud's account is *au fond*
social. It is constituted and develops only insofar as it finds itself in a
world of others. There is no "one" without "two" or more. Thus,
even our private concerns and judgments have social origins and
implications.

But if the self is socially constituted, it hardly follows, as Rorty says
here, that "Freud, in particular, has no contribution to make to social
theory" (11). (Nor does it follow for Darwin, as Rorty also seems to
imply.)

Rorty confuses the dominant thrust of Freud's therapeutic and
theoretical intentions, his relative indifference to social and political

arrangements, with the implications of Freud's work as they have been developed by others and with the "social foundationalism" implicit in Freud's own work.[17] Rieff's *Triumph of the Therapeutic* is largely devoted to dissecting the attempts of post-Freudian thinkers to develop a normative social and cultural theory that derives from Freud. Rorty (and Rieff) may think that such efforts have been unenlightening or failures, as demonstrated by Rorty's dismissive comments on Adorno's *The Authoritarian Personality.* It is difficult to know what success or failure along these lines would look like. But certainly the work of the Frankfurt School, Wilhelm Reich, Erich Fromm, Paul Goodman, Norman Brown, and Erik Erikson, to name a few, provides prima facie evidence against the irrelevance of psychoanalytic theory for social and political concerns.[18]

To be specific, consider briefly a Freudian concept that Rorty mentions but fails to bring to bear on this point—repression. Surely Rorty would not want to claim that it is a purely descriptive term, for then he would embrace a kind of fact/value, descriptive/normative distinction that he generally scoffs at. Whether one assumes that repression is necessary or assumes that under certain circumstances it can be significantly minimized (Marcuse and sometimes Freud) or abolished (Brown), to use the concept at all implies crucial judgments about the origin, strength, and function of repression. This is the very stuff of normative political and social theory. To talk about repression is implicitly to have a notion of justice as well as of personal self-realization.[19]

Further, Rorty characterizes Freud's domain as concerned with "the portion of morality that cannot be identified with 'culture'; it is the private life, the search for a character, the attempt of individuals to be reconciled with themselves" (11). This strange concept of private morality is a contradiction in terms; rhetorically, it is oxymoronic. No matter what a person might eventually decide—to become a "virtuoso of the self" (Rieff) or to live for others, to become a "rich aesthete" (Rorty, 15) or to mount the barricades—morality is always about more than the self. To ask how it is with one's self is necessarily to ask how it is with others. Rorty's morality of the private self sounds suspiciously like an inverted Kantian adherence to principle ("realize yourself") or, as he admits, a Kierkegaardian aestheticism. But as Alasdair MacIntyre has pointed out, morality is less a matter of adhering to abstract rules than of engaging in various practices of a community, a view that Rorty generally accepts. More pertinently, Rorty's morality of the private self echoes James's emphasis in *Varieties of Religious Experience* on the personal, not the social or institutional, implications of the religious experience. Thus, because Rorty's notion of the self lacks social grounding or implication, it lacks moral weight.[20].

But the real problem with Rorty's analysis is that his separation of private morality from social and political morality depletes rather than enriches our vocabulary of "self-realization" *and* of "justice." No description of the self that neglects the *public* opportunities for self-realization can be considered adequate. It is just this loss of a culture that maintains the connection between communal imperatives and private desires that Rieff associates with the triumph of the therapeutic. Clearly, Rorty does not accept Rieff's (or MacIntyre's) negative evaluation of our cultural situation. Nor do I think he has to entirely. But it is difficult to see how Rorty can accept so much of Rieff's framework without confronting such areas of deep disagreement.

Finally, there is Rorty's account of Freud's description of the internal relationships among the quasi-persons making up the self. As we have seen, the unconscious for Rorty is rational (internally coherent) and creative, a view that bears a certain resemblance to the Lacanian concept of the unconscious. But however old hat the view might be that the unconscious is the seat of the passions, Rorty passes too easily over, or at least radically underplays, the disruptive effects of the unconscious. Here, again, Rorty has opted for the Jamesian position on the unconscious as a largely beneficial repository of creative urges and impulses. Whatever "feeds us our best lines" hardly deserves to be throttled. This is a partial "truth" about the unconscious, but it fails to do justice in Freudian terms to the disruptive effects of the unconscious.

But Rorty's characterization of the unconscious fits well with his larger purpose of seeing the self as made up of "interlocuters" who "offer different versions" of things. However cut off from others Rorty's private self may be, internally it is nothing if not social. And this reminds one in turn of Rorty's favorite trope—the conversation. His description of the internal relations within the self mirrors his social and cultural ideal. Now, Rorty is aware that this view of the self might seem "too sweetly reasonable." But it still needs saying that whatever Freud's description of the self might have been, the *last* thing it resembles is a conversation. Here Rorty posits a false dichotomy—between a nontechnical way of talking about conflicts within the self—for example, "candidates for admission into one's set of beliefs and desires" and "self-description in terms of cathexes, libidinal flow, and the like" (22–23). This is a false dichotomy because there is another Freudian vocabulary that talks of the self in dynamic terms by deploying such terms as censorship, repression, and defense and making use of the trope of hostile and quasi-warlike relations between states to characterize the self's internal relationships. (The last thing a genuine conversation should allow is "censorship.")

Thus, the Freudian description of the relationship among the constituent parts of the self quite often makes use of the language of power not persuasion, of resistance not "admission." It is not just a matter of humanizing what the "tradition thought of as divine inspiration" (8) but of finding a vocabulary consistent with the spirit of Freud's description. As it stands, Rorty takes the bite out of Freud's description of the self. Where Rorty sees a conversationally pluralist self as the basis for an analogous political and cultural order, for Freud, the conflicted self mirrors a conflict-ridden political and cultural order. The pathos of the relationship Freud sees between the individual and the collective consists in the difficulty the self has in participating in the conversation that should be at the center of our common life.

To summarize: in neglecting the social origins or implications of the self, Rorty cuts the self off from an essential dimension of morality and of politics. In redescribing the self's internal constituents in benign form (a move that is much more at odds with Freud's intentions than the distinction between private and public morality is), he trivializes the unconscious and minimizes intrapsychic conflict. The conversational trope offers a worthy social, political, and cultural ideal, but it is hard to figure out how Rorty can get from his description of the self, deriving from *his* Freud, to his ideal of "solidarity." It is to that issue that I now turn.

Solidarity as Discovery and Solidarity as Choice

Though social and political thought was not Rorty's original interest, his recent work has moved in that direction. And though his sympathies lie broadly with the "left," he provocatively (and puckishly) identifies himself as a "postmodernist bourgeois liberal." What this means concretely, according to Rorty, is that there are neither metanarratives (e.g., Marxism) nor metaphysical foundations (e.g., rights-based political theories) that will ground our political preferences and justify our interventions (1983b, 583–89).[21] Rather, Rorty's moral and political thought centers on the ideal of "solidarity." Solidarity, for Rorty, is an attitude that affirms the possibility of locating oneself in a community of thought, judgment, and action and being answerable to that community and its informing traditions. This implies that not all positions, not all world-views, are live options for us. We must, in short, be "ethnocentric." Morality and political judgment are the results of communal, not universal, standards, versions of Hegelian *Sittlichkeit,* not Kantian *Moralität.*[22]

To be more specific, Rorty insists that neither our political institutions nor the regulative concepts of political life, whether conservative, reformist, or revolutionary, are transhistorical or universal. He rejects the notion that "rights" are justifications for our political and legal practices, and instead claims that they are "summaries" of desirable legal and political practices. Within our political culture we should proceed by "convention and anecdote," not by following rules that have alleged metaphysical foundations (1983b, 585, 587). Moreover, Rorty suggests that ethnocentrism is less likely to sanction cultural or political imperialism than claims to transcultural truths or principles. The latter—for example, the laws of history—are forms of rhetorical self-congratulation generated by our culture, ways of claiming we know better. As such, these putative transcultural principles are more likely to "colonize" other cultural communities than would a frank admission of loyalty to our own political and moral principles.

In particular, Rorty has recently attacked intellectuals who refuse to identify themselves with any determinate social or political order for fear of being "coopted." "There is no 'we' to be found in Foucault's writings," he writes, and the result is a "facelessness" in his critical stance (1984b, 40). Americans who justified their opposition to the war in Vietnam by appealing to abstract moral principles prepared the way for a "separat[ion] of the intellectuals from the moral consensus of the nation rather than [altering] that consensus" (1983b, 588). Rorty suggests that the obsession of continental philosophers from Kant through Nietzsche to Habermas with "subjectivity" and "self-grounding" has been of little importance to the men and women engaged in actual political struggle (1984b, 38–39).

All of this is delivered in a kind of throwaway style by Rorty. One objection would be that Rorty fundamentally accepts the basic structures of power in advanced industrial society. This is true in the sense that Rorty believes that in countries where elections and the press are free: "serious politics is reformist" (1985, 584). Foucault, he notes, engaged in efforts at prison reform in France, even though his own analysis suggested that such action reinforced the dominant institutions of power (1984b, 40). Another objection to Rorty's position would be that in contextualizing all political and moral values, he undermines the possibility of a privileged "rational" position from which to criticize existing values or institutions. But Rorty would maintain that no such unsituated vantage point exists. To think otherwise is an illusion. Our ideas of justice come from within our historical situation and are all we have to work with. The charge of relativism implies that someone occupies a "God's-eye view" from which to measure all particular positions. Again, no such view exists, and thus relativism is a red herring. Finally, it might be objected that the use of the term *ethnocentrism* is an unfortunate one, since it evokes a whole history of racism and cultural imperialism that has marked Western culture. There is something to this criticism, but Rorty's point here would be that our tradition of moral and political thought provides the ideas with which to combat such pernicious notions. Generally, traditions must be seen as changing not toward some point of static perfection, but toward diversity and complexity (1983a, 19). The hopes and aspirations of the Enlightenment are worthy ones, but the foundational claim underlying them "isn't doing its job" (1983a, 31).

Still the nagging question remains, how does Rorty get from the Freudian self to a postmodernist bourgeois liberal self—to what I have called the judging self? Or can you get there from here? Does it matter? Even if we accept the broad outlines of Rorty's political and social thinking, he has not made the connection. In the space remaining I would like to sketch in a way of linking the two in a more convincing way than Rorty has achieved.

One answer Rorty might give to the question of how to get from Freud to the judging self would go as follows. Freud's description of the private self, the seeker for self-realization, simply fails to shed any light on the nature of the judging self. That is, how we act privately, what the constitution of the psyche prompts us to do, has no essential connection with our role as citizens. Our self-image as a citizen (or as a revolutionary) does not depend on our self-image as a private self. There is no more contradiction here than between describing a person as a citizen and describing him or her as a collection of molecules. Different descriptions fit different purposes.

This position has been most elegantly set forth in John Rawls's "Kantian Constructivism in Moral Theory" (1980). According to Rawls we must distinguish the conception of the person we assume for the purposes of constituting just political institutions from a general theory of human nature. The former is normative; the latter is descriptive. Rawls assumes, for instance, that the citizen is a "human being capable of taking full part in social co-operation, honoring its ties and relationships over a complete life" (571). But a theory of human nature (or changes in such a theory due to "new" knowledge) is only relevant in reference to our attempts to "imple-ment . . . institutions and policies" (566). Thus, Rawls might say that to discover that human beings do not completely control their intentions or the effects of those intentions should not lead us to jettison the notion of the autonomous agent as crucial for our political institutions or practices. At most it should lead us to design certain institutions or modify certain practices so as to minimize the unfortunate effects of this new discovery. For instance, the insanity plea in criminal cases recognizes an exceptional case to the general assumption of personal responsibility for criminal behavior. But it does not cause us to abandon that assumption.

Now, Rorty would certainly reject the Rawlsian idea that there is such a thing as human nature or that we "discover" any new knowledge about ourselves. He would also reject Rawl's separation of the self and its attributes, since for Rorty the self is only its attributes, intentions, and beliefs. But he might not find Rawl's general argument uncongenial, if it is understood as a refusal to ground our social or political selves in some prior or more firm reality, even if that reality is social rather than ontological.

Yet, neat though this sort of solution might be, it is unsatisfactory. In fact, as we have seen, Rorty implicitly grounds his ideal of the conversation of culture in a psyche that engages in conversation among its constituent parts. Moreover, Freud's description of the private self can and should be linked with a self that makes social and political judgments. Indeed, that judging self can be enriched by Freud's description of the private self, while the private self can be given weight by linking it with social and political roles.

The central idea in such a mutual enrichment is self-narration, one that Rorty explicitly takes from MacIntyre and implicitly from Freud himself. This seems to me precisely the bridging concept between the private and the social self, between self-realization and solidarity. But I would part company with Rorty by claiming that although we construct and reconstruct a narrative of our lives, although we make our own histories, as it were, and become a self in that way, what we *discover* (rather than construct) by this self-narration is the fact that we are not merely externally related to others. Rather, to construct a narrative is to discover that we are always already social beings, that the building blocks of our narratives—our experience, action, values, sense of the world and its possibilities—are derived from the social world. Our narrated/narrating self, which is never fixed or defined once and for all, has social foundations.

This means that solidarity must be thought of on two levels. The first-order sense refers to the fact that our private self is never just private or individual. But later we may consciously choose our partners in solidarity according to shared political, moral, philosophical, and aesthetic preferences. Rorty uses solidarity in this second-order sense of the term. But second-order solidarity is only plausible and given full weight by our registration of the fact of first-order solidarity, that our narrating/narrated self only finds its footing in a world of others. To be sure, there is no automatic move from the realization of first-order solidarity to a second-order solidarity of shared practices and values. But the latter position makes more sense if one is grounded in the notion of first-order solidarity.

Further, and more to the political point, it is not *in spite of* Freud's description of the self as a collection of contentious, defensive personages but because of that "fact" that we need others to whom we can try to narrate our story. In transforming "thing" presentations into "word" presentations, our conflicting impulses are made public, apprehended by others and by ourselves for what they are—often fascinating, usually confusing and disruptive, and sometimes, as Rorty would have it, enriching. In this sense, the analytic situation is a simulacrum of the public space. Its defining condition is power; its optimal destination is conversation among equals. Talk from and about the personal experiences or repressions of the body point by analogy to talk from and about the collective experiences and repressions of the body politic. "Private" interests are articulated and, ideally, brought into line with the "public" interest. This is not to say that all citizens should be psychoanalyzed, and certainly is not to suggest that politics should serve as individual or group therapy. The former is neither possible nor desirable; the latter is a recipe for disaster. But it is to suggest that psychoanalysis provides a kind of anticipatory justification for and model of speaking in public to others.

But it is just on this matter of "publicness" that the analogy between psychoanalysis and the ideal political order breaks down. In one sense, to speak even to one other person is to speak publicly. But in a more traditional sense, speaking in public involves a speaker before an audience of equals concerned with matters having to do with the constitution and survival of the public realm of speech and action. Second, that public speech aims at persuading others to a certain position or course of action.[23] On such matters psychoanalysis has little or nothing to say. As Carl Schorske has noted, psychoanalysis was for Freud an alternative to politics (1980). It did, as Rieff and Rorty insist, valorize the private and cast doubt upon the distinction between acting and "acting out." At best, it might be said that where a successful analysis ends, the possibility of political speech and action begins.

Rorty's notional ideal of a "conversation" is strong where the psy-

choanalytic model is weakest. In its political dimension, "the pragmatic utopia is not one in which human nature is emancipated, but
rather one where each has the chance to propose various ways of
building a world society." "Tolerance rather than emancipation" is its
central value; "persuasion," not "force," is the means to a "free
consensus" of judging selves (1985, 570–71). But as I have indicated,
Rorty's conversation is weak where psychoanalysis is strong—in insist-
ing on the presence of "force" as a factor in speaking to and with
others. And this is true not only in the intrapersonal description of the
self but also in the relationship among individuals, groups, and institutions.

But this criticism is not aimed at any lack of realism on Rorty's
part—that is, that he does not realize that knowledge and power,
theories and institutions, are in fact intimately connected. Rather, it
concerns his utopian ideal, in which persuasion produces and then
maintains a free consensus. As Lyotard has observed: "To persuade is
a rhetorical operation, and the Greeks knew that this operation used
deception, intellectual violence" (582). In response Rorty countered
that the "traditional Greek distinction between rhetoric and logic"
could not be maintained, once the "metanarrative" of "authentic
human emancipation" has been abandoned. The best way to tell
whether persuasion or force characterizes a society is to notice "the
presence or absence of secret police, journalists, television, etc."
Deciding whether "a discourse is free" is not a profoundly philosophical matter but a matter of "examining the multitude of concrete
symptoms of freedom" (Rorty in Lyotard 1985, 584)

Although Rorty's rejoinder to Lyotard is convincing on one level—
freedom is a political and social issue, not a philosophical one—he
does beg several questions of importance. First, freedom is not just a
matter of possessing a status in a legal and political order—the right to
speak freely and participate in the political process. It also involves
having citizens who are capable of persuading and of being persuaded. Thus, freedom has a substantive as well as a formal dimension. Second, Rorty fails to emphasize sufficiently that it is not just a
matter of the number of voices or *what* is said in the cultural and
political conversation but also of *who* says it. The power of institutions
such as journalism and television may shape the conversation in ways
that mystify rather than clarify issues of importance. Finally, the activity of free conversation that arises from the community of free partici-
pants is not self-enforcing and may have to be defended by force.
Until Rorty more fully accounts for and delineates the function of
power and force in our private and public lives, his conversational
ideal will remain abstract and utopian in a negative sense.

Notes

1. I take "public morality," not justice, to be the crucial term here, since the latter has a relatively specific sense in recent political thought.

2. I use Derrida and Foucault as primary points of comparison and contrast with Rorty throughout this essay. In general, Rorty, it seems to me, has more to learn from Foucault than Derrida. Similarly, Rorty comes close to, yet differs importantly from, Jürgen Habermas and Jean-Francois Lyotard. Typically he responds by splitting the difference with his opponents, taking X while rejecting Y.

I am also well aware that the "learning from" / "learning about" dichotomy is an oversimple one, that most thinkers display a mixture of the two, and that each term can be pushed to the point of self-deconstruction, at which point it becomes the other.

3. I am not sure that *pretheoretical* is the right term here. It might be called an *attitude* or something like a *transcendental*. The point is that it is an assumption that is not subject to proof of any sort.

4. See Cavell's fascinating *Pursuits of Happiness.*

5. The Czech novelist Milan Kundera offers a version of this dichotomy in *The Book of Laughter and Forgetting,* where he talks of two different kinds of laughter—one that arises from joy at the plenitude of things and one that ruefully points to the inadequacy of creation (61–62).

6. One might also add: "If anyone really believed that the worth of psychoanalysis depends upon the worth of its metapsychology.. . . ."

7. A standard charge against relativism or historicism is that it is self-contradictory. See, for instance, Putnam, 161. One response would be that a historicist can more easily grant this than a foundationalist, allowing that at some future (or past) time, foundations could be discovered, but not at present. This is not, I think, Rorty's position. His point would be that the pragmatic method is no guarantee of success but the result of a judgment. More generally, Rorty's claim is that the charge of relativism only makes sense from a "God's-eye" perspective; otherwise it carries no weight.

8. I use *judgment* and *judging* throughout to refer to "something we do when we seek to decide about a course of action, that is, in practical deliberation. This calls for *phronesis* or practical wisdom" (Beiner, *Political Judgment,* 7). See also Bernstein, *Beyond Objectivism and Relativism,* and the work of Hannah Arendt. A judgment is neither purely subjective nor deducible from a set of rules. It seeks to establish itself by persuasion, not proof, of correctness and implies a community that exists to be persuaded.

9. I do not specifically address the thought of Habermas or Gadamer here. Both, according to Bernstein, display affinities with Rorty. Also, in France Paul Ricoeur's thought, however stimulating, does assume a foundational subject.

10. See also Harry Frankfurt, "Freedom of the Will and the Concept of a Person." Connolly and Taylor are among the few thinkers in the Anglo-American tradition who address the questions raised by the French.

One major problem with this essentially Kantian language of agency and responsibility is its neglect of other ethical and political values such as courage, friendship, fraternity or solidarity, the common good, and political freedom. Only the civic humanist (republican) tradition, and at times Marxism, attempt to do justice to these other values.

11. The terms here are Foucault's. The best single work on Foucault is Dreyfus and Rabinow, *Michel Foucault.*

12. Most indications are that Derrida and Foucault are (were) rhetorical radicals and practical socialists, much marked by the "events of 1968." See Jean-Francois Lyotard, "Discussion entre Jean-Francois Lyotard and Richard Rorty," for his explanation for the different styles of French and Anglo-American political culture. According to Lyotard the difference traces back to the regicide of 1792 and the omnipresence of the "question of legitimacy" in French political thought. Lyotard's comment came in response to Rorty's wonder at the lack of French support for parliamentary democracy.

13. Besides Taylor and Connolly, this emphasis upon the situated self can be found in Michael Sandel, *Liberalism and the Limits of Justice,* and is paralleled by an emphasis upon the "community" of judgment in Beiner and Bernstein. I am grateful to Professor Richard Flathman of the Johns Hopkins University for introducing me to this line of thinking.

14. For Rorty (as for Dennett), mind is not separable from its attributes and functions and differs in degree, not kind, from the power of computers. It is an "impure" semantic engine.

15. This is Rorty's claim in "Freud, Morality, and Hermeneutics," where he suggests that we resist assimilating Freud's language to our common language of morality and emotion, not because of any dehumanizing effect Freud might have, but because a rephrasing of Freud would obscure what is different in his thought. Further, on first glance, the rise of psychobabble and the therapeutic ethic, beginning in the 1960s as a mass phenomenon, would seem to give the lie to Rorty's claim that we have not yet absorbed Freud's language. Yet the tradition of cultural criticism that emphasizes the triumph of the therapeutic and variations thereon, from Rieff through Christopher Lasch, can be seen as an analysis not only of the hegemony of therapeutic self-descriptions but also of the cooption and corruption by popularization of the psychoanalytic language game.

16. By "conservative" I mean a position emphasizing the importance of stable structures of cultural authority and a distrust of the ethics of self-realization. For MacIntyre's position see *After Virtue.* Rieff's readings of Freud can be found in *Freud: The Mind of the Moralist, Triumph of the Therapeutic,* and *Fellow Teachers.*

17. "Social foundationalism" is the phrase William Connolly uses to suggest the conformist cast to Rorty's position. The term is useful, but Connolly's judgment is overly harsh in reference to Rorty's work as a whole. It is more apt in reference to Rorty's lecture on Freud. See Connolly, "Mirror of America" (132).

18. See Paul Robinson, *The Freudian Left,* and Richard King, *The Party of Eros,* for analyses of several of these figures.

19. A similar line of analysis would certainly apply to the concept of culture. It is not a value-neutral term, however it is defined.

20. For MacIntyre on morality see *After Virtue,* chaps. 16 and 17. I should emphasize that I am not denying that it may be necessary to take one's self into

primary account on certain occasions. Such a decision may even have a significant political dimension, if it is directed against some all-pervasive social or political power that threatens to destroy the private sphere or sense of individual self altogether. This is a dominant theme of Milan Kundera's fiction. Still, the fact remains, I think, that the self is social in origins and its choices involve it necessarily with others. If Rorty wants to defend a line of thought like the one I have sketched in here, then he is uncharacteristically obscure on the matter.

21. What Rorty takes from Lyotard is the concept of "metanarrative," which refers to any view of history in terms of an origin, subject (whether individual or collective), or goal. As Lyotard says, "We have paid enough price for the nostalgia of the whole" (1984, 80). It should be said that no one has believed in metanarratives outside of France for years. Indeed, one would have assumed that Albert Camus's work was nothing if not directed against the pernicious ethical and political influence of metanarratives.

22. These positions are developed in Rorty's "Relativism" and "Habermas and Lyotard on Post-Modernity."

23. This formulation concerning political speech is drawn generally from Hannah Arendt's thought, especially *The Human Condition.*

References

Arendt, Hannah. *The Human Condition.* Garden City, N.Y.: Doubleday Anchor, 1959.

Beiner, Ronald. *Political Judgment.* London: Methuen, 1983.

Bernstein, Richard. *Beyond Objectivism and Relativism.* Oxford: Basil Blackwell, 1983.

Cavell, Stanley. *Pursuits of Happiness.* Cambridge, Mass.: Harvard University Press, 1981.

Connolly, William. *The Terms of Political Discourse.* 2d ed. Oxford: Martin Robertson, 1983a.

———. "Mirror of America." *Raritan,* 3 (Summer 1983b): 124–35.

Dennett, Daniel. *Elbow Room.* Oxford: Clarendon Press, 1984.

Derrida, Jacques. "Structure, Sign, and Play." In Derrida, *Writing and Difference.* Chicago: University of Chicago Press, 1978.

———. "Signature Event Context." In Derrida, *Margins of Philosophy.* Chicago: University of Chicago Press, 1982.

Dreyfus, Hubert, and Rabinow, Paul. *Michel Foucault.* Chicago: University of Chicago Press, 1982.

Foucault, Michel. *Language, Counter-Memory, Practice.* Edited by Donald Bouchard. Ithaca, N.Y.: Cornell University Press, 1977.

———. *Power/Knowledge.* Edited by Colin Gordon. New York: Pantheon, 1980.

Frankfurt, Harry. "Freedom of the Will and the Concept of a Person." *Journal of Philosophy* 68 (1971): 5–20.

James, William. *Varieties of Religious Experience.* New York: Collier Books, 1961.

King, Richard. *The Party of Eros*. Chapel Hill: University of North Carolina Press, 1972.

Kundera, Milan. *The Book of Laughter and Forgetting*. New York: Penguin, 1981.

Lyotard, Jean-Francois. *The Postmodern Condition*. Minneapolis: University of Minnesota Press, 1984.

———. "Discussion entre Jean-Francois Lyotard and Richard Rorty." *Critique* 41 (1985): 581–84.

MacIntyre, Alasdair. *After Virtue*. Notre Dame, Ind.: University of Notre Dame Press, 1981.

Macksey, Richard, and Donato, Eugenio, eds. *The Structuralist Controversy*. Baltimore: Johns Hopkins Press, 1972.

Polan, A. J. *Lenin and the End of Politics*. London: Methuen, 1984.

Putman, Hilary. *Reason, Theory, and History*. Cambridge: Cambridge University Press, 1981.

Rawls, John. "Kantian Constructivism in Moral Theory." *Journal of Philosophy* 77 (1980): 515–72.

Rieff, Philip. *Freud: The Mind of the Moralist*. Garden City, N.Y.: Doubleday Anchor, 1961.

———. *Triumph of the Therapeutic*. New York: Harper & Row, 1966.

———. *Fellow Teachers*. New York: Harper & Row, 1973.

Robinson, Paul. *The Freudian Left*. New York: Harper & Row, 1969.

Rorty, Richard, ed. *The Linguistic Turn*. Chicago: University of Chicago Press, 1967.

———. *Philosophy and the Mirror of Nature*. Princeton: Princeton University Press, 1979.

———. "Freud, Morality, and Hermeneutics." *New Literary History* 12 (1980): 177–85.

———. *Consequences of Pragmatism*. Minneapolis: University of Minnesota Press, 1982a.

———. "Contemporary Philosophy of Mind." *Synthese* 53 (1982b): 323–48.

———. "Relativism." Howison Lecture, Berkeley, Calif., January 31, 1983a.

———. "Postmodernist Bourgeois Liberalism." *Journal of Philosophy* 80 (1983b): 583–89.

———. "Signposts along the Way that Reason Went." *London Review of Books* 6 (February 16–29, 1984a): 5–6.

———. "Habermas and Lyotard on Post-Modernity." *Praxis International* 4 (April 1984b): 32–44.

———. "What's It All About?" *London Review of Books* 6 (May 16–June 6, 1984c): 3–4.

———. "Deconstruction and Circumvention." *Critical Inquiry* 11 (September 1984d): 1–23.

———. "Le Cosmopolitanisme sans Emancipation: En Réponse à Jean-Francois Lyotard." *Critique* 41 (1985): 569–80, 584.

Sandel, Michael. *Liberalism and the Limits of Justice*. Cambridge: Cambridge University Press, 1982.

Schorske, Carl. "Politics and Patricide in Freud's *Interpretation of Dreams.*" In Schorske, *Fin de Siècle Vienna.* New York: Alfred A. Knopf, 1980.

Taylor, Charles. "Responsibility for Self." In Amelie Rorty, ed., *Identities of Persons.* Berkeley and Los Angeles: University of California Press, 1976.

———. *Hegel and Modern Society.* Cambridge: Cambridge University Press, 1979.

———. "Foucault on Freedom and Truth." *Political Theory* 12 (1984): 152–83.

3 Primitive Guilt

Joseph H. Smith

Many elements of the conventional vocabulary of moral deliberation are largely alien to the psychoanalytic lexicon. *Moral, ethical, virtuous, righteous,* and their opposites are words that seldom appear in the theory or the clinical dialogue. We do work with envy, jealousy, guilt, and reparation, but even so central a concept as guilt tends to have a special technical (and essentially nonmoral) meaning. The concept usually refers not to guilt as such but to a failed capacity to experience guilt. This failure occurs in the depressive whose "guilt feelings" are more a desperate effort to placate tenuously internalized parental objects, and in the sociopath who is seemingly heedless of them and thus unburdened, at least overtly, by either guilt or guilt feelings.

It is similar with *right* and *wrong.* These are general terms that have application in many regions where they carry either the meaning that something works or does not work or the morally neutral meaning of correct or incorrect. The analysand may present a moral dilemma, but the analyst's interpretation is either correct or incorrect, even though, if correct, the interpretation may be a significant step in clarifying the moral dilemma.

Overtly—with the large exception that the analyst practices what he or she does not preach—the analyst's position is morally neutral. By overlooking this exception and the reasons for it, psychoanalysts can be taken as passively fostering the notion that, morally, anything goes. This popular interpretation is an essentially uninteresting trivialization of the meaning of analytic neutrality.[1] It is aided and abetted by a similarly popular understanding of Freud's account of how repressed sexuality and aggression enter into civilization and its discontents and by a simplistic understanding of psychic determinism (Smith 1978).

The analyst is neutral not only about moral decisions but also about what is correct or incorrect regarding decisions the analysand faces in any region. On several counts, neutrality here does not mean passivity. One purpose of neutrality is to ensure that all sides of a conflict gain a hearing. Thus the analyst's position is, as Anna Freud put it, equidistant from the id, ego, and superego, a stance that the analysand also gradually assumes. A more encompassing purpose and a prime source of the dramatic tension in the dialogue is that the analyst's neutrality and abstinence signal from the beginning a respect for the analysand's developing autonomy. The analytic situation is charged by the fact that at the same time that it invites regression and dependency, it points toward separateness and independence. The analyst not only does not take sides in conflict but also signals from the start that the final arbiter regarding decisions as to how the analysand's life will be conducted will always be the analysand. The work of the analyst is directed toward enhancing the analysand's capacity to decide on the basis of a maximum understanding of himself or herself and the situation—an understanding that derives primarily from the mutual work of clarifying the relationship between analyst and analysand.

The Analytic Attitude

One consequence of analytic neutrality is that the analyst's concept of health does not occupy center stage. It is implicitly conveyed in general form as Freud's characterization of health as the capacity to love and to work through the attention given to inhibitions and symptoms that hamper these capacities. But the work is guided by the latter, beginning with the analysand's chief complaint. Analysts do not tell analysands what they ought to be concerned about but join them in the clarification of what they are concerned about, including their moral dilemmas.

Of course, this position would be taken by many as an ethical stance and, ultimately, it may be motivated by concepts of what is good and what is healthy in the culture of both analyst and analysand. However, at least proximally, the analyst's position is not determined by such considerations but by the understanding that whatever symptoms the analysand presents constitute his or her best effort at the moment to deal with dangers so far as the analysand's psychic reality is concerned—dangers as yet consciously unknown to both analysand and analyst. What appears to the observer as malfunction may be, for a time, the best possible solution. How it is that some set of symptoms constitutes such a solution is the issue to be investigated. The clarity that ensues allows leeway for the analysand to find other and better solutions. Thus the proximal motive for the analytic stance or attitude (Schafer 1982) is that it is right in the sense that it works. It has been found to be correct for the task at hand.

The task at hand, the alleviation of individual suffering by means of a one-to-one dialogue, and the analytic stance that facilitates the accomplishment of the task, are cardinal points to bear in mind regarding interpretations of Freud and psychoanalysis. The fact that psychoanalysis is not proximally guided by precepts of health but by whatever is of concern to the analysand allows for both variousness of application and variousness of interpretation. With this purpose and this stance in mind, Rieff's assertion, for instance, that Freud "wanted merely to give men more options than their raw experience of life permitted. . . . He had no interest in creating a doctrine of the good life, nor one of the good society. . . . Freud's object was personal capacity, not general cure" (1966, 57), can be read as true to Freud's task—as Rieff, I think, meant it to be read—rather than a veiled criticism of his negligence of another possible task.

Because of its variousness of application and interpretation, psychoanalysis may, at times, foster an aesthetic way of life, as Rorty suggests in the essay in this volume. But, depending on the individual, it may also at other times foster development of the purity of heart to will one thing, a Kierkegaardian notion that Rorty refers to in the same article. Effectively pursuing either direction would require an individual to be relatively unhampered by symptoms—to have worked through, for instance, the depressive tendencies associated with primitive guilt that I shall here consider. Psychoanalysis does not prescribe values, goals, or a way of life. It enhances the capacity of persons to choose such. However, to have greater freedom is not necessarily to have a greater number of "options" in crucial matters. The capacity for neurotically unhampered choice is the capacity to strive more clearly for the *right* choice, not only in regard to one's desires and potentialities but also in the light of one's dominant values (Smith 1978).

The foregoing has outlined reasons for believing that the impact of psychoanalysis on the vocabulary of moral deliberation is more a measure of its stance and the clinical theory of technique that justifies that stance than it is of its specific interpretations or its general theory. It is a point that an intellectualized reading of Freud's case histories and his general theory can easily miss. Interpretations are responsive to particular analysands. In content, they are morally neutral, as is the general theory. One cannot look to psychoanalysis for answers to the question of what the good life would be. Psychoanalysis invariably turns the question back into something like "let us see if we can better understand what hinders you from leading a life that you would consider good." Nor can one summarize some consensus of the good life that runs across the way people live after they and their analysts agree the treatment is no longer required, and take that to be the notion of health that psychoanalysis advocates. At best, what one would get from that would be whatever could be said about the way most people who seem reasonably happy and fulfilled in our culture live their lives. But individuals get nowhere trying to model themselves directly on any such consensus. They must start where they are with whatever ails them and with whatever constitutes their own idiosyncrasies and see what they can do with that. One could rightly look upon beginning in that way as an implicit precept of the analytic stance.

Genesis and the Varieties of Guilty Experience

Let me begin again. How can psychoanalysis be taken as morally neutral when its stance steadily fosters automony in the sense of separateness, self-definition, being responsible, and being able to love and work? Furthermore, where is moral neutrality in all those texts that speak of pathological guilt, a pathological absence of guilt, failed guilt in the form of guilt feeling, criminals from a sense of guilt, the negative therapeutic reaction, archaic superegos, superegos corrupted by the id, the ego as sycophant and liar, and so on? What did Freud mean when he wrote to Putnam, "I do not agree with Socrates and Putnam that all our faults arise from confusion and ignorance" (in Jones 1955, 182)? How are we to understand from the last page of his dream book the reference to "the much trampled soil from which our virtues proudly spring" (S.E. 5:621)? Would not taking a bearing from all these vantage points bring into view a clear concept of what is good and what is healthy that psychoanalysis particularly advocates? Is not this talk of neutrality only pretense or self-delusion covering an attempt by psychoanalysts to influence analysands in the direction of conforming to the model of whatever we or our culture extol as the good life? Furthermore, even in the absence of such texts, is not identification of the child with parent and the analysand with analyst surely an important determinant of what sort of person the child or analysand becomes, no matter how much the analyst, say, attempts to veil his or her own values?

As for the last question, the answer can only be yes. But there is a difference in parent or analyst making himself or herself available for identification, on the one hand, out of love and respect for the development of another person, and, on the other, out of the narcissistic motive to shape the other in one's own image to the detriment of the child's or the analysand's separateness and autonomy. In the latter case, difference in the other tends to be neither acknowledged nor affirmed. The neutrality of the former means the kind of love that allows one to be available and at the same time free of any impulse to jump in and take over.

As for moral neutrality generally, the question is what would a morally neutral study of morality be? When Freud responded to the question of the dreamer's responsibility for his or her dreams by saying, in effect, "Who else would be?" (*S.E.* 4:133; see also *S.E.* 5:620), he was not telling us that we *ought* to be responsible but just that we are. My dreams are mine, just as is my morality or the lack thereof.

Psychoanalytic narratives tend to be narratives of genesis, so my beginning again might as well be the beginning. One can reasonably assume that the forerunners of any moral sense of right or wrong are, in the infant, states of satisfaction (fulfillment, safety, and bliss), in which things are "right," and states of need (discomfort, danger, panic, and potential death), in which things are "wrong." This is the beginning polarity in which, no doubt, all of our currently much criticized proclivity for dualistic thinking is rooted. It maintains a claim at every level. As basic context for all that is constructed, it persists through every deconstructive move. In this primitive sense, good and evil are introduced as the context for understanding the development of the drives, ego functions, and the superego—that is, of everything. The urgency of adult specifically moral concerns derives from the infant's states of danger and the infant's imperative need for satisfaction.

Brickman (1983) has reviewed the psychoanalytic literature on the preoedipal development of the superego. I shall attempt here to add to that some outline of how the moral sense might arise from the viewpoint of the need/satisfaction polarity. But having touched on genesis, let me frame that discussion by going directly to one further way in which the most advanced shape of that sense comes back to its beginning. In early childhood "things being wrong" tends to be interpreted as "I am bad," and specifically in the eyes of one's parents. With the oedipal consolidation of the superego and the internalization of parental values, a gradual depersonification (Freud, *S.E.* 20:223) begins. The voice of conscience is no longer a parental one. Except in moments of moral crisis, the sense of urgency and danger is diminished or absent. One lives out values that have been made one's own without even thinking about them. In this more neutral mode wrongdoing is not experienced only as badness, but partakes of the original wrong as unfitting, incorrect, at odds with one's dominant values. Acts that are at odds may be rejected, specially justified, or require a revision of the dominant values. In any event, the gradient in the process of superego depersonification is in the direction of this more neutral self-appraisal.

Neutral here implies a maximum openness to reality from id, ego, and superego points of view, in the service of self-preservation in the sense of preserving the developed and developing self (Fingarette 1963; Modell 1984). Neutral does not necessarily mean unimpassioned. Although it is true that our conduct is ordinarily guided by our dominant values in effortless, uncharged fashion, in a moral crisis a person confronts the possibility that one can self-destruct in ways other than by actual suicide. Too often we are guided by the usually reliable rule of thumb that affective intensity is a measure of regression—of a person out of the driver's seat and taken over by id or superego factors and primary process functioning. But some dilemmas remain as highly charged dilemmas even after a maximum openness to all sides of a question has been achieved, which is to say that some dilemmas are real dilemmas and not just states of mind suffered because one does not rightly understand the situation. The urgency that characterizes such crises in the preservation of the self is modeled on the urgency that basically characterizes biological self-preservation.

Such dramatic crises are overt manifestations of the covert ongoing dramatic tension in development or in an analysis. Accounts of development and analysis are, among other things, stories of the achievement of separateness or the lack thereof, narratives of mutual letting-go in relatively successful or unsuccessful fashion. There is a master-slave element in this struggle, just as there is between every parent and child and every in and out group. The conflict is universal, in us and between us. To be aware of it is what I am calling a neutral position. What we do about it or how we deal with it involves action or inaction that will reflect our moral and political decisions and stance.

In the following pages I consider this conflict with respect to both development and analysis from the point of view of how guilt and guilt feelings enter into it, beginning with a discussion of peripheral awareness and inner awareness of awareness.

Awareness and Awareness of Awareness: Piaget, Chomsky, and Freud

Stern (1983) has shown that the neonate has, along with a striking number of other capacities, a remarkable prewired competence to differentiate the mother from others by smell, sound of voice, or

appearance. This has led Stern to question the idea of an undifferentiated and symbiotic phase of development. It is my assumption, however, that this competence of the infant is of a different order from the
differentiation achieved at eight months or that which is marked by
the advent of language and object constancy (Smith 1983b, 29). such
early competence would be a part of the cognitively unconscious
knowledge stressed by Piaget (1973) and Chomsky (1978). Its demon-
stration is an additional bit of hard evidence that the infant's mind is
not a tabula rasa. No doubt this level of awareness has some guiding
role in the development of awareness of awareness (Rapaport 1957,
329), but it is the latter and the structural development that allow for
such awareness of awareness that is at stake so far as development of
the self is concerned. As for how that development comes about one
must still rely, in large part, on assumptions based on inferences from
states of regression. Although the neonate demonstrates prewired,
reflex "knowledge" of who the mother is, there is much reason to
believe that this "knowledge" occurs and is effective without the
infant having or needing to have any awareness that it possesses this
competence. Knowledge comes to be experienced as "my" knowledge through the establishment of an I. In this regard, one assumes
an undifferentiated, symbiotic state from which the self-object differentiation is gradually established.

One takes the content of prelinguistic thought or ideation (as
opposed to perception) to be, as in dreams, images—presumably in
infancy, fragmentary images—of what in later development will come
to be known as absent objects of need or interest. Even though the
infant's world is as yet without temporal dimensions and without
differentiation of self and object, one can infer that the direction of
thought is toward the object and, since this is based on the memory of
a prior satisfaction, that the object, as it comes into view, has a
positive valence. In brief, consciousness begins in some form of awareness of the hoped-for object and not with the self or with the inner
sources or mechanisms of mind (Smith 1976, 149). So far as ideation
is concerned, a "silent" lack or need evokes a wish for the object. The
lack or need itself is not in focus ideationally but is manifested by the
affective distress at critical moments. Inner need evokes hope for the
object because need is a danger.

Prior to any capacity for defensive splitting, and certainly prior to
any capacity for being morally good or bad, the infant and his or her
world just *is* either right or wrong, good or bad. But, since awareness
is evoked by inner need as a danger, what is inner—the locus of what
will eventually be the established self—first comes into view with a

negative valence (Smith 1980, 394). Let us call this state, prior to any capacity for wrongdoing, original guilt.

The preceding two paragraphs contain the basic assumption to be elaborated herein. Before proceeding to the possible implications for the adult, one might pause to consider the grounds for assuming that from the primitive either/or, good *or* bad, undifferentiated self-object, arises first a partially differentiated self more associated with the bad and a partially differentiated object more associated with the good. Is it reasonable to assume, that is, that this would precede and, as I will also assume, in some way mark the fully differentiated position that is characterized (ideally, anyway) by an awareness of self as both good *and* bad and of the object as both good *and* bad?

This small question has, of course, large precedents and large consequences. As for the precedents, the issue is whether this is a way to investigate the question that might open options between or other than the received truths of either the Greek or Judeo-Christian sources of Western thought—that is, between or other than the Greek doctrine that any problem of ethics is only a problem of ignorance that calls for enlightenment and the Judeo-Christian doctrine of original sin that calls for salvation.

When the question is placed in that context a large part of my own response—and I assume that of most of my colleagues—is to want to turn away, get back to work in my own field, and leave such issues for the philosophers and theologians. As Freud mentioned in the letter to Putnam cited earlier (in Jones 1955, 182), analysis cannot do everything. It should achieve a unity but not necessarily make people good. And in so writing Freud dissociated his project from both the Socratic (overcoming ignorance need not yield goodness) and the Judeo-Christian.[2]

However, the matter was more complicated than that. In other places Freud wrote of two reasons for being good—one where Eros prevailed and the other, much less reliable, based on fear of authority. It was in Freud's nature, that is, to disclaim any effort to make people good, but it was also in his nature not to flinch from the observation that fortunate development (or successful analysis) results in a more reliable ethical stance. Finally, it was in his nature to leave it to us to ponder the real or apparent inconsistency.

This might, at least, give the psychoanalyst reason to think that, in getting back to work, one might find that some of what one knows or discovers could be pertinent even to so large a context. The experiments designed in current research to "ask questions" of preverbal and even neonatal events, referred to here earlier, yield information and provide the model for further information about both the infant's knowledge and affective experience. It may become possible to ask questions about the possibility of a partially differentiated phase with a tendency toward experiencing the self as bad and the object as good.

Much of the remainder of this chapter is an effort to marshal the evidence as to whether our present knowledge and beliefs provide sufficient grounds for the assumption of such a possibility. The obvious basic principles here are that development is from the simple to the more complex and that conscious realization—with the exception of affect—begins with a more peripheral focus. The neonate "knows" the mother by smell and sight but not yet itself even on that simple basis, and not yet that the mother and itself are separate entities. Similarly, it seems reasonable to assume that primitive affective experience is simple in the sense of either good *or* bad prior to the capacity to experience more differentiated and complex affects.

The peripheral focus of early conscious knowledge, already mentioned, should be fully specified, because that is the main framework to which I wish to tie the assumption of a differential gradient in affective response toward experiencing the object (or preobject) as good and the self (or preself) as bad. *Tie,* however, is too strong a word because it might suggest an effort to coordinate cognitive knowledge with affect, value, aesthetics, and ethics in a way that has defied, to date, all science and all philosophy. The effort is instead to take some small steps toward highlighting how the capacity for gradually more differentiated affect response might follow and be made possible by development from primitive to more advanced thought and structure.

So far as conscious knowledge is concerned, its peripheral focus appears to be a point of interdisciplinary agreement. Piaget (1965) wrote: "Conscious realization starts from the peripheral result of actions before turning to their inner mechanism, which, moreover, it never completely attains" (47–48). This is not to say, of course, that concepts derive purely from perception, but that the schemas and complex structuring upon which they evolve come to be known only later and partially (see 51, 54, 56, 57–58, 60, 108, 134)—that is, "Consciousness proceeds from the periphery to the center and not inversely" (135). In such conscious realizations "we perceive at first the intentions and results of acts before being able to grasp their complete mechanism" (160).

At the level of language acquisition and use the whole gist of Chomsky's understanding parallels the idea of the relative inaccessibility of complex mental acts underlying actual performance (e.g.,

1968, 26, 43, 103, 173). Of course, *any* consciousness of one's language is self-reflective knowledge, but what comes first in such performance is language applied to external objects and events. Saying "me" comes later and, though a person through introspection "may accumulate . . . evidence . . . determined by the rules of the language . . . there is no reason to suppose that he can go much beyond this surface level . . . so as to discover, through introspection, the underlying rules and principles" (103–4).

The correlative Freudian passages are in the seventh chapter of *The Interpretation of Dreams*. The first of these is of particular interest because it attributes a peripheral focus to consciousness with, primitively, the single exception of inner excitations of pleasure and unpleasure.

> Consciousness . . . is capable in waking life of receiving excitations from two directions. In the first place, it can receive excitations from the periphery of the whole apparatus, the perceptual system; and in addition to this, it can receive excitations of pleasure and unpleasure . . . [from] the inside of the apparatus. All other processes in the ψ-systems, including the *Pcs.*, are lacking in any psychical quality and so cannot be objects of consciousness, except in so far as they bring pleasure or unpleasure to perception. (*S.E.* 5:574; passages also in accord with those of Piaget and Chomsky are on 611 and 615–16).

Although certain portions of these formulations by Piaget, Chomsky, and Freud are debatable, they reflect, at a minimum, a general consensus regarding development from the simple to the complex both in thought and affect, together with a primitive peripheral focus of consciousness, with the exception of affect. This, then, is the framework. The remainder of this article attempts to justify within this framework that affective development proceeds from primitive either/or experience through a phase in which the good is associated with the evolving object and the bad with the evolving self.

Origins of the Self as Guilty

What has been called primitive guilt in the preceding paragraphs, from an adult point of view, could be only guilt feeling (though not, as in the adult, defensive guilt feeling) and not guilt. It is indigence—neediness—and not wrongdoing. But from an infant's point of view, these are differences that cannot make a difference. They are differences that can only be sorted out in later development. Through that development, the child harbors, I am suggesting here, a mostly silent suspicion of inner badness that goes beyond any actual wrongdoing in deed or fantasy. Even the preoedipal and oedipal fantasies of murder and incest may, in some measure, already represent the child's involvement in fantasied criminality from a sense of guilt. The lack of differentiation together with original guilt constitutes the child's negative grandiosity in the form of a readiness to believe that anything bad that happens in the child's world is because of his or her badness.

I have argued that the either/or, good/bad nature of primitive experience means that affective response involves no gradation of good or bad attributable to either self or object. As self-object differentiation proceeds, the good is more associated with the fulfilling object and the bad initially more with the developing self. Gradually the infant, by internalizing aspects of the relationship with the object, also achieves a sense of its own goodness and is on the way toward a tolerance for ambivalence and variousness in seeing itself and its object as both good and bad in a variety of ways. But the structure of the relationship between the self and its objects is such that parity is never fully achieved. A bias toward experiencing the self as bad and the object as good remains. Needs, whether cyclical or ongoing, are always there, and wished-for objects are "good" because they promise satisfaction of needs.

With fortunate development, needs are no longer primarily experienced as danger. Indigence can be acknowledged as such without a sense of badness. But most of us achieve this only imperfectly. At some level, we remain marked by the primitive tendency to respond in moments of regression to any misfortune with guilt. The issue then becomes whether such moments of regression trigger depression or some other defense or whether they can be in the service of the ego. In the latter case, such moments signal the necessity for scanning the possibility or degree of one's personal responsibility for misfortune as a basis for decisions regarding future conduct. If one's defenses were such as to preclude all such regressive moments simply because they are regressive, it would not mean a better but a less adequate attunement to one's situation.

This line of reasoning would suggest that original undifferentiated negative affect, the precursor of all affect that will subsequently signal or signify negative experience, is marked at the start of self-object differentiation by a tendency toward the guilt feeling experienced by the adult depressive. Study of the structure of depression should shed light on guilt and guilt feeling as universal aspects of development and the variety of defensive and nondefensive modes of guilt mitigation or atonement. That is, even though the guilt feeling of the adult depressive may be the closest analogue to original guilt in the infant, if such primitive guilt is, as I have argued, a universal, then it is an issue in every person's development, whether toward normality or toward any of the psychiatric syndromes, and, thereby, a task to be confronted and reworked in every analysis. It would be important background for understanding the depressive position but would also be there earlier as an influence in primitive projections and introjections. The grandiose self or idealized object of narcissistic disorders derives partly from the normal narcissism consequent to infantile experiences of satisfaction and bliss, but grandiosity and idealization become fixed as disorder by virtue of an unrepaired defensive tendency to turn away from lack, danger, and the self as indigent even as the self is being constituted. The intensity of such fixed grandiosity or idealization is a measure of the intensity of guilt and danger being thus warded off. Inattention to this meaning of grandiosity and idealization has marred our understanding of the source and intensity of narcissistic rage (Smith, Pao, and Schweig 1973, 343) and of depressive narcissistic despair consequent to the breakdown of these defenses.

These speculations go counter to the usual understanding of Freud's pleasure ego (*S.E.* 12:223–24; *S.E.* 14:134, 136), wherein everything pleasurable is introjected and everything painful is projected. But Freud also wrote of "the original 'reality-ego' " (*S.E.* 14:136) that "cannot avoid feeling internal instinctual stimuli for a time as unpleasurable" (135). It is this original reality-ego that, in his 1915 view, "changes into a purified, pleasure-ego" (136), that in turn undergoes subsequent modification into the reality ego we ordinarily think of (*S.E.* 12:224). Hartmann's ideas on broad and narrow reality principles (1939, 43–45; 1956, 33) carry a similar meaning, as does Piaget's assertion that what is censured "is never unconscious except with the subject's connivance" (1965, 135).

I don't want to press my own, or Freud's, or Hartmann's, or Piaget's speculations too far—only far enough to suggest it is plausible that that from which all grandiosity and idealization stem is an unconsciously registered unpleasure or pain that has a role in eventually marking the inner as inner. Obviously, my argument does not amount to an airtight case. Unpleasure or pain is inner, but so is pleasure. Besides, in the purely undifferentiated state there is no inner or outer anyway. Again, it seems to me reasonable, notwithstanding all the lack of clear-cut boundaries, that as these boundaries form and the undifferentiated state changes to a partially differentiated state, inner pleasure is associated with fantasied wish fulfillment or actual gratification and thus with the fantasied or real objects of gratification, and unpleasure with an unfulfilled or ungratified wish or desire, tied to a need that constitutes actual danger.

The Mitigation of Guilt

No doubt certain individuals are genetically predisposed toward a heavier burden of guilt feeling than others. However, we must assume, until or unless it is proven otherwise, that not all such predisposed persons fall ill with depression as the most direct adult analogue of primitive guilt feeling. In the main, reasonably good parenting should mitigate original guilt. To understand how this mitigation is effected or not effected, or even to understand fully the nature of genetic predisposition, would be to understand what ails or hinders the achievement of the differentiation and integration that allow for the tolerance of ambivalence toward the self and object. Such tolerance would involve a sense of the self and object as separate, each both good and bad, and thus a sense of agency that allows for experiencing guilt consequent to wrongdoing but in a world where good and bad are never total and thus in a world with hope of reparation. What evidence we currently have of genetic predisposition is as yet very gross in the sense of being tied directly to the outcome of depressive illness. We do not yet have information about how such predisposing factors might interfere with specific aspects of development that could otherwise be reasonably expected to mitigate guilt feeling.

At the same time, such specific understanding from a psychological point of view is similarly lacking. Eventually, discoveries along these lines in the field of either neurobiology or psychology will no doubt focus research in the other field. What can reasonably be assumed from a psychological point of view is that one factor that determines the extent to which original guilt is mitigated, regardless of degree of predisposition, depends on the ratio of good to bad experience early in life. Repeated and prolonged experience of intense need can result in marasmus and infantile death. Short of this extreme, neglect can hamper development in a number of ways.

When need is at a peremptory level less learning goes on. Attention is riveted on images of the object of need in an atmosphere of danger or panic. Introjections and projections are on an emergency basis. By contrast, the capacity to regard the object (and later the self) in terms of aspects not immediately related to intense need is possible in the wake of need satisfaction. The nonperemptory mode allows for internalization of aspects of the relationship with the object (or whatever goes in that direction prior to the establishment of boundaries between self and object) in something like an optional rather than an enforced mode. It is learning in this mode that goes toward the establishment of boundaries and the structuring of the object and the self as separate in a context of trust.

When the peremptory mode dominates too much in development, identifications wrought in emergencies tend to persist in the form of archaic and punishing precursors of the superego. But also persisting is too large a quotient of the primitive sense of badness, wrongness, or deficit, not just as a consequence of having an archaic superego, but as the sense of badness that preceded and evoked the primitive identifications—the badness that only an archaic superego could match. Then the sense of badness and the archaic superego perpetuate each other and, as we learn in the analysis of the depressive, any attempt to alleviate directly either the sense of badness or the correlative superego harshness is misguided.

Depression can be viewed as an inability to mourn (Smith 1971), an inability that implies all the failures of differentiation and integration that I have outlined here in connection with a too high or a too fixed quotient of original guilt. Mourning requires a basic caring for oneself. One needs to be able to feel sympathy or even love for oneself rather than guilt or shame, as if any loss one has experienced or any danger one faces is a deserved punishment and any success or good fortune an undeserved reward and thus an occasion for intensified guilt, often defended against by either manic reactions, depression with guilt feeling, or, in analysis, the negative therapeutic reaction.

I have attempted to tie this adult guilt feeling to primitive guilt feeling by assuming that early distress (later discriminated as need, loss or danger) is equated with the bad. This seems to me more likely than the possibility that early guilt results from the inheritance of memory traces of primordial murder of the father or the impulse to do so that Freud (*S.E.* 13:158–60; *S.E.* 23:99–102; *S.E.* 23:206–7) assumed or that it is simply and directly consequent to adultomorphic fantasies of the kind that Melanie Klein attributed to infants. In addition, it is a formulation that I believe is more useful in understanding depression and the negative therapeutic reaction.

The Negative Therapeutic Reaction

The negative therapeutic reaction (Freud, *S.E.* 22:49) was associated with several crucial questions that arose in the history of psychoanalysis. Is masochism primary? Is aggression first of all toward the self and only secondarily—and, primitively, as a defense—toward the object? Does the urgency of primitive guilt and dependency mean that aggression toward the object intensifies rather than alleviates distress and thus compels a return of aggression toward the self as the compounded guilt and self-punishment of secondary masochism?

Freud came to grips with these questions and finally acquiesced to affirmative answers in an effort to understand those patients who responded to insight by becoming worse rather than better—what he called the negative therapeutic reaction—and to those character types who could be wrecked by success. These responses seemed to him to contradict the pleasure principle and the assumption that the aim of psychoanalysis was simply to make the unconscious conscious. They thus led to radical revision of his theory in which the structural point of view (or the second topography), centered in the concepts of id, ego, and superego, was superimposed on the topographic model of unconscious, preconscious, and conscious. The idea of "an" or "*The* Unconscious*" was relinquished since not only the repressed but also repressing forces could have the quality of being unconscious.

The Ego and the Id (Freud 1923) is not so much about the ego or the id as it is about guilt and that grade within the ego that came to be named the superego. Analysis moved from what in retrospect could be called an id psychology to an ego psychology wherein the dominant task was to understand the complexity of unconscious repressing forces and the defensive and nondefensive aspects of ego and superego functioning generally. The line of thought that began with the negative therapeutic reaction was then extended to primary masochism and the death instinct—matters "beyond" the pleasure principle as Freud understood it at the time (Smith 1977). Most analysts believe that with the death instinct he went too far, but that may reflect a reluctance to concede that any problems are insoluble or that work upon them might yield solutions directly at odds with utopian wishes. In any event, most analysts do agree to the extent that the product of this line of Freud's thinking placed aggression on a par with sexuality in human development.

So far as the death instinct is concerned, it may be, dramatic as it sounds, that in Freud's usage it was too neutral a name to refer to the universality of a self-punishing tendency. The idea of a general, conservative tendency to return to a prior state or a state of rest at least strikes me as empty of explanatory value and far removed from the underlying dynamics of primitive guilt that I assume central to self-punitive behavior. Besides, these tendencies can hardly be said to be motivated by the aim of death (Smith et al. 1973, 343), even though death becomes, for some individuals, the mode of enacting the aim of self-punishment. Both terms in Freud's concept of a "death instinct" were, in any event, to convey, and to convey powerfully, his conviction of the universality of such tendencies. This intention was also embodied in his speculations regarding the phylogenetic consequences of murder of the primordial father and implicit in his theories of primal repression and primary masochism. On the assumption that Freud's conviction was on the mark, the question becomes whether there is a better way of understanding and conveying this universality embedded in his texts on the negative therapeutic reaction and primary masochism that led to his concept of the death instinct.

What Freud was reaching for was a way of understanding guilt that preceded and exceeded that which could be accounted for by any and all personal wrongdoing. I have suggested previously here that the source and universality of this guilt can be understood in terms of the primitive lack of differentiation of guilt as a consequence of wrongdoing and simply feeling bad because things are not right—not right in a variety of ways ranging from moderate neediness to panic in the absence of the object. No individual avoids such experiences, and thus the universality of primitive guilt feelings. The degree to which such guilt takes hold of and shapes the destiny of an individual depends on several obvious variables. These are the innately given frustration thresholds together with the ratio of good or bad care plus the extent to which later events can alter the effects of good or bad early experience.

It is true that if early experience is dominantly good an individual will be less guilt prone, and if dominantly bad more guilt prone, provided "guilt prone" could be extended to cover those whose experience and development were so flawed as to preclude the capacity for the conscious experience of either guilt or guilt feeling. Further, those with dominantly good experience will be better able to sort out the badness of misfortune—things being not right—from the guilt of wrongdoing. Their differentiation and their capacity to differentiate such matters will proceed more smoothly. However, this is about as obvious and about as useless as asserting simply that differences of response indicate innate givens pertaining to frustration thresholds in infants. What is needed in both instances is more detailed and specific understanding. As I have indicated, evidence of a genetic predisposing factor for depression has its main import in leading to the investigation of precisely what the innate factors are and how they enter into the developmental process. Knowing this would sharpen our psychological understanding, which, in turn, would provide the basis for formulating more precise questions for genetic and neurobiologic research (Smith and Ballenger 1981). Similarly, such an obvious, general rule of thumb that the product of predominantly good experience in early life is a less guilt-prone individual does not take one very far into understanding the significance of the universality of guilt. To be guided only by such a rule of thumb might lead to the notion that an ideal of development would be a completely guilt-free individual or that all superego functions are to be considered neurotic manifestations. In opposition to such short-circuited conclusions, I am here pursuing the hunch that something like that which Freud named or misnamed the death instinct is universally operative and that our best chance of elucidating the referent of that concept is in tracing out and extending as best we can the understanding of guilt embedded in the texts on depression, primary masochism, and the negative therapeutic reaction. The consequence, it can be hoped, will be the achievement of a better position to intervene in the treatment of the negative therapeutic reaction at the core of every depression (Modell 1971, 340).

Primal Repression and Primary Masochism

In the concepts of both primal repression and primary masochism Freud was attempting to formulate processes that preceded any self-object differentiation. Primal repression can be taken as an automatic turning away or "flight" from need as danger prior to any capacity to know of a self or a self in danger, and primary masochism an automatic response to need as badness also prior to the emergence of a self. Such processes have to be assumed by inference from their later forms as factors that begin the organization of self and the differentiation of self and object. However, since the dominant dangers of the infant are what will come to be known as inner needs, these needs are, at an early stage and perhaps always at a certain level, experienced as bad. In that world, they are the ideationally unknown evil—an evil known only by virtue of affective distress.

Primal repression in this view would refer to processes like primitive disavowal or denial that we would now call precursors of repression. It consists in simply turning away from danger—that is, "an excessive degree of excitation" (Freud, *S.E.* 14:137; *S.E.* 20:94; Smith et al. 1973, 341), and toward the object of need. In that world, need satisfaction and the object that provides that satisfaction is the good.

With these definitions of primal repression and primary masochism, I am attempting to frame something of what Freud was pointing toward when he referred to certain quotas of the death instinct not "bound by the superego" (*S.E.* 23:242) deriving from an earlier era, and "at work in other unspecified places" (242). At the primitive level, with only "a little inexactitude" (*S.E.* 19:164)—that is, not differentiating sadism and aggression (LaPlanche 1976, 85–102)—the "death instinct," "primal sadism," and "original masochism" (*S.E.* 19:164) are one. Sources of disequilibrium are at once both dangerous and bad. After an initial experience of satisfaction, they initiate a turning toward the object of need in both anxiety and in what I have here chosen to call original guilt.

Depression and Mourning

Of course, the difficulty is in thinking of self and object prior to their differentiation. We are actually referring to processes that precede and shape such differentiation. Nevertheless, the primitive processes I have outlined here would affect how the self and object would come into view as they are constituted. They are reasons for believing that the bad would be more associated with the self and the good with the object. In what might seem a paradox, the intensity of this coloration of the self as bad and the object—the mother—as good is intensified to the extent that mothering is inadequate. In that situation if needs are too often or too long at a peremptory level, the danger is greater and the primitive defenses are more intensely deployed. The dominance of such primitive defenses sets the stage for identifications to be of the identification with the enemy type wherein the "badness" of the mother is internalized in a desperate effort to maintain the actual object, as it comes into view, as good.

This is the special way in which the shadow of the object falls on the ego of the melancholic. It can, in later development, constitute such a burden of guilt that there is a turning away from the object, a guilty renunciation or a negative reaction to any hope for the good, with an exclusive focus on the self as bad. Even where the seeming opposite obtains—accusations and chronic blaming of the object or the pseudo self-accusations that are really reproaches of the object that Freud wrote of in "Mourning and Melancholia" (1917)—it is motivated in the depressive by unacknowledged self-accusation. Here blame always connotes self-blame. The focus is so exclusively on the negative that Freud's irony regarding the melancholic's self-accusations—even if "he is speaking the truth" (*S.E.* 14:246–47), a person would have to be ill to say so—would also apply to accusations toward the object.

But blame, the clamorous protestation of guilt feelings, self or object accusation, or self or object condemnation, all fall short of experiencing guilt as such. Freud noted in "Mourning and Melancholia" that if it were guilt, the person might be expected to be less insistently communicative about it (247). Depression indicates a dependence upon and a not yet accomplished differentiation from the object. It is a protestation of guilt feelings with the unconscious aim of placating or reproaching the object. Guilt as such is more akin to mourning—it is to mourning as guilt feelings are to depression. The capacity to be guilty is a product of differentiation and also fosters further differentiation. It implies having achieved the autonomy to choose between good and evil, to conduct oneself in right or wrong ways in accordance with one's established values.

The question here is how it is that a person achieves the separateness to so choose. From the foregoing, it might be inferred—wrongly, I believe—that such separateness is achieved at a point in development where cognitive functions permit an intellectual sorting out of indigence or misfortune from actual wrongdoing. But I believe the move from guilt feelings to guilt arises first from a different and less defensive mode of experiencing guilt feelings themselves. Before being able to sort out misfortune from wrongdoing, it is as if the child or the depressive has to do a double-take on his or her self-accusations—something like "What if everything I am saying about myself were true?" Such moments can be sobering turning points. However, they do not, first of all, yield a release from guilt feelings. The first step seems to be a taking on of the whole burden of guilt and guilt feelings—both the guilt of wrongdoing and the original guilt of primitive indigence. It is not a moment of sorting out what one is to be blamed for or not blamed for, but simply "I am guilty." Guilt feelings are experienced as guilt. Paradoxically, such giving up of all claims on the object, the giving up of any "right" to be loved as a precondition for experiencing oneself as lovable, can probably only occur in a context of being loved, and it might come in the wake of having freely committed an unrationalized wrong—that is, an act of open defiance rather than one unconsciously motivated to evoke chastisement (Freud, *S.E.* 19:169). However, it is a giving up that can allow for differentiating indigence and wrongdoing and for achieving reparation and self-forgiveness for the latter. It is a movement that transcends defensive blaming.

Preoedipal Taboo

The series of danger situations in early life constitute nodal points for an accentuation of both anxiety and primitive guilt. In *New Introductory Lectures on Psycho-Analysis* (1933), Freud listed these as "the danger of psychical helplessness . . . the danger of loss of an object (or loss of love) . . . the danger of being castrated . . . and finally fear of the superego." The last, fear of the superego, "should normally never cease" (88). The first, psychical helplessness, I take to be the danger of the object being absent, prior to self-object differentiation.

Although I would suggest that it is in this earliest danger situation that the bedrock of the incest taboo is laid down, obviously each situation would pertain to taboo, castration particularly so.

The series begins with need and the absent object, which initiates early undifferentiated forms of love and hate manifested in anxiety, demand, desire, and guilt. My argument is that the danger situation becomes primitively interpreted as meaning the subject is bad—guilty—and the object is good. At this level, if one is in danger one is also in guilt; if needy, guilty. Of course, this would not be represented initially in such discretely formed mentation. However, the global affective experience indicates and subsequent conscious guilt and unconscious need for punishment affirm a developmental bias toward believing that whatever bad happens is the fault of the subject, and whatever good by virtue of the object. This, then, is the foundation for experiencing the murderous and sexual extremes of one's impulses toward the object as taboo. That tendency in early mentation can, I believe, be drastically enhanced or drastically mitigated, depending upon the mother's way of responding to the infant's demands (Winnicott 1971, 86–94), but not erased. Some burden of guilt is inevitably building toward marking the extremes of primitive aggressive and libidinal impulse as taboo.

One, still preoedipal, culminating point in this development comes when the advent of language and self-object differentiation coincide in the formation of the depressive position. In terms of guilt and danger, this phase marks the transition from the danger of absence of the object when in primitive need, to fear of the loss of the object or loss of the object's love by reason of guilty action or guilty fantasy. At this point the child can own its actual or fantasied wrongdoing, and that becomes the conscious explanation for guilt. The previously established taboo on the extremes of aggressive and libidinal impulses becomes more urgent just because the impulses are now claimed by the subject as "mine." Of course, in the development leading to this capacity the stages, each with its typical danger situation, overlap. It is through repeated primitive experience of presence and absence of the object that self-object differentiation occurs.

So far as differentiation is concerned, being able to claim one's impulses (and one's thoughts, feelings, and acts) as one's own is the crucial matter. But further development will also allow the subject to recognize various ways in which the claim is excessive. For Lacan (1977, 1–7; see also Muller and Richardson 1982, 26–41), what the child achieves in the self-object differentiation toward the end of the first year of life is an imaginary unity—the language achieved is as yet literal and the unity of the self claimed is falsely based on the bodily unity revealed in the mirrored image.³ The claiming of impulses as one's own overlooks the fact that the aggressive and libidinal drives are formed and shaped in the early interaction with the mother. The consciously clamorous claim that one's guilt or guilt-feeling is consequent to actual or fantasied wrongdoing overlooks the unconscious equation of indigence and badness as a still operative source of a certain quotient of guilt. This is what I meant earlier by raising the question of whether, in some measure, fantasies of wrongdoing seen at this stage might be criminality from a sense of guilt.

Children whose guilt *is* largely consequent to actual or fantasied wrongdoing are the lucky ones. Where this covers what is largely primitive guilt based on equating need, indigence, weakness, vulnerability—ultimately finitude—with badness, the situation is considerably more complicated and predisposes the individual to affective disorder. The former children are bad because they have committed or fantasied a wrong act; the latter are bad just because they are.

The point here is that guilt not attributable to *conscious* acts or fantasies of wrongdoing cannot simply be taken as consequent to *unconscious* fantasies of wrongdoing (Freud, *S.E.* 12:225). The second group of children may have more guilt but even less unconscious fantasy because of primitively established taboo, a state of affairs that could abort any reasonable transition into and through the phallic stage and the oedipal era.

In the oedipal era, castration, felt or feared, is judged to be punishment—punishment for desiring the always already tabooed object. But the two levels of guilt are still operative here also. It is believed that castration has occurred or might occur because of guilt-laden wishes, but also the original equation of guilt and indigence now centers on having or not having a penis, and the degree of original guilt the child carries into the oedipal era will affect the degree of castration anxiety or penis envy experienced.

The overcoming of castration anxiety and penis envy depends, in part, on making the transition from the literal to the symbolic use of language—in Lacan's terms on achieving entry into the symbolic order. Rather than being the "bed-rock" that Freud took them to be (*S.E.* 23:252), castration anxiety and penis envy represent a literality that falls short of comprehending that the penis becomes in early childhood the symbol of an original unity lost in separating from the mother. Its lack is a symbol for that more crucial lack in the girl, and, in the boy, its presence is a symbolic denial of a loss that has already occurred—a denied loss that is then transformed into anxiety over a future danger (Smith 1980, 395).

What I am suggesting here is that the depressive position is one phase in working through the loss of symbiotic oneness with the mother and that the oedipal era involves, in part, a more definitive, more final reworking at a higher level of that same loss. The imaginary unity of the depressive position occurs in the context of a grandiose self/idealized self-object dyad—virtually a fantasied persistence of the original symbiosis—established, in part, to deny or disavow lack, danger and guilt. Successful oedipal resolution involves recognizing one's finitude, including the finitude of one's gender to a point that lack, need, indigence, and finitude are not experienced—or at least minimally experienced—as reasons for guilt. This would require the recognition, at some level, of the symbolic meaning of having or not having a penis. This is not to learn that neither gender is indigent, only different; it is instead to learn that both genders are indigent and finite. It is also to learn that this kind of learning, thenceforth under the aegis of the oedipally consolidated superego, will continue through all eras of life. At issue throughout, for example, will be the ongoing test of the extent to which one anticipates the infirmities of aging and eventual death as a measure of one's finitude or the extent to which they are anticipated as punishment still consequent to original guilt.

I have emphasized that the child with the greatest burden of original guilt can be expected to have the greatest difficulty in achieving these transitions. However, it should also be noted that the child with the greatest burden has at least a chance of finally achieving the deeper insight.

If the foregoing is a plausible interpretation of early development, it seems to me also plausible to assume the bedrock of the incest taboo to be located in this aspect of the mother-infant relationship for both genders, prior to the oedipal appearance of the father. Both the boy and girl are barred from merger with the object, and they tend to interpret the reason for the bar to be their own guilt. They are, from this particular garden, forthwith expelled. Libidinal development is then covered over and becomes a private individuating matter. Guilt and shame can thus have a constructive role in development, but they are anchored in processes that precede the infraction of parental no-saying. Although there are no doubt numerous factors that ensure the incest taboo at various levels, its cross-cultural universality would suggest that it basically derives from processes of primitive differentiation prior to all cultural variation in childrearing practices and prior to the major consolidation of the oedipal phase.

A further preoedipal factor is that development for the child is significantly development into the linguistic order. In a partially literal sense the child is called forth to its selfhood (cf. Brickman 1983, on linguistic competence and the "auditive"). That the mother is a language-speaking animal with a linguistically ordered, remembered past and a linguistically ordered, anticipated future means that she can also be more concerned with her own and her child's future than with the gratification of her own or her child's immediate wishes. This concern is not only a moral dimension but at the same time one that carries phylogenetic survival value and no doubt ensures at that level the universality of the incest taboo being anchored in the preoedipal era.

A final preoedipal factor—really a deeper aspect of all those discussed here—has to do with the effects of the achievement of awareness of the mother (and self) as separate. This can be phrased as awareness of the mother as absent even when present. The mother, even though present, comes into view in her aspect of "unassimilable . . . thing," as Freud put it in the Project (*S.E.* 1:366; see also 328, 331, 334). This confrontation with a preordained, never-to-be-overcome absence of the mother from oneself, oneself from one's mother, and, by virtue of that lack as compared with the prior symbiotic unity, a certain lack or absence of oneself from oneself, is considerably more awesome than merely the actual, literal, bodily absence of the mother. For Lacan this lack of being or lack in being is the fundamental castration to which all are subject. It is the cause of desire and the ultimate incitement to impossible incest. Incest, that is, at this level, is barred prior to taboo and more profoundly than by guilt. It is incited because barred, and out of that dilemma guilt, taboo, and the laws of marital exchange arise.

The horror of incest is, in part, horror in the face of the impossibilities of incest, even where that is denied by actual literal cross-generational consummation of the sexual act. The common mode of dampening—defending against—the horror of incest is to be guilty about the desire to overcome the fundamental lack of separateness. This is the basic indigence—the original indigence—of the subject. Although guilt feelings defend against horror, they also thereby partake of the horror. The whole complex is attenuated by a universal experience of taboo as if it is an externally—eventually an internally—imposed bar to a possible infraction. In that sense we take an unjustified pride in our civilizing, superego or ego controls and—at the expense of being untrue not merely to our fundamental desire but also to the original and ongoing indigence that incites desire—live as if we have overcome the lack within and between us.

Summary

Rorty has expressed grave doubts about the usefulness of understanding adults by extrapolation from demonstrable or inferred primitive states in infants. Although appreciating that, I must also keep in mind that Rorty has not worked with seriously ill adults. Though it would be folly to directly ascribe psychotic processes to infants, it would no doubt also be folly to assume that the regressed positions of schizophrenics and psychotically depressed patients have nothing to teach us about primitive thinking and primitive affective experience, an assertion with which Rorty, I believe, would agree.

I have relied here heavily on such inferences about early states in a discussion of how primitive guilt might enter into development, depression, the negative therapeutic reaction, and taboo. I have argued the plausibility that in the early partially differentiated phase, primitive guilt enters in the form of a gradient toward associating the bad with the differentiating self and the good with the differentiating object. Although of particular pertinence in the to-be-depressive, I have also taken this as a universal in development. The fact that in fortunate development or in successful analysis the individual can come to know the difference between primitive guilt (indigence) and the guilt of wrongdoing, and on the basis of that knowledge overcome depression, seems to be a partial affirmation of the Socratic doctrine that human problems are problems of ignorance. However, that overcoming primitive guilt *is* a developmental task and not purely a cognitive achievement seems a partial affirmation of the Judeo-Christian doctrine of original guilt or original sin.

Notes

1. For a comprehensive discussion of analytic neutrality, see the panel report by Leider (1984).

2. The doctrine of an inclination to evil in every person—I rely on Kirn's article in the not-so-new (1911) *New Schaff-Herzog Encyclopedia of Religious Knowledge*—is in the later Judaic literature, but analogous conceptions were there earlier in Genesis 4:7 (following Genesis 3, where it all began by eating from the tree that brought knowledge of good and evil). Sin "lieth at the door" in wait for all. In Jeremiah 17:9, the heart is naturally evil, "deceitful above all things and desperately wicked." Other instances of the treatment of sin as universal, sometimes as a correlate of human frailty, are in Job 4:18, 9:2, and 14:4, and in Isaiah 6:5 and Psalms 41:5.

The Christian emphasis on the doctrine of original sin began with Pauline teaching and was variously elaborated by Augustine and Thomas Aquinas. The interpretation nearest to the concept of primitive guilt presented here is that of Duns Scotus, who reduced "original sin to the absence of a long-lost good" (Kirn 1911, 436).

3. The reference to Lacan at this point should not be taken to mean that the conceptual framework of my argument coincides with his. For the general contrast, see my "Lacan and the Subject of American Psychoanalysis" (259). In regard to the subject matter under discussion here, Lacan specifically discards (1968, 83) or excludes from his field of study (1977, 21) the concept of primary masochism. However, the gist of what I am here presenting in my own terms might be recognized in the final two paragraphs of his "Aggressivity in Psycho-Analysis" in *Ecrits*, 28–29). There he writes of the

> assumption by man of his original splitting *(déchirement)*, by which it might be said that at every moment he constitutes his world by his suicide, and the psychological experience of which Freud had the audacity to formulate, however paradoxical its expression in biological terms, as the "death instinct."
> In the "emancipated" man of modern society, this splitting reveals, right down to the depths of his being, a neurosis of self-punishment, with the hysterico-hypochondriac symptoms of its functional inhibitions, with the psychasthenic forms of its derealizations of others and of the world, with its social consequences in failure and crime. It is this pitiful victim, this escaped, irresponsible outlaw, who is condemning modern man to the most formidable social hell, whom we meet when he comes to us; it is our daily task to open up to this being of nothingness the way of his meaning in a discrete fraternity—a task for which we are always too inadequate.

References

Brickman, Arthur. "Pre-oedipal Development of the Superego." *International Journal of Psycho-Analysis* 64 (1983): 83–92.

Chomsky, Noam. *Language and Mind*. New York: Harcourt Brace Jovanovich, 1968.

———. "Language and Unconscious Knowledge." In *Psychoanalysis and Language,* edited by Joseph H. Smith. Vol. 3 of *Psychiatry and the Humanities.* New Haven: Yale University Press, 1978.

Fingarette, Herbert. *The Self in Transformation.* New York: Harper & Row, 1963.

Freud, Sigmund. *The Standard Edition of the Complete Psychological Works of Sigmund Freud.* Edited and translated by James Strachey. 24 vols. London: Hogarth, 1953–74.

Project for a Scientific Psychology (1895), vol. 1.

The Interpretation of Dreams (1900–1901), vols. 4, 5.

"Formulations on the Two Principles of Mental Functioning" (1911), vol. 12.

Totem and Taboo (1913), vol. 13.

"Instincts and Their Vicissitudes" (1915), vol. 14.

"Mourning and Melancholia" (1917), vol. 14.

The Ego and the Id (1923), vol. 19.

"The Economic Problem of Masochism" (1924), vol. 19.

"Inhibitions, Symptoms, and Anxiety" (1926), vol. 20.

"The Question of Lay Analysis" (1926), vol. 20.

New Introductory Lectures on Psycho-Analysis (1933), vol. 22.

"Analysis Terminable and Interminable" (1937), vol. 23.

Moses and Monotheism (1939), vol. 23.

An Outline of Psycho-Analysis (1940), vol. 23.

Hartmann, Heinz. *Ego Psychology and the Problem of Adaptation.* New York: International Universities Press, 1939.

———. "Notes on the Reality Principle." *Psychoanalytic Study of the Child* 11 (1956): 31–53.

Jones, Ernest. *The Life and Work of Sigmund Freud.* Vol. 2. New York: Basic Books, 1955.

Kirn, Otto. "Sin." In *New Schaff-Herzog Encyclopedia of Religious Knowledge,* edited by Samuel M. Jackson and George W. Gilmore. Vol. 10. New York: Funk & Wagnall, 1911.

Lacan, Jacques. *The Language of the Self.* Translated by Anthony Wilden. Baltimore: Johns Hopkins University Press, 1968.

———. *Ecrits.* Translated by Alan Sheridan. New York: W. W. Norton, 1977.

LaPlanche, Jean. *Life and Death in Psychoanalysis.* Translated by Jeffrey Mehlman. Baltimore: Johns Hopkins University Press, 1976.

Leider, Robert. "The Neutrality of the Analyst in the Analytic Situation. Report of the 1981 Panel Chaired by Ernest S. Wolf." *Journal of the American Psychoanalytic Association* 32 (1984): 573–85.

Modell, Arnold. "The Origin of Certain Forms of Preoedipal Guilt and the Implications for a Psychoanalytic Theory of Affects." *International Journal of Psycho-Analysis* 52 (1971): 337–46.

———. "Self-Preservation and Preservation of 'the Self.' " Lecture presented at joint meeting of Washington Psychiatric Society and Washington Psychoanalytic Society, Washington, D.C., January 13, 1984.

Muller, John, and Richardson, William. *Lacan and Language: A Reader's Guide to Ecrits.* New York: International Universities Press, 1982.

Piaget, Jean. *Insights and Illusions of Philosophy* (1965). Translated by Wolfe Mays. New York: World Publishing, 1971.

———. "The Affective Unconscious and the Cognitive Unconscious." *Journal of the American Psychoanalytic Association* 21 (1973): 249–61.

Rapaport, David. *Seminars on Elementary Metapsychology.* Edited by Stuart Miller. Stockbridge, Mass.: Austen Riggs Center, 1957. Mimeographed.

Rieff, Philip. *Triumph of the Therapeutic.* New York: Harper & Row, 1966.

Schafer, Roy. *The Analytic Attitude.* New York: Basic Books, 1982.

Smith, Joseph H. "Identificatory Styles in Depression and Grief." *International Journal of Psycho-Analysis* 52 (1971): 259–66.

———. "Language and the Genealogy of the Absent Object." In *Psychiatry and the Humanities,* edited by Joseph H. Smith. Vol. 1. New Haven: Yale University Press, 1976.

————. "The Pleasure Principle." *International Journal of Psycho-Analysis* 58 (1977): 1–10.

————. "The Psychoanalytic Understanding of Human Freedom: Freedom from and Freedom For." *Journal of the American Psychoanalytic Association* (1978): 87–107.

————. "Fathers and Daughters." *Man and World* 13 (1980): 385–402.

————. "Lacan and the Subject of American Psychoanalysis." In *Interpreting Lacan*, edited by Joseph H. Smith and William Kerrigan. Vol. 6 of *Psychiatry and the Humanities*. New Haven: Yale University Press, 1983a.

————. "Rite, Ritual, and Defense." *Psychiatry* 46 (1983b): 16–30.

Smith, Joseph H., and Ballenger, James. "Psychology and Neurobiology." *Psychoanalysis and Contemporary Thought* 4 (1981): 407–21.

Smith, Joseph H., Pao, Ping-nie, and Schweig, Noel. "On the Concept of Aggression." *Psychoanalytic Study of the Child* 28 (1973): 331–46.

Stern, Daniel H. "The Early Development of Schemas of Self, Other, and 'Self with Other.' " In *Reflections on Self-psychology,* edited by Joseph Lichtenberg and Samuel Kaplan. Hillsdale, N.J.: Analytic Press, 1983.

Winnicott, Donald W. *Playing and Reality.* London: Tavistock, 1971.

4   Identification and Catharsis

James W. Earl

The relation of the audience to the tragic hero is an intractable problem, because every member of the audience is unique, and his relation to the hero is in large part private. The Greek tragedies were public religious and civic performances, and Aristotle assumed they illustrated moral principles—*hamartia* in essentially good characters. But their powerful effect on the audience can hardly be explained in moral terms—except perhaps that often they just outrage all our common notions of morality and justice. Public as they are, and Aristotle notwithstanding, there is little agreement about the moral principles operating in plays like *Oedipus* and *Prometheus Bound;* and it is just as hard to imagine an Athenian audience as it is a modern one leaving the theater murmuring to each other "Well, *that* made sense!" and "Yes, he certainly deserved *that!*" Rather, our response to the plays is individual and psychological. That everyone responds to *Oedipus* in his or her own way is not interesting in itself, of course; but since Aristotle we have suspected that underlying our various responses there are principles to be described. I bring to this ancient problem the psychoanalytic theory of *identification,* a concept unknown to Aristotle, who speaks instead of imitation, sympathy, and catharsis. *What can identification tell us about catharsis?*

For several reasons, our response to tragedy is more obviously a concern of psychoanalysis than of literary theory or philosophy. First, tragedy is *acted out* rather than expounded, because, as Ricoeur says (1967, 211–31), its essential themes are *unspeakable*—which is to say they are repressed, in the audience as well as in the play; and to make them conscious requires the sort of analysis best suited to unconscious ideas. Second, although Shakespeare knew well enough the value of the drama as a metaphor for life, it has assumed a new metaphorical value after Freud, now that we understand how our own characters and roles in life are acted out largely under unconscious direction. "Character is fate" has a new depth of meaning in an age when it is understood that, as Freud says, "the ego is not the master of his own house." Richard Rorty, in chapter 1 in this volume, explains how different this new image of the self is from the pre-Freudian picture of the intellect under the sway of the passions. And so, for example, Wollheim's discussion of identification (1974) adopts the drama as a natural explanatory model, dividing the self into author, character, actor, and spectator.

Third, and more to my point in this essay, the tragedy resembles in essential respects psychoanalysis itself: it is a strictly delimited, intense psychological process, which, if Aristotle is right, results in the particular therapeutic effect he calls catharsis. In both cases, this effect proceeds from an identification (with the hero or the analyst) that is highly disruptive psychologically, but ultimately resolved. Freud himself, in his early work with Josef Breuer, performed what he called "cathartic analysis." Though he never discusses the relation of his use of the term to Aristotle's, I will follow this terminological clue; this chapter discusses the "madness" of our identification with the tragic hero, and its cathartic cure, on the analogy of the psychoanalytic drama of identification called the transference, and the termination of analysis.

Catharsis

The "madness" of identification with the hero was first discussed by Plato. Socrates asks Ion, who is a rhapsode, a reciter of Homer:

> When you produce the greatest effect upon the audience in the recitation of some striking passage, such as the apparition of Odysseus leaping forth on the floor, recognized by the suitors and shaking out his arrows at his feet, or the description of Achilles springing upon Hector, or the sorrows of Andromache, Hecuba, or Priam,—are you in your right mind? Are you not carried out of yourself, and does not your soul seem to be among the persons or places of which you are speaking, whether they are in Ithaca or in Troy or whatever may be the scene of the poem? (1975, 18–19)

"Are you in your right mind?" *Sympatheia* and *ecstasis* so undermine reason that poetry is exiled from the Republic. The poet, after all, "has been inspired and is out of his senses, and reason is no longer in him" (18), and the reader's identification with the hero, though Plato does not exactly call it that, is too much like madness to suit the philosopher.

Aristotle's approach is more psychological. The theory of catharsis is presented quite clinically in *The Politics:*

> An emotion which strongly affects some souls is present in all to a varying degree, for example pity and fear, and also ecstasy. To this last some people are particularly liable, and we see that under the influence of religious music and songs which drive the soul to frenzy, they calm down as if they had been medically treated and purged. People who are given to pity and fear, and emotional people generally, and others to the extent that they have similar emotions, must be affected in the same way; for all of them must experience a kind of purgation [catharsis] and pleasurable relief. (1958, xv–xvi)

In his definition of tragedy in *The Poetics,* Aristotle says simply "through pity and fear it [tragedy] achieves the purgation [catharsis] of such emotions" (12). So if Plato believes that poetry *causes* madness, Aristotle believes it *cures* it. The theory assumes, of course, that the audience is already emotionally disturbed, unbalanced, overemotional, and that, as with physical ailments, a laxative is the obvious treatment. Not everyone has this problem—certainly not philosophers; but as Aristotle sees it, it is endemic in the lower classes, who should be given regular doses of tragedy and cathartic songs to keep them calm—in the same cynical spirit as our cities sponsor summer concerts to relieve the furies of our frustrated, uneducated, unemployed, disenfranchised, poor, and angry youth. (Aristotle assumes, by the way, like Plato and most of us, that cathartic musicians are just as unbalanced as their audience.)

Paradoxically, then, the unbalanced, manic audience is not given a model of sanity to identify with, but by way of inoculation and immunization is presented with madness to exhaust them: terrifying plots, and characters driven to insanity by the gods. And not only tragic heroes are mad; Achilles is also mad, in the sense that he is angry, and anger too is a form of possession, an unbalancing, a loss of *sophrosuné* and reason. Madness, therefore, in the Greek sense, is actually a requirement of a good plot, tragic or epic. A good plot will enter the irrational so squarely that even in summary it will evoke terror and pity. "The story should be so constructed that the events make anyone who hears the story shudder and feel pity even without seeing the play. The story of Oedipus has this effect" (Aristotle 1958, 26–27). The unbalancing of the emotions is thus a sine qua non of good narrative art, and has a therapeutic effect on emotional disturbances endemic in the audience.

Except for this medical metaphor of purgation, however, Aristotle does not explain *why* this treatment should work, though he knows from observation that it does. If he is right, and the unbalancing performance does somehow relieve common emotional disturbances, then one should be able to describe the process psychoanalytically.

There has been a continuous and ever-widening stream of commentary upon Aristotle's few sketchy remarks about catharsis, and every age has had its own understanding of the process. "It would not be difficult," says Laín Entralgo, "to compose a history of European feeling and thought following the thread of this immense philological and exegetical hodgepodge. The Renaissance commentators were accustomed to interpret the favorable effect of tragic catharsis as a hardening to the vicissitudes of life produced by familiarity with spectacles that fill us with fear and compassion. The French preceptors and playwrights of the seventeenth century, more devout, extend the cathartic process to all the passions and interpret it as a purification of the individual" (1970, 186). Goethe dismisses the problem altogether by taking catharsis as a feature of the play itself, rather than the mind of the spectator, though to do so he has to claim that the discussion in *The Politics* is irrelevant to *The Poetics* (Eissler 1971, 545). The distinctively *modern* interpretation understands *catharsis* as a term borrowed from Greek medicine—"a designation transferred from the somatic to the affective in order to designate to the treatment of a sufferer a treatment with which the endeavor is not made to transform or repress the aggrieving element but to excite and foster it in order thus to bring about the relief of the sufferer" (Jacob Bernays, quoted in Laín Entralgo 1970, 187).

Jacob Bernays was an eminent Viennese classicist whose *Zwei Abhandlungen über die Aristotelische Theorie des Drama* was published in Berlin in 1880. According to Laín Entralgo, "Hardly had the study by Bernays been published than it gave rise to no less than one hundred and fifty works for or against it" (1970, 186). Widespread interest in the subject extended to the Viennese salons, where, it has been argued (Dalma 1963), Josef Breuer's first patient in cathartic analysis, Anna O., heard of it, and so was able to help Breuer rediscover catharsis as a medical treatment in his treatment of her during the years 1880–82. In 1882, Freud was engaged to Martha Bernays, Jacob's niece, and Freud's sister Anna was to marry Martha's brother, Eli Bernays. It is not hard to conclude from these connections that Aristotle's theory, as understood by Bernays, was not just "in the air" but was a strong influence on Freud and Breuer's development of the "cathartic method," the subject of their joint volume, *Studies in Hysteria* (1895).

This method treated hysterical symptoms by encouraging the patient to recall the traumatic events that had triggered them, and to release the repressed emotions attached to those memories. The socially appropriate response to a traumatic event, like the death of a parent or loved one, often does not allow for an adequate affective reaction; in cathartic analysis these events are reexperienced in the relative security of the therapeutic setting, and an "abreaction" provoked, resulting in relief. Freud soon decided, however, that although the cure worked, its effects proved temporary, and he abandoned it. Breuer had already abandoned it in a panic after Anna O., his only patient, fell in love with him during the course of her treatment. In the final pages of *Studies in Hysteria,* Freud speculates briefly on this first case of the transference, which he was quick to recognize as an inevitable hazard of the method, but which at this early stage he describes simply as a "false connection" (*S.E.* 2:301–4). He was only beginning to understand the complexities of the analyst's role in the patient's shifting identifications during the analytic process.

Though Freud abandoned the cathartic method, it has elements of permanent value. It remains as a residue in Freud's later work, and in fact still persists in various forms today, from the fully psychoanalytic "re-grief therapy" of Volkan (1975) and the cathartic psychotherapy of Nichols and Zax (1977), to the California pop therapy of Scheff (1979). What does cathartic therapy, as Freud and these latter-day exponents practice it, have to tell us about *tragic* catharsis, if anything?

It would seem to suggest that tragedy reexposes the audience to commonly repressed traumas, and that the resulting catharsis is a sort of collective abreaction to universal features of psychic life. Perhaps (if we were to elaborate this idea freely with elements from Freud's later work) tragedy briefly reawakens the oedipal crisis, or the other losses and humiliations suffered in growing up, the repression of instinctual love and violence that constitutes the discontents of a civilized audience. Perhaps the tragic hero, like the epic or folk hero Freud discusses in *Group Psychology and the Analysis of the Ego* (1921), is reenacting the murder of the primal father: "hearers understand the poet, and in virtue of their having the same relation of longing toward the primal father, they can identify themselves with the hero" (137).

Perhaps; but I reject this whole train of thought as too simple, just as Freud rejected the cathartic method. It is veering too sharply into the universal, and neglecting the clinical variety one should expect in individuals. It could only be a blunt instrument of analysis. Besides, although the great tragedies clearly do concern these great themes, their heroes are anything but epic. The tragic hero is *destroyed* in the tragedy, for what Aristotle assumes is his hamartia, his *fault*—which complicates our identification with him considerably. If he represents an ego ideal, it is a guilty one; if he is a wish-fulfillment, it is at least partially a death-wish. It is not likely that all spectators identify with the hero in the same way, and considering the hero's tragic end, it is not likely that the identification can be maintained in any simple way throughout the play. So these first suggestions will appear only as residues in my own conclusions after I have explored the nature of these identifications in more detail.

Identification

The term *identification* was introduced into literary criticism by Shelley, who elegantly expresses the modern common-sense attitude toward the hero:

> Homer embodies the ideal perfection of his age in human character; nor can we doubt that those who read his verses were awakened to an ambition of becoming like to Achilles, Hector, and Ulysses:. . .the sentiments of the auditors must have been refined and enlarged by a sympathy with such great and lovely impersonations, until from admiring they imitated, and from imitation they identified themselves with the objects of their admiration. Nor let it be objected that these characters are remote from moral perfection, and that they can by no means be considered as edifying patterns for general imitation. (1821, 486)

But that is precisely my objection. No one in his right mind would choose to be Achilles, not to mention Oedipus, Hamlet, or Lear. One would not want to shoulder their agonies outside the text, and one would be mad to do so.

We do identify with the hero, of course; but Freud taught us there are forms of identification that do not stem from admiration and imitation. The tragic hero, a figure of towering proportions and often terrifying features, whose character is idiosyncratic and flawed, whose story is after all tragic, is an ideal we can identify with only indirectly, or in a highly specialized sense. Our identification is complicated by unconscious factors; for example, the hero is likely to inspire guilt in us for our own inadequacy.

> No! I am not Prince Hamlet, nor was meant to be.
> ("Prufrock," T. S. Eliot)

Nor am I Oedipus, nor Achilles—though Prufrock's guilt-ridden, hesitating ambivalence is the one quality he *does* share with Hamlet, whose madness, like that of many tragic heroes, eases our temporary mad identifications with them.

In short, our relations to these heroes have some of the murky complexities of our everyday relations to parents, priests, teachers, leaders, doctors, gangsters, and all the other figures stalking about in the superego. As ego ideals they are critical, fearsome, and bound up with our guilt.

Notice how Shelley shifts the focus of the analysis from plot to character. Whereas Aristotle says "the plot is the first essential and the soul of a tragedy; character comes second" (14), for Shelley it is the hero who bears the meaning. Perhaps that misconception leads to his other errors. Psychoanalysis, however, will refocus our attention on plot: for all of Freud's interest in character, he never treats it as other than a development, a case history. Identification too is a development, an act with a structure—a beginning, middle, and end.

Among psychoanalytic concepts, the dramatic structure of identification is especially well understood, because it is at the heart of the psychoanalytic relationship itself, in which the development of the patient's identification with the analyst, his or her transference, is used as a route to cure. So analysis is a drama of sorts, too, a therapeutic drama of identification with a beginning, middle, and end.

What is the "drama" of identification?

Pope says the audience at a tragedy will "live o'er each scene, and be what they behold"—which is not wholly true, of course, since we identify only with certain characters, especially the hero. To observe characters, even to sympathize with them, is not necessarily to identify with them, in the psychoanalytic sense; just as in our personal relations, even to love someone is not necessarily to identify with him or her. A child may love both parents, for example, and identify with only one. Not every strong attachment is an identification, which I will define here simply as *an extension of the self that fails or refuses to distinguish itself from an object*. Such identification is in fact generally incommensurate with mature object-love, since it denies the object its own being. It is immature in the sense that it is regressive, because in identifying with the object the ego recaptures some of its infantile narcissism, that first stage of mental development in which the world is not yet clearly distinguished from the self.

This is a highly simplified definition of identification. As with so many of Freud's original concepts, which are always elegantly simple, a subsequent half-century of clinical practice has revealed numberless forms of identification, and has generated theoretical distinctions to account for them, culminating in Schafer's "Identification: A Comprehensive and Flexible Definition" (1968, 140–80). The near-byzantine complexity of the concept in the post-Freudian literature is due to the fact that any part of the self (id, ego, or superego) may identify with any or all aspects of the object (e.g., desired, feared, or even hated characteristics), resulting in a wide array of effects and disorders. In general, primary-process and in toto identifications tend to be neurotic in adults (Smith 1971, 1975), although the most fundamental of all primary-process identifications, the formation of the superego during childhood, is paradigmatic of later identifications, and is especially useful in understanding the mechanics of the transference. It is the latter forms that concern us here, and to describe them I adopt a simple model for relatively normal adults, similar to Loewald's (1962, 1973).

In normal development, identification takes a number of forms, in a sequence beginning with infantile narcissism. At this early stage, the two complementary types of identification that are to emerge later, *projection* and *internalization,* cannot usefully be distinguished (Smith 1975). But the first to evolve is probably projection, in which aspects of the self are projected into the world and attached to objects. A child may identify with a doll in this way, as if it were herself, or herself as she wishes to be. As the ego slowly learns to distinguish its own states from those of others, it comes to accept the separateness and objectivity of others and the world: the doll is after all only a doll, so you need not cry if your brother sticks his tongue out at it. But the world will always remain something of a mythological funhouse to the unconscious, so projection remains active in many forms in the adult. We catch ourselves at it every day. A familiar example is paranoia, in which the fearful, guilty ego finds the world's most innocent gestures threatening; many a lover has discovered to his dismay that the beloved's encouraging gestures were only the projections of his own desire; and our sense of bodily violation when our home has been broken into, or our car wrecked, also bespeaks our projective identifications with these things.

Of special interest to us are the temporary narcissistic fantasies that come into play in art, such as our daring identifications with the hero, which can also be a type of projection. We may identify with a character as an externalization of some aspect of our own ego, a projection of our desire, or a figure of ourselves as we would like to be, or imagine ourselves to be, or fear we are. I am Tarzan, Michael Jackson, Oedipus, King Lear. In our relations to works of art, which even for adults occupy that psychological playground of "transitional objects" between the clearly subjective and clearly objective worlds, we can venture into identifications without fear of the chastisement, disillusionment, and loss that inevitably attended our infantile identifications, which had to be renounced more or less unwillingly as we discovered that our dolls—and our parents too—were not merely extensions of ourselves, not merely parts of *our* world.

If, as adults, we are to be chastised or disillusioned for our identification with a literary hero, it must happen in the work itself, since normally such an identification lasts only so long as we are engaged with it. Don Quixote and Walter Mitty are pathological exceptions to prove the rule. As readers of romances, their identifications become a form of madness when carried beyond the act of reading; as heroes themselves in their own romances their madness is only typical, and is the basis of our own identification with them, mad readers that we are. We identify with heroes whose madness is that they identify with heroes in the same way. Their humiliations are their chastisement and ours too. But the book comes to an end, or we put it down, and unlike them we can terminate our madness. We are not crazy, after all.

We are taught this danger early, in stories like *Peter Pan:* we must always return to reality, and deal with our real father, bastard that he is, after we have projected our murderous rage for him onto Captain Hook and made him walk the plank; we cannot remain in Peter's world of infantile wish-fulfillment, though it is painful to leave. It is our fate to grow up. The inferior forms of art we now call "escapism" are perhaps distinguished by the conspicuous absence of this theme, inviting us to form identifications that are then not resolved within the work. At the other extreme is tragedy, in which our projective identification is both guilt-ridden and conspicuously terminated by the destruction of the hero, thus forcing its internalization—the last act in the drama of identification.

Narcissistic projections outside of art are usually pathological and laden with guilt, since the infantile desires we fulfill in this regressive way are usually unattainable in reality, and often illicit to boot. As our projections are broken, as reality forces us to renounce our narcissistic demands that the world serve, reflect, and embody us, this idealized past is internalized. Internalization (or introjection) is something of a reverse projection, in which our relations to renounced or otherwise-lost objects are retained as ego-structures, as relations among components of the self. The grandest identifications of this sort occur in the internalization of our oedipal relations, once we have renounced them, by which the superego is formed. The awesome, idealized parents of our infancy become inner agencies, ideals against which the ego is constantly being measured and found wanting. The consequent guilt is normal and socially useful: it makes us moral and self-critical.

To call internalization a form of identification is perhaps misleading, for it is not regressive and narcissistic. "The ideal outcome of

internalization is identity in the sense of self-sameness as an individual, and not identification and identity with objects" (Loewald 1973,
84–85). It is by internalization that our inner world is constituted and
distinguished from the external world; it is the only road to normal,
healthy object-relations. New identifications and new internalizations
always force a psychic reorganization to one degree or another, as the
inner world grows and shifts its many relations into new patterns of
coherence. Analysis and tragedy are calculated means of such growth
and reorganization.

Projection, relinquishment, internalization: this is the normal
drama of identification, the beginning, middle, and end of the oedipal, as well as the analytic and tragic cures. Childhood, analysis, and
the tragedy must all come to an end; the parents, the analyst, and the
hero must be relinquished, our relations with them internalized with
our other *daimones.*

So the audience does not simply identify with the hero, and then
live through the plot with him; the form of our identification changes
as the plot develops toward its inevitable ending—just as our identifications with our parents develop, or the analytic transference, or any
other narcissistic bond that reality forces us to relinquish. Lear must
die—though nothing will be learned from his death except that it was
inevitable. That is enough to learn.

Others have noted that our relation to the hero changes during the
course of the tragedy. The change is commonly described in terms of
the two emotions Aristotle repeatedly links, terror and pity: our terror
turns to pity as the play progresses. This is in fact a common-sense
interpretation, which itself implies a shift in identification. Suppose
we were to see an old lady being beaten with a tire iron on the street,
for example: we feel terror, identifying with her; when it is over,
however, her attacker fled and she stunned and dying, our terror turns
to pity, as we stop identifying with her and come to see her objectively
as a woman who has been injured and needs our help. Simon Lesser
(1957) suggests a similar shift in the tragedy; at the end of the play we
are led to a point of detachment, when we no longer identify with the
hero but with the cosmic order that has punished him, and our terror
with him turns to pity *for* him. But although we can come to accept
and even understand Fate, I am not so sure we can identify with such
an abstraction unless a clear image of it is provided, such as Teiresias,
into whom we can project ourselves.

Be that as it may, it is surely not enough to say that our identification with the hero has simply been terminated. Identification with
someone who is guilty and is being punished so extravagantly involves
us in a drama of the superego, which cannot be so cleanly resolved by

just shifting our identification to the punishing agency. At best we will end by saying "Yes, I certainly deserved *that!*"

We cannot speak of relinquishing a powerful identification without internalization, which is best understood as the mechanism of super-ego formation. Loewald's analysis of this oedipal process adopts the termination of analysis as an especially illuminating analogue, because "experiences purposefully and often painfully made explicit in analysis usually remain implicit in ordinary life."

> Analysis, understood as the working out of the transference neurosis, changes the inner relations which had constituted the patient's character by promoting the partial externalization of these internal relationships, thus making them available for recognition, exploration, and reintegration. By partial externalization, psychic structures in their inner organization are projected onto a plane of reality where they become three-dimensional, as it were. However, the analyst, as was the case with the original parental figures, is only a temporary external object in important respects. The relation with the analyst, like that with parental figures in earlier ego development, has to become partially internalized. . . . The pressure of the impending separation helps to accelerate this renewed internalization. (1962, 259–60)

Projection, relinquishment, internalization: Loewald sees in this process a general law of mental life, which will bring us back to the drama.

> Emancipation as a process of separation from external objects. . .goes hand in hand with the work of internalization, which reduces or abolishes the sense of external deprivation and loss. Whether separation from a love object is experienced as deprivation and loss or as emancipation and mastery will depend, in part, on the achievement of the work of internalization. Speaking in terms of affect, the road leads from depression through mourning to elation. (263)

As in analysis, so in the tragedy: the hero, too, is a temporary object promoting the partial externalization of internal relationships, thus making them available for recognition, exploration, and reintegration. The *temporary* nature of our relation to the hero is important to note. The plot comes to an end, and so does the hero. The pressure of his fated destruction accelerates the reinternalization of what we have projected upon him.

From depression through mourning to elation: this is to speak of the process, as Loewald says, in terms of affect. This is the clue to an achieved understanding of catharsis in tragedy and in psychoanalysis that encompasses far more than Aristotle, Bernays, Anna O., Breuer, or the early Freud could have conceptualized. Catharsis as more than transient cure is not simply the unlocking and venting of pent-up emotion. Instead it is participation in the drama of recognition, exploration, and reintegration that I take to be the highest mode of identification. The affective concomitants bear witness to the underlying dynamics of the structural changes in process.

The early idea that curative catharsis was merely the release of emotion is related to Freud's early understanding of anxiety as the consequence of repressed libido. Cure was simply un-repression. The understanding of catharsis subsequently achieved is the product of his revised theory of anxiety in *Inhibitions, Symptoms, and Anxiety* (1926), where anxiety is taken to be a response to danger, together with a deeper understanding of the developmental factors that enter into the dynamics of structural change, of which the drama of identification is the central theme.

Conclusion

It is more than fortuitous that in 1897 Freud first glimpsed his model for the drama of superego formation in *Oedipus* and *Hamlet* (Freud 1985, 272–73): the significant plot is borne in tragic dramas, where our evolving identification with the tragic hero recapitulates our most private drama. Catharsis is a successful working-out of the complex. It is psychologically therapeutic, as Aristotle realized, although not exactly like a laxative.

I have at last to consider the *content* of our identification with the hero. The foregoing discussion has centered on plot, not character, following Aristotle's assertion that plot is more important. But who *is* the hero we identify with? If he is an ego ideal, why is he flawed? And why must he suffer so? What can identification tell us about hamartia?

Hamartia is notoriously difficult to define or translate, and often difficult to find, much less analyze, in the plays themselves. Is it a flaw, an error, or a misstep? And what hamartia do we see in Oedipus, or Prometheus, or Hamlet, or even Lear? Does not criticism usually show them as powerful but enigmatic characters crushed ruthlessly and unjustly by the gods? Is not their fault really our feeling that they *must* be guilty to suffer such punishment, or the projection of our own guilt? For all his power, is not the hero's character really a cipher?

Perhaps the clue to character in these plays is that mysterious mask. The tragic mask is as blank as the imperturbable face of the analyst, as blank a screen for our projections, our transference. Catharsis, one should never forget, is a matter of plot, not character. As I said at the beginning of this chapter, everyone in the audience is different, and our identifications with the hero will be different. Think of Hamlet, as rich a character as any tragic hero, yet paradoxically as enigmatic as a blank mask. To Eissler (1971, 22, 47, passim) this radical ambiguity is the essential feature of the play and the source of its power. Sane or mad, moral, devious, incapable, young or old, male or female even— anyone can play Hamlet, anyone can identify with him—there are any number of interpretations of his character, because he is the perfect object of our temporary transference.

But each of us must finally relinquish his or her other narcissistic oedipal fantasies and internalize them. The play must have an end. Tragedy, and literature generally, helps us master this process, which repeats itself endlessly in our psychic lives, by inviting us to enter into a drama of controlled regression and development. From another angle, of course, it will always look a little like madness.

References

Aristotle. *On Poetry and Style*. Translated by G.M.A. Grube. Indianapolis: Bobbs-Merrill, 1958.

Dalma, Juan. "La Catarsis en Aristoteles, Bernays y Freud." *Revista de Psiquiatria y Psicologia Medical* 4 (1963): 253–68.

Eissler, Kurt. *Discourse on Hamlet and "Hamlet": A Psychoanalytic Inquiry.* New York: International Universities Press, 1971.

Freud, Sigmund. *The Standard Edition of the Complete Psychological Works of Sigmund Freud.* Edited and translated by James Strachey. 24 vols. London: Hogarth, 1953–74.
Studies in Hysteria (1895), vol. 2 [with Josef Breuer].
Group Psychology and the Analysis of the Ego (1921), vol. 18.
Inhibition, Symptoms, and Anxiety (1926), vol. 20.
————. *The Complete Letters to Wilhelm Fliess.* Edited and translated by Jeffrey M. Masson. Cambridge, Mass.: Harvard University Press, 1985.

Laín Entralgo, Pedro. *The Therapy of the Word in Classical Antiquity.* Translated by L. Rather and J. Sharp. New Haven: Yale University Press, 1970.

Lesser, Simon. *Fiction and the Unconscious.* Chicago: University of Chicago Press, 1957.

Loewald, Hans. "Internalization, Separation, Mourning, and the Superego" (1962). "On Internalization" (1973). In Loewald, *Papers on Psychoanalysis.* New Haven: Yale University Press, 1980.

Nichols, Michael, and Zax, Melvin. *Catharsis in Psychotherapy.* New York: Gardner, 1977.

Plato. *The Ion.* Translated by B. Jowett. In *Criticism: The Major Statements,* edited by Charles Kaplan. New York: St. Martin's Press, 1975.

Ricoeur, Paul. *The Symbolism of Evil.* Translated by E. Buchanan. Boston: Beacon Press, 1967.

Schafer, Roy. *Aspects of Internalization.* New York: International Universities Press, 1968.

Scheff, Thomas. *Catharsis in Healing, Ritual, and Drama.* Berkeley and Los Angeles: University of California Press, 1979.

Shelley, Percy Bysshe. "A Defense of Poetry" (1821). In *Shelley's Poetry and Prose,* edited by D. Reiman. New York: W. W. Norton, 1977.

Smith, Joseph H. "Identificatory Styles in Depression and Grief." *International Journal of Psycho-Analysis* 52 (1971): 259–66.

———. "On the Work of Mourning." In *Bereavement: Its Psychosocial Aspects,* edited by Bernard Schoenberg and Irwin Gerber. New York: Columbia University Press, 1975.

Volkan, Vamik. "Re-Grief Therapy." In *Bereavement: Its Psychosocial Aspects,* edited by Bernard Schoenberg and Irwin Gerber. New York: Columbia University Press, 1975.

Wollheim, Richard. "Identification and Imagination." In *Freud,* edited by Richard Wollheim. Garden City, N.Y.: Doubleday Anchor, 1974.

5   The Moral Perils of Intimacy

Annette Baier

Richard Rorty has said that "the problem is that love (and therefore courage and cowardice, sacrifice and selfishness) looks different after one has read Freud. It is not that we have learned that there is no such thing, but rather that it has been described in ways which make it difficult to use the notion in moral reasoning" (1980, 180). But this will be a problem only for those who have tried to use the notion of love in their moral reasoning, or have relied on it in their moral sentiments. A striking feature of modern moral *philosophy* is the avoidance of the concept of love. It is as if our great moral theorists, since Hobbes, have tried to formulate a morality acceptable to unloving and unloved persons, an impersonal morality that is to govern relationships between persons seen as essentially strangers to one another, ones having no natural interest in each other's interests. Should there be closer ties between any particular moral agents, these are then thought to superimpose extra rights or duties on the rights and duties of strangers among strangers.

The so-called core morality governs relations between aloof adult strangers, and this core may be supplemented but not supplanted by special duties to children, friends, or loved ones. In the dominant Western liberal moral tradition, a person is, morally speaking, first of all an autonomous individual (or a potential one, or an ex-one), whose privacy and freedom are to be respected, and only after that and compatibly with that a lover, friend, parent, child, or coworker. For such moral reasoning as Hobbes and Kant have taught us to engage in, the transformation of the concept of love will have no consequences whatever, since it figures there only incidentally and peripherally. Such sacrifice and selfishness as our modern moral philosophers have been led to consider are linked not to love, but only to self-love and its overcoming. And as David Hume emphasized, self-love is not love "in a proper sense" (1978, 329). Nor is that love of humanity, or of truth, or of intellectual freedom that Rorty thinks supplanted love of God as the driving force in liberal secular morality. To find any accounts of morality in which love in a proper sense figures centrally, one must turn to Christian moralists, and among philosophers to Christian moral theorists such as St. Augustine, St. Thomas Aquinas, and Bishop Butler. (But Butler's discussion of love of one's neighbor, like Nietzsche's words on love of one's nonneighbor, do not really make love in a proper sense central to anything they thought of much importance for morality, or for what lies beyond it.)

Rorty says, just before the previously quoted passage, that "neither the religious nor the secular and liberal morality seem possible, and no third alternative has emerged" (1980, 180). That, I think, is to ignore not merely Hegelian and Marxist moral theories but also to overlook the distinctive contribution of Hume's moral philosophy. For Hume offers us a basis for a secular morality that is free of the false psychology and bad faith of liberalism, and it is a moral theory that both gives love in a proper sense a very important moral role and treats love quite "anatomically" and realistically. Humean heroes and heroines not only can but must be both ironists and lovers (as Hume himself was). And Humean love needs no unmasking, since whatever masks it may wear are appreciated by Humeans for what they are.

Hume discusses love at great length, and, unlike many other moral theorists, does not see it as merely a *psychological* possibility, to be contrasted with moral necessities. But his subtle account of love is no *more* essential a preliminary to his account of the moral sentiment and morality than is his account of pride, of avidity, and of a "sympathetic" communication of passions that presupposes no love, so it would be an exaggeration to see his moral theory as love-based. To the extent that his moral philosophy relies on the actuality of love between parents and children, between friends, and between lovers, more than do most modern moral theories, the transformation of our understanding of love that Freud wrought seems to me to strengthen rather than weaken Hume's moral philosophy. This is because Hume's own version of psychic energy, of love, and of the dependencies and interdependencies love produces and is produced by, itself in some ways anticipates Freud. Hume has no starry-eyed romantic conception of love, vulnerable to more realistic revisions. He is both a clear-headed moral "anatomist," seeing human love and its variants as special cases of animal or more specifically mammalian love, grounded in physical needs and dependencies, and also a subtle discerner of all the delicate refinements, variations, and vulnerabilities peculiar to love between those who have human understanding as well as human needs and human feelings.

Hume is a tireless reporter of the oddities of human affection—that a son's tie to his mother is weakened by the mother's remarriage, but his tie to his father weakened "in a much less degree" by the father's remarriage; that "a mother thinks not her tie to her son weaken'd, because 'tis shared with her husband: Nor a son with his parent, because 'tis shared with a brother," whereas having to share it with a stepbrother and a stepfather is another matter (Hume 1978, 355–57). These "pretty curious phenomena" attending our "love of relations" are noted by Hume, and explained by him in terms of his association-ist theory, itself a theory of "relations" between ideas and impressions that he himself has just associated with "one *relation* of a different kind," namely, "the relation of blood" (352). Although some of his associationist explanations of the vagaries of our affections may seem strained and overintellectualized, they assume a rather different com-plexion when one bears in mind the close relation Hume forges between relations of ideas and impressions and that "relation of blood" which forges "the strongest tie the mind is capable of, in the love of parents for their children" (352).

My purpose here, however, is not just to represent Hume as a moralist who offers an alternative both to liberalism and to a religion-based morality, and who does not need to be sheltered from the insights Freud gave us, but more particularly to direct attention to the fact that Hume is atypical among moral philosophers in the modern period in seeing any need to discuss love in order to understand our specifically moral beliefs and attitudes. I also want to raise the ques-tion of why it is that most of our great modern moral theorists do *not* find love to be of any particular moral importance, and so do not, presumably, need to revise their conclusions in the light of anything Freud has taught us about love.

One explanation of the "lovelessness" of modern moral theory in the dominant Western tradition is suggested by the recent findings of Carol Gilligan regarding differences between typically male and typi-cally female moral development, or rather of the development of the conceptions of morality in men and women. For our great classical moral theorists not only are all men but are mostly men who had minimal adult contact with women. Hume, Hegel, and Sidgewick are the exceptions among a groups of gays, misogynists, clerics, and puri-tan bachelors (the status of J. S. Mill and of Bradley is unclear). If Gilligan is right about male understanding of morality, in its usual mature form it takes morality to be more or less what Kant takes it to be—a matter of respect for the more or less equal rights of free autonomous persons who have learned to discipline their natural self-assertiveness and self-aggrandizing tendencies in order to make it possible for many such natural self-seekers to coexist without mutual destruction or unnecessary mutual frustration. The male "genius" in moral matters, according to the story Gilligan gives, is the capacity to arrive at, institute, and obey rules regulating competition among selfish individualists. Girls, by contrast, seem initially both less self-assertive and competitive, and less willing or able to institute rules to control or arbitrate such interpersonal conflicts as naturally develop. They see themselves as born into ties to others, as having responsibilities for the preservation of these "natural" ties, not as inventors or even very good respecters of humanly forged, formal rule-dependent relations between persons.

The conflicts that Gilligan's women want a satisfactory morality to avoid or resolve are not so much conflicts between self-interested persons as conflicts that present themselves to a single other-centered person finding herself with incompatible responsibilities to a variety of persons. The situation of a woman who tries to care both for her aged mother and for her husband whose psychosomatic health troubles are aggravated by the aged mother's presence (or by his wife's attention to her mother) is *not* like that of someone who has to arbitrate a head-on conflict of wills between a demanding old woman and a demanding middle-aged man, both competing for one woman's attention and care. If the woman loves both her mother and her husband, she cannot take up the position of an impartial arbitrator, and no Solomonic wisdom can settle the matter for her. For even if she knows that her husband's intolerance of her mother's company and need is unreasonable, she will, if she loves him, prefer to tear herself in two rather than refuse to try to partially satisfy his needs and wishes, however unreasonable.

The women in Gilligan's abortion study (1982, chaps. 3 and 4), who unwillingly and with lasting ill effects in their own lives decided for abortion to try to please their men and to prolong their relations with them, are melancholy testimony to the typical female unwillingness to resolve a conflict of emotional demands by cutting ties with the less "innocent" of the two demanders. The usually futile effort is somehow to have it both ways, to share oneself between those making competing calls upon one. No list of rights, and no techniques of arbitration, will settle such emotional and moral conflicts. It is noteworthy here that men writing on abortion tend to address the issue in terms of the right (or lack of right) of the fetus to life and of the woman to control of her body, while women often find all such talk beside the point. The point, for them, is not what they or others have a right to, but whom, among those they *want* to care for, they should reluctantly abandon or neglect in these conflict situations, where none of these persons need be seen as having any *right* to their care. The morality that solves or avoids such dilemmas will need different concepts and will encourage a different sort of moral reflection from those liberal ones that have evolved to resolve disputes between egoists.

It is sometimes claimed that the altruists' dilemmas are of essentially the same sort as the egoists' (so-called prisoner's dilemma),[1] namely, a matter of conflict between the best interest of one person and the parallel and incompatible best interest of another. But the altruist, torn between continuing to support her mother and her husband, or between keeping her mate and keeping her unborn child, is *not* in the position of a judge asked to arbitrate between the conflicting interests of different parties, for her own interest and her own wishes are also part both of the problem and of most possible solutions. She must choose not just who is to be hurt or harmed by her action but what sort of person she herself is to become—a child-abandoner or a mate-abandoner, a mother-neglecter or a husband-neglecter. Her own future, as well as that of those she wishes to care for, is at stake. The sort of wisdom needed to avoid, or to best make and live with such choices, is different from that needed by the judge, peacemaker, or referee. But since none of our moral theories have come from women, nor been articulated to "rationalize" such womanly moral wisdom as may exist on such matters, all we have, as yet, are old wives' tales, not alternative moral *theories* giving intellectualized voice to women's insights into what seem to be typically female moral issues.

It is possible, of course, that women's moral insight is intrinsically resistant to theoretical reconstruction—that we old wives are essentially antitheorists. If men can detach intellect from passion more readily than women, and put more value on such passionless intellect, and if theories are purely intellectual products, then it is to be expected that moral theory will continue to be a typically male product, independent of the degree of liberation, wisdom, power, or self-consciousness of women. (I myself have in the past given voice to some antitheoretical sentiments,[2] but I am uncertain whether the impetus was antitheoretical, or merely antagonism to the style and content of the currently dominant theories.)

There are, as already acknowledged, some male moral philosophers who do not see the main moral problems and solutions in the dominant modern way as arising out of clashes of perceived self-interest. Both some Marxists, who look forward to a realm of freedom where communal pursuits fulfilling to all parties replace competitive individualism, and some Hegel-influenced non-Marxists, such as Alasdair MacIntyre (1981), see the central problem not as what to do to achieve fair settlement of interpersonal clashes of interest, but rather as what form of life to institute so that interpersonal conflicts are avoided, and so that the propensity to those narrowly self-interested and self-indulgent pursuits that usually lead to such conflicts is overcome. Such a theory is, like Hume's, an important alternative to liberalism. It does not take relationships between mutually disinterested strangers as morally central, but directs attention to relationships between persons of unequal authority and expertise who are united in a common but nonuniversal practice, in pursuit of a shared substantive and to some extent esoteric good.[3] MacIntyre's voice in moral theory can, as much as Hume's, be more easily tuned to harmonize with the "other voice" Gilligan has heard than can the liberal male voice. But MacIntyre shares, with liberalism, a conception of morality as discipliner of desire, including desires attendant upon love, rather than as any sort of development or fuller expression of naturally arising love, so his theory, as much as that of liberals, seems untouched by anything Freud has taught us about love. At most Freud will have informed all such male moral theorists of some interesting details about the genesis and ancestry of the passions a rational morality has to control.

Of more consequence to all such "disciplinary" conceptions of morality will be Freud's account of the origins and nature of the superego, the impetus to self-discipline, and self-denial. Had Rorty said that the *disciplining* of desire, along with the associated concepts of conscience and duty, look different after Freud, and are now less easily invoked in moral reasoning, his remarks would have applied more tellingly to the moral reasoning of most modern philosophers, liberal and antiliberal. The courage and sacrifice needed to obey conscience and deny desire are at least as transfigured by what Freud taught us as are the courage and sacrifice that love sometimes entails. A version of morality, like MacIntyre's, that demands of us a willingness to let our tastes be reformed and our desires disciplined by some authoritative tradition, will be received with some suspicion by those who have learned from Freud that self-proclaimed authoritative voices tend to be those of jealous fathers or their envious imitators and epigones.

The idea of a practice into which novices get initiated, receiving at each point what is due to them in virtue of their position and their performance there, and such that conflicts of interest (or at least of what comes eventually to be accepted as true interest) are avoided—

thus needing no or minimal machinery for settlement—would be an appealing one did not the shadow of the tyrannical patriarch darken its promise. The assurance that we are being disciplined for our own real good, forced to be truly free, denied so that we can be better satisfied, has been too often the drug used on the victims of patriarchs, oppressors, and brainwashers.

It is not, of course, impossible that there should be a form of life that really did offer self-transformation without exploitation, guidance by authoritative experts without dictatorship, dominion without domination. But given the record of such promises, it will not be surprising if we are suspicious of those who, like MacIntyre, tell us that we cannot expect to see the justice or the good of what we are to undergo until we have undergone it. The same thing has been said to those burnt at the stake for their souls' and their creator's sake, by slave owners to slaves, and by males to the females trained to serve them (and trained to train other females to continue that service).

If the debit side of the liberal morality is, as MacIntyre has vividly portrayed it, the danger of anomie and noncommunication, the debit side of MacIntyre's alternative is the danger of patriarchal (or patriarch-supplanters') oppression. Obedience and self-denial are dangerous virtues, both for those who possess them and for their fellows. They invite, on the part of others, tyranny and self-aggrandizement, and they poison both communication and communion. "Lo, here is fellowship; one cup to sip; and to dip in one dish faithfully, as lambkins of one fold. Either for others to suffer all things; one song to sing in sweet accord, and maken melodie. Lo, here is fellowship." A fine ideal, except that sheep come with shepherds, choirs with music directors and conductors, who tend to sip first and dip more deeply in the common dish than their followers.

The moral heritage of our patriarchal past includes not only the myth of the paternal omniscient authority but also that of the *loving* father. Moralities that require of us that we love, and respond to love, can be equally apt to encourage tyranny and coercion. "Whom the Lord loveth, He chastiseth." The claim "You won't like this, but I do it for your own good, and one day you will be glad I did it," is made not just by superiors to novices and teachers to pupils, but also by loving parents to children. Parental love, paternal or maternal, is as dangerous a central concept for ethics as is expert wisdom. Should some of Gilligan's females whose moral genius it is to successfully sustain, combine, and express their love of their corevolutionaries, friends, lovers, parents, and children have the wish to produce a moral theory that does justice to their conception of morality, then *they* will be the ones who will need to heed what Freud, his followers, and his critics have taught us about the love between parents and their young children, and its relation to other loves. Rorty's claim will be tested only when we have some fully articulated love-based account of moral reasoning and moral feeling. Like MacIntyre's, such theories will face the difficult task of steering between the Scylla of empty formal rights and the Charybdis of substantive exploitation in communal activity. The challenge for any moral theorist today is to find a recipe for avoiding the loneliness and anomie for which the liberal morality of "civil society" is the breeding ground, and also the intrusive and smothering closeness of life in a tyrannical family, be it a natural, a communist, or a religious "family."

What, after all, did Freud teach us about love? That it begins in dependency, that its first object is the more powerful but loving mother who has been the loving infant's whole world, and who remains the source of nourishment, security, and pleasure. The pathologies of love all develop from this initial situation of unequal dependency. Motherlove, if it is to be good of its kind, has to avoid both exploitation of the mother's immensely superior power and that total self-abnegation that turns the infant into the tyrant. Love between unequals in power is good of its kind when it prepares the less powerful one for love between equals. It fails when what it produces is either a toleration of prolonged unequal dependency or a fear of any dependency, rather than a readiness for reciprocal and equal dependency. As Nancy Chodorow's important work (1978) has shown, motherlove in our society tends to prepare sons for independence rather than for reciprocal dependency, and to prepare daughters both to accept continued unequal power (with parents, and, later, husbands) and to use their eventual power over their own children to perpetuate this pattern of both crippling male adult inability to accept the dependencies of love, and crippling female adult inability to assert themselves enough to become equals to their male fellows in politics, love, war, and peace. We urgently need a new assignment of social roles, and a new morality, whether or not it is backed by a new moral theory, to enable us to stop maiming each other in the way we have long been accustomed and trained to do. Such a morality would give us guidance where no current moral theory even attempts to guide us, and where currently received moralities misguide us—on how to treat those close to us so that closeness, chosen or not chosen, can be sustained without domination or mutual suffocation, as well as on how to respect the rights of strangers, so that distance does not entail moral neglect. Only when intimacy becomes morally decent, and when moral decency braves the perils of intimacy, will we have achieved a morality worth trying to present, for those with intellectual tastes, in the form of a new, different, and better moral theory.

Notes

1. After writing this I was pleased to read Ian Hacking's negative assessment of the popular big boys' game of prisoner's or prisoners' dilemma in his review in the *New York Review of Books* (June 28, 1984) of Robert Axelrod's *The Evolution of Cooperation*.

2. See my "Doing Without Moral Theory?" and "Theory and Reflective Practices," in my *Postures of the Mind*.

3. See MacIntyre's "Rights, Practices, and Marxism: A Reply to Six Critics," for a clear statement of his position on this point.

References

Baier, Annette. *Postures of the Mind*. Minneapolis: University of Minnesota Press, 1985.

Chodorow, Nancy. *The Reproduction of Mothering*. Berkeley and Los Angeles: University of California Press, 1978.

Gilligan, Carol. *In a Different Voice*. Cambridge, Mass.: Harvard University Press, 1982.

Hume, David. *A Treatise of Human Nature*. Edited by L. A. Selby-Bigge and P. H. Nidditch. New York: Oxford University Press, 1978.

MacIntyre, Alasdair. *After Virtue*. Notre Dame, Ind.: University of Notre Dame Press, 1981.

———. "Rights, Practices, and Marxism: A Reply to Six Critics." *Analyse und Kritik* 1 (1985).

Rorty, Richard. "Freud, Morality, and Hermeneutics." *New Literary History* 12 (1980): 177–85.

6   The Politics of Ethics: Freud and Rome

David Damrosch

Freud's treatment of ethics is marked by an ironizing of Judeo-Christian conceptions in favor of a far more pagan psychology and philosophy of ethics. As programmatic as Freud's contrasts of pagan and Judeo-Christian ideas are, however, their relations are in fact extremely complicated in much of his work. Freud is neither so purely secular as Philip Rieff and Steven Marcus suggest, nor as thoroughly Jewish at heart as David Bakan and Susan Handelman claim.[1] I wish to examine the interrelations of Judaism, Christianity, and classicism as they contribute to Freud's ethics, particularly as seen in his treatment of Rome. As I hope to show, Rome is a remarkably rich "nodal point," in *The Interpretation of Dreams* and elsewhere, the center of many of Freud's ambivalences both about religious culture and about classicism. As a result, the image of Rome shows many of the complexities of politics and history underlying Freud's redefinitions of ethics.

The valorizing of classicism against the Judeo-Christian religious tradition is a recurrent theme in Freud's *Traumdeutung*. Thus, in introducing his discussion of Oedipus and Hamlet, Freud polemically contrasts Judaism and classicism on a scale of mysticism and blindness versus rationalism and insight. It is our religious upbringing, he tells us, that has prevented us from observing the "real relations" between parents and children so suggestively delineated by Greek myth. He continues:

> The sanctity which we attribute to the rules laid down in the Decalogue has, I think, blunted our powers of perceiving the real facts. We seem scarcely to venture to observe that the majority of mankind disobey the Fifth Commandment. Alike in the lowest and in the highest strata of human society

filial piety is wont to give way to other interests. The obscure information which is brought to us by mythology and legend from the primaeval ages of human society gives an unpleasing picture of the father's despotic power and of the ruthlessness with which he made use of it. Kronos devoured his children, just as the wild boar devours the sow's litter; while Zeus emasculated his father and made himself ruler in his place.

(*S.E.* 4:256)

As such passages show, Freud is engaged in a fundamental redirecting of ethics, one that goes beyond a desire for rationalism as opposed to mysticism. Underlying the contrast is the fact that classical ethics is fundamentally a branch of politics. Thus Aristotle opens his Nicomachean Ethics by locating the study of ethics as a branch of political science:

Most people would regard the good as the end pursued by that study which has most authority and control over the rest. Need I say that this is the science of politics? . . . This is not to deny that the good of the individual is worth while. But what is good for a nation or a city has a higher, a diviner, quality.

Such being the matters we seek to investigate, the investigation may fairly be represented as the study of politics.

(1953, 26–27)

In Judaism, by contrast, politics is rather a branch of ethics, and ethics is a basic constituent of Jewish religious life, not the predominantly secular concern it is in Plato, Aristotle, and Freud. The "real relations . . . between parents and children" that Freud sees as the basis for all morality have, then, a double quality: not only are they natural (and hence lie in the field of science), but, equally, they are political, and hence lie in the realm of secular moral philosophy.

Like any Freudian displacement, however, the translation of religion into political economy does not free Freud from the inheritance of Jewish mysticism, but rather opens up new territory for his ambivalence toward authority. In fact, religion and politics are often virtually indistinguishable in Freud, and provide complementary fields of struggle. As a Jew, Freud is a member of both a religious and a political/social minority, and Rome, as the seat both of Catholicism and of the original Western empire, is an object of intense and ambivalent interest for Freud.

The Archaeology of Imperialism

The two major metaphors in the *Traumdeutung* for Freud's project of psychic exploration are a mountain walk and an archaeological excavation. I return to the theme of the mountain walk later; as for the archaeological metaphor, it is notable how frequently it is associated with Rome. Thus, hysterical symptoms "stand in much the same relation to the childhood memories from which they are derived as do some of the Baroque palaces of Rome to the ancient ruins whose pavements and columns have provided the material for more recent structures" (492). Several such passages in the *Traumdeutung* foreshadow the long comparison early in *Civilization and Its Discontents*, in which we are invited to imagine the mind on analogy to "the Eternal City." There,

> all these remains of ancient Rome are found dovetailed into the jumble of a great metropolis which has grown up in the last few centuries since the Renaissance. There is certainly not a little that is ancient still buried in the soil of the city or beneath its modern buildings. This is the manner in which the past is preserved in historical sites like Rome.
>
> Now let us, by a flight of imagination, suppose that Rome is not a human habitation but a psychical entity with a similarly long and copious past. . . . This would mean that in Rome the palaces of the Caesars and the Septizonium of Septimius Severus would still be rising to their old height on the Palatine. . . . But more than this. In the place occupied by the Palazzo Caffarelli would once more stand—without the Palazzo having to be removed—the Temple of Jupiter Capitolinus; and this not only in its latest shape, as the Romans of the Empire saw it, but also in its earliest one, when it still showed Etruscan forms and was ornamented with terracotta antefixes.
>
> (*S.E.* 21:70)

Philip Rieff challenges this metaphor on two grounds. First, he claims that the analyst, unlike an archaeologist, is far from neutral toward the material he excavates (a point to which I will return). Further:

> The comparison of analyst with archaeologist is invalidated on another count as well—that psychological history cannot be represented spatially. . . . Beneath the mild exercise of classical erudition a major issue of Freud's psychological theory is involved. When "we try to represent historical sequence in spatial terms," we face an apparent absurdity: that of envisaging several contents occupying the same space. . . . Freud's implication is that psychology had better avoid, as misleading and simplifying, any sustained recourse to spatial metaphors.
>
> (1979, 45–46)

Noting in passing the amusing irony that Rieff uses the same archaeological spatialization that he decries (in his evocation of the real meaning "beneath" the classical erudition), one may wonder how one is to dispense with spatial metaphor. To be sure, Rieff is following Freud, who closes his evocation of Rome, the most extended such spatialization in his work, by asserting its impossibility:

> There is clearly no point in spinning our phantasy any further, for it leads to things that are unimaginable and even absurd. If we want to represent historical sequence in spatial terms we can only do it by juxtaposition in space: the same space cannot have two different contents. Our attempt seems to be an idle game. . . . It shows us how far we are from mastering the characteristics of mental life by representing them in pictorial terms. . . . A city is thus *a priori* unsuited for a comparison of this sort with a mental organism.
>
> (*S.E.* 21:70–71)

Clearly, Freud protests too much here, and one is presented with a typically Freudian moment of asserting the impossibility of what he has actually just done. The issue of space and time is already openly debated at the end of the *Traumdeutung* (610–11), where Freud both advances his "topographical" representation of the mind, and urges that such a model be rejected in favor of a "dynamic" (i.e., temporal) model, on the grounds that one is dealing not with systems but with processes. At the same time, he preserves his spatial models intact, and constantly returns to similar spatializations in his later work. Both in the *Traumdeutung* and in the passage just quoted from *Civilization and Its Discontents,* there is a positive value for Freud in remaining "far . . . from mastering the characteristics of mental life"; mastery is something Freud clearly both seeks and shies away from, and this hesitancy is one factor behind the innumerable assertions of incompleteness and inadequacy in his work in general.

The acceptance/rejection of the metaphor of Roman archaeology exhibits the same tension found in Freud's attitudes toward political power in his references to Rome. Writing the *Traumdeutung* in his early forties, Freud speaks of his longing to visit Rome, which, however, he has never seen. "For a long time to come, no doubt, I shall have to continue to satisfy that longing in my dreams: for at the season of the year when it is possible for me to travel, residence in Rome must be avoided for reasons of health" (*S.E.* 4:193–94). This is a rather surprising obstacle—the *doctor* has to avoid the capital of Italy for his *health?* Lest one suppose that Freud's concern is really for his family's well-being, one should note the footnote added in later editions, in which he puts his triumph over this danger in purely personal terms: "I discovered long since that it only needs a little courage to fulfil wishes which till then have been regarded as unattainable; and thereafter became a constant pilgrim to Rome." Clearly, the medical reason given is only a part of Freud's reluctance to become "a constant pilgrim" to the Eternal City. A number of further reasons will emerge later in this paper, but Freud's ambivalence toward mastery—political, religious, and intellectual—is a central factor.

The archaeological comparison quoted earlier clearly shows the essential ethical enterprise: to expose the pagan foundations of the Christian capital. At the same time, the excavation goes a step further and reveals the Etruscan foundations of Imperial Rome (with their terra-cotta antefixes, or as we might say, their feet of clay). Freud's ambivalence toward Rome is perhaps the muddiest of all the ambivalences in the *Traumdeutung,* and considerably complicates Freud's attempts to construct a political ethics.

In "Politics and Patricide in Freud's *Interpretation of Dreams,*" Carl Schorske has shown that the idea of Rome is closely linked to Freud's ambivalence both toward political power and toward his father. Frustrated in his early hopes for a political or military career, Freud turned to science, and gradually developed a "counterpolitical psychology," in which politics, and even social history at large, could be reduced to "an epiphenomenal manifestation of psychic forces" (Schorske 1973, 342, 329–39).

Freud is fairly clear about his turn from such childhood models as Hannibal and Oliver Cromwell to an adult role as an apolitical scientist. What is surprising is the vehemence with which he denies any adult political ambitions in his chosen sphere of professional activity. A good example of this is seen in the dream following his encounter with Count Thun, then prime minister, who grandly brushes past the ticket-taker at the train station where Freud is about to leave on holiday. Freud tells us that this incident affected his mood for the rest of the day:

> The whole evening I had been in high spirits and in a combative mood. . . . And now all kinds of insolent and revolutionary ideas were going through my head. . . . I thought, too, of how our malicious opposition journalists made jokes over Count Thun's name, calling him instead "Count Nichtsthun." Not that I envied him. He was on his way to a difficult audience with the Emperor, while I was the real Count Do-nothing—just off on my holidays.
>
> (*S.E.* 4:208–9)

What is surprising here, I think, is not the displacement of ambition onto science but the claim that Freud does not feel ambition even there: he would rather take a vacation than stay at home and work. No one with any awareness of Freud's devotion to his work will find this disclaimer credible, and it is not the only such claim. What is involved here is not so much a political problem as an ethical dilemma: a discomfort with ambition itself. In his desire to deny the emotions of ambition and envy that most people feel from time to time in their professional lives, Freud is driven to complicated rhetorical maneuvers, as when he denies a wish for a professorship even though it is "a rank which in our society turns its holder into a demigod to his patients" (S.E. 4:137). Tragically, anti-Semitism has prevented several of his colleagues from achieving this status. Knowing this, Freud tells us, "I therefore determined to meet the future with resignation. So far as I knew, I was not an ambitious man. . . . Moreover there was no question of my pronouncing the grapes sweet or sour: they hung far too high over my head" (137). Here already we may wonder how much resignation needs to be summoned in order to bear doing without something one does not want; but the situation becomes further complicated when Freud returns to this issue later on. Denying the manifest appearance of ambition in the dream about his colleagues, he tells us:

> If it was indeed true that my craving to be addressed with a different title was as strong as all that, it showed a pathological ambition which I did not recognize in myself and which I believe was alien to me. I could not tell how other people who believed they knew me would judge me in this respect. It might be that I was really ambitious; but, if so, my ambition had long ago been transferred to objects quite other than the title and rank of *professor extraordinarius*.
>
> (S.E. 4:192)

Every line of this passage is odd. Freud begins by synecdochically reducing the many advantages of a professorship to the minor fact of "a different title" and then concludes that a desire for that must show a "pathological" ambition (*einen krankhaften Ehrgeiz*). Not content with this, he grudgingly admits that other people might judge him differently, though, like Quixote with his pasteboard helmet, he does not venture to test the hypothesis. He further protects himself in advance by the note that at best others can only "believe" that they know him.

Having done everything he can to resist the hint of an after all quite moderate ambition, Freud ignores his own arguments, or rather continues as if he had just established the contrary: "What, then, could have been the origin of the ambitiousness which produced the dream

in me?" He then recalls a pair of quite remarkable fairy-tale prophecies, one from a fortune-teller and one from an itinerant poet, that he
would grow up to be a great man (S.E. 4:192–93).

Freud's reluctance simply to admit his ambition openly has to do
with the fact that ambition is the motive he most closely associates
with imperialistic behavior, and he hardly wishes to allow himself to
be like those who are keeping him from power. The association of
ambition with imperialism, and specifically with Roman imperialism,
is clearly seen in the discussion of a later dream, in which Freud is
again supplanting former colleagues, notably his "friend and oppo-
nent P." Searching for a model for such ambivalence, Freud asks:

> Where was an antithesis of this sort to be found, a juxtaposition like this
> of two opposite reactions towards a single person, both of them claiming
> to be completely justified and yet not incompatible? Only in one passage
> in literature—but a passage which makes a profound impression on the
> reader: in Brutus's speech of self-justification in Shakespeare's *Julius Cae-
> sar,* "As Caesar loved me, I weep for him; as he was fortunate, I rejoice at
> it; as he was valiant, I honour him; but, as he was ambitious, I slew him."
> (S.E. 5:423–24)

The "one passage" in literature with this theme connects ambitious
rivalry not only with ancient Rome but also with the modern German
Empire, and with Freud's childhood as well. Freud is brought to this
passage by way of a Latin phrase in the dream just mentioned, which
he recalls having seen on a monument to Kaiser Josef; "Caesar"
clearly recalls the modern Kaiser. Josef is a particularly appropriate
Kaiser here, since, as Freud elsewhere tells us, "It will be noticed that
the name Josef plays a great part in my dreams. . . . My own ego finds
it very easy to hide itself behind people of that name, since Joseph was
the name of a man famous in the Bible as an interpreter of dreams"
(S.E. 5:484, n.2).

So Freud is Caesar/Kaiser Josef at the same time that he is Brutus,
and, "Strange to say, I really did once play the part of Brutus" (S.E.
5:424)—acting out a scene with his nephew John (a year older than
he) playing Caesar. Here he describes John as "my tyrant," and he
later tells us that John formed the pattern for all his future relationships both of love and of hatred (483).

Rome, then, provides a symbolic link between the national politics
of Freud's adult life and the familial politics of his childhood, and in
the process is highly charged with Freud's ambivalence toward what
he elsewhere refers to as his "suppressed megalomania" (S.E. 5:448,
on naming his son after Oliver Cromwell). One should not conclude,
however, that Freud is deluding himself when he describes his dream

after seeing Count Thun as expressing only an ancient emotion, "an absurd megalomania which had long been suppressed in my waking life" (*S.E.* 4:215). Freud knows better than anyone that ancient emotions do not vanish under the power of repression. Here again Rome figures significantly as a locus of displacement for the soon-to-be constant pilgrim: for Freud displaces a good deal of his criticism of imperialism onto religion.

It is for this reason that, in *Moses and Monotheism,* Freud makes the surprising claim that the Jews could not have developed monotheism on their own because they were not an imperial power:

> It is time to raise the question of whether there is any need whatever to call in the influence of [an Egyptian] Moses as a cause of the final form taken by the Jewish idea of God, or whether it would not be enough to assume a spontaneous development to higher intellectuality during a cultural life extending over hundreds of years. . . . In Egypt, so far as we can understand, monotheism grew up as a by-product of imperialism: God was a reflection of the Pharaoh who was the absolute ruler of a great world-empire. With the Jews, political conditions were highly unfavourable for the development from the idea of an exclusive national god to that of a universal ruler of the world. And where did this tiny and powerless nation find the arrogance to declare itself the favourite child of the great Lord?
>
> (*S.E.* 23:64–65)

An unpersuasive argument, to say the least; both in Egypt and in Rome, the development of empire led to an enhanced, syncretic polytheism rather than to monotheism, for centuries of imperial rule. In Egypt, for example, well before the brief period of Akhnaten and the Amarna regime, the worship of Astarte had been successfully introduced from the new Asiatic colonies, much as the worship of Isis would in turn spread in the later Roman Empire. Despite its historical weakness, Freud's argument is valuable for his overall theory, for religion, like ethics, becomes a branch of politics, and especially of imperialistic politics, with all its negative social consequences: "along with the belief in a single god religious intolerance was inevitably born, which had previously been alien to the ancient world and remained so long afterwards" (*S.E.* 23:20).

Thus one can say that Freud's concern is to combat the ethics of imperialism, whether political or religious, and to counter such ethics with the recognition of a pluralistic internal economy. Within the psyche, the Emperor is clearly the conscious ego, which time and again is represented as undercut by the downtrodden populace, identified either with the unconscious itself or with its fabrication, the dream. Thus, in an analogy to the fairy tale of the *Emperor's New*

Clothes, the pseudo tailor "is the dream and the Emperor is the dreamer himself" (*S.E.* 4:244). Similarly, the dream is compared to the feigned madness of Hamlet as he tries to survive in his uncle's hostile court (*S.E.* 5:444). Elsewhere, the sleeping consciousness is a citadel whose watchman has grown careless (568), or an unpopular autocrat whose people are rebelling (*S.E.* 4:144–45). In an Italian analogy:

> The state of things is what it was after some sweeping revolution in one of the republics of antiquity or the Renaissance. The noble and powerful families which had previously dominated the scene were sent into exile and all the high offices were filled with newcomers. Only the most impoverished and powerless members of the vanquished families, or their remote dependants, were allowed to remain in the city; and even so they did not enjoy full civic rights and were viewed with distrust.
>
> (*S.E.* 5:516)

This passage is particularly interesting for its difference from the earlier analogies, in which a suppressed revolution is brewing; here, one sees the political unrest as the result of an earlier revolution, in which the original powers have been driven into exile; and exile is a recurrent theme in the *Traumdeutung.*

The idea of the dream as the trace of an already-ended battle is also seen in what may be the eeriest analogy in the book: a seemingly happy dream "reminds one of the peace that has descended upon a battlefield strewn with corpses; no trace is left of the struggle which raged over it" (*S.E.* 5:467). It will be noted that this image of the ended battle, like the image of the exiled nobles, is an image of defeat rather than of victory. In theory, most battles should have a victor as well as a vanquished; Freud always gives us the latter perspective.

This pattern clearly paves the way for Freud's later myth of Moses as the Egyptian noble fleeing into exile after the collapse of the Amarna regime, and Moses is only one of many such political outsiders for Freud.[2] As suggestive as comparisons between Freud and Moses are, from the point of view of the war against imperialism it is equally interesting that Freud sees Bismarck as identifying himself with Moses as well. One of the few dreams Freud adduces from another analyst, quoting the analysis in full, is a dream of Bismarck's as reported and discussed by Hanns Sachs in 1913, which Freud added to the *Traumdeutung* in 1919 (*S.E.* 5:378–81). In the dream, Bismarck finds himself trapped on a narrow Alpine path, hemmed in by a precipice and a wall of rocks. With his whip, which grows to a great length, Bismarck strikes at the wall of rock, calling on God as he does so; the rocks fall away, revealing a wide landscape and a Prussian army. As Sachs notes:

The whole episode of a miraculous liberation from need by striking a rock and at the same time calling on God as a helper bears a remarkable resemblance to the Biblical scene in which Moses struck water from a rock for the thirsting Children of Israel. . . . Of the two prophecies made by God to Moses—that he should see the Promised Land but that he should not enter it—the first is clearly represented as fulfilled . . . while the second, highly distressing one was not mentioned at all.

(in *S.E.* 5:380–81)

If God is Bismarck's guide here, it is Freud who is Hanns Sachs's guide, as Sachs twice cites his mentor as providing the basis for an understanding of the dream ("Freud's theory of wish-fulfilment fully suffices"; the wish is fulfilled "just as is postulated by Freud" [379]). This guidance along the path of the dream brings the whole insertion into a close relation to the extended mountain-walk analogy at the start of chapter 3, where it is the reader who is to be guided by Freud: "When, after passing through a narrow defile, we suddenly emerge upon a piece of high ground, where the path divides and the finest prospects open up on every side, we may pause for a moment and consider in which direction we shall first turn our steps . . ." (*S.E.* 4:122). In a letter to Fliess, Freud expanded on this analogy:

The whole thing is planned on the model of an imaginary walk. First comes the dark wood of the authorities (who cannot see the trees), where there is no clear view and it is easy to go astray. Then there is a cavernous defile through which I lead my readers—my specimen dream with its peculiarities, its details, its indiscretions and its bad jokes—and then, all at once, the high ground and the open prospect and the question: "Which way do you want to go?"

(122, n.1)

The analogy is factitious, however, since Freud is not actually offering us any choice as to our direction. Rather, he is like Virgil leading Dante from the "dark wood . . . where there is no clear view and it is easy to go astray" through the cavernous defile and out to the high ground. In the *Traumdeutung* as in the *Commedia* there is finally only one viable path.

Dante indeed seems to be in the background at several points in the book, and provides a cautionary perspective for those critics who argue for the purely Jewish religious roots of Freud's interpretive methods. It appears that Freud's debt to Gentile culture may extend beyond secular scientific method to the Christian exegetical tradition as well. To stay only with Dante, we may note that according to Freud, "Wild beasts are as a rule employed by the dream-work to represent passionate impulses of which the dreamer is afraid" (*S.E.* 5:410); elsewhere Freud more than once adopts the view that the left hand is used in dreams for forbidden acts, while the right hand symbolizes proper action.

Equally, Freud's fourfold scheme of interpretation, by which dream elements are to be read antithetically, historically, symbolically, or linguistically (*S.E.* 5:341), shows less resemblance to rabbinic interpretation than to medieval Christian hermeneutics as practiced by Dante, among many others. Insofar as Handelman's distinction holds between univocal Christian interpretation and multivalent Jewish interpretation, Freud stands more on the Christian side of the scale than on the Jewish side. His pathway metaphor offers us the image of free choice, but in the end only a single path is shown us. This restricted choice should not, however, be seen simply as a covert return of the authoritarianism of an imperialistic interpreter, for finally Freud no more ranks himself with an Augustine than with an Akiba. Rather, Freud is himself circumscribed in his choices, and in his powers of insight, like Virgil in Dante.

The limited abilities of our guide, which are repeatedly emphasized in the text, are first announced as early as the title page of *Die Traumdeutung,* again in relation to Virgil. The epigraph to the volume, quoted in Latin without attribution, is taken from the *Aeneid:* "Flectere si nequeo superos, Acheronta movebo," "If I cannot bend the higher powers, I will move the infernal regions." Freud quotes this line again near the end of the volume, also adding in 1910: *"The interpretation of dreams is the royal road to a knowledge of the unconscious activities of the mind"* (*S.E.* 5:608).

How are we to understand Freud's epigraph? He wrote in 1925 that "this line of Virgil is intended to picture the efforts of the repressed instinctual impulses" (608, n. 1). Encountering the line on the title page, the reader is more likely to view Freud as the speaker; both readings should be kept in mind in looking at the epigraph's context.

In the *Aeneid* (7.312), the speaker is Juno, who is enraged that Aeneas has finally reached the mouth of the Tiber and is about to go upstream and conquer the region, marry the Latin king's daughter, and pave the way for the founding of Rome. She has been unable to persuade her husband, Jove, to prevent this, and she declares in wrath that at least she can make Aeneas's path difficult. King Latinus has greeted the arrival of Aeneas with friendship, bowing before fate and offering his daughter Lavinia in marriage. Juno now causes Latinus's wife, Amata, to become inflamed with rage. When Amata fails to move Latinus by mere words, she goes on the rampage, stirring up the Latin women to a Bacchic frenzy; by the time they are done, the attempt at peace is destroyed and Aeneas will only win access to Lavinia and the site of Rome by a protracted battle. Thus Juno, unable to influence her own husband, engineers by a truly Freudian displacement an overturning of the *mortal* husband's will by the wife's madness, with Bacchic revels representing precisely the uncontrollable instincts.

Here, then, Freud—who wore a ring set with an intaglio engraving of Jove—takes over Juno's words, and appears to ally himself with the feminine instinctual forces of the unconscious that indirectly thwart the masculine imperial will. This is the context in which one should read the rhetorical question Freud poses a few pages after the return to the Virgil line: "But what part is there left to be played in our scheme by consciousness, which was once so omnipotent and hid all else from view? *Only that of a sense-organ for the perception of psychical qualities*" (*S.E.* 5:615). The destabilizing, even the overthrowing, of the imperial conscious self is a project at the heart of Freud's ethics. To reach a position from which one can undermine the ego, however, a journey of exploration is required.

Winckelmann and the Road to Rome

In the passage just quoted, the consciousness was represented not only as the omnipotent tyrant but as a mountainous form that blocks the view—like the cliff in Bismarck's dream, like the narrow defile out of which Freud will lead the reader. The way out of the mountain impasse for Freud is not, however, Bismarck's Moses-gesture of striking the rock. Rather, Freud means to dig further down, to expose the Titans buried at the mountain's roots: "These wishes in our unconscious, ever on the alert and, so to say, immortal, remind one of the legendary Titans, weighed down since primaeval ages by the massive bulk of the mountains which were once hurled upon them by the victorious gods and which are still shaken from time to time by the convulsion of their limbs" (*S.E.* 5:553).

Thus the metaphor of the journey over the mountain paths merges well with a metaphor of "mythical" archaeology. The figure Freud most clearly identifies as his precursor on the mountain road to Rome is Hannibal, who comes not to excavate but to conquer. Hannibal, Freud tells us, was "the favourite hero of my later school days. . . . And when in the higher classes I began to understand for the first time what it meant to belong to an alien race, . . . the figure of the semitic general rose still higher in my esteem. To my youthful mind Hannibal and Rome symbolized the conflict between the tenacity of Jewry and the organization of the Catholic church" (*S.E.* 4:196). This recollection leads in turn to the famous episode of Jacob Freud's mild response to the anti-Semite who knocked off his cap, and young Freud's wish to have his father act more like Hannibal's father in urging his son to take vengeance on the oppressor.

This much is discussed by Freud himself with almost unique auto-biographical fullness and poignancy, and it has often been remarked on. It appears, however, that Hannibal serves as a stand-in for a somewhat different fantasy, one rather nearer to home for Freud and hence only hinted at and not discussed. Hannibal is introduced in the following way:

> It was on my last journey to Italy, which, among other places, took me past Lake Trasimene, that finally—after having seen the Tiber and sadly turned back when I was only fifty miles from Rome—I discovered the way in which my longing for the eternal city had been reinforced by impressions from my youth. I was in the act of making a plan to by-pass Rome next year and travel to Naples, when a sentence occurred to me which I must have read in one of our classical authors: "Which of the two, it may be debated, walked up and down his study with the greater impatience after he had formed his plan of going to Rome—Winckelmann, the Vice-Principal, or Hannibal, the Commander-in-Chief?" I had actually been following in Hannibal's footsteps.
>
> (*S.E.* 4:196)

Freud develops the comparison to Hannibal at length, but passes over the actual subject of the quotation, Johann Winckelmann; yet it is actually Winckelmann whom Freud most closely resembles. Winckelmann (1717–68) was the founder of modern archaeology and art history, and on these bases alone is clearly a figure of interest to Freud. But in fact virtually everything about Winckelmann has particular resonance for Freud's interests generally, and especially for his project in the *Traumdeutung*. Winckelmann performed for art history and archaeology precisely the function Freud wished to perform for the study of dreams and of the psyche: to transform impressionistic and amateurish fields of study into modern science.

Winckelmann did this chiefly in two enormously influential works, an essay on the imitation of Greek art in painting and sculpture (*Gedanken über die Nachahmung der griechischen Werke in der Malerei und Bildkunst,* 1755), and a history of classical art (*Geschichte der Kunst des Altertums,* 1764). His *Geschichte* was the first to attempt to study classical art on analogy with human development, with periods of youth, maturity and decline—in effect, to construct a social psychology of art history. In the field of archaeology, after visits to Herculaneum and Pompeii, he wrote a series of critiques of the treasure-hunting that then passed for archaeology, and helped to introduce scientific order to the excavations.

The more general philosophy of classicism in Winckelmann's works was as influential as his specific remarks on art history and archaeology, and the evocation of Greek culture in his *Gedanken* had an enormous impact on Lessing, Goethe, and many others. Specifically relevant to Freud is Winckelmann's assertion that the greatness of Greek art was intimately tied to the sexual freedom he saw in the period—in an age of little prudery, Winckelmann writes, artists constantly had beautiful nude bodies to observe, at sporting events and even at religious festivals (1755, 11–15). We have here a clear precursor to the Freudian plea for the importance of the open recognition of our physical selves, an argument for the importance of recognizing the hidden "lower" self, which is actually indissolubly bound to the highest manifestations of culture. Here it should be pointed out, against Rieff's objection to the archaeological analogy in Freud, that Winckelmann was by no means objective or neutral as regards his material. Freud certainly has a much more complicated view of the "primitive" elements in the psyche than Winckelmann's roseate classicism, but a kind of academic objectivity toward one's findings is nowhere seen in Winckelmann or in his nineteenth-century followers.

As intriguing as these parallels are, given Freud's interest in the lives of those he admired it is remarkable how readily Winckelmann's life admits of parallels to Freud's. Before becoming an art historian, he had studied first theology and then medicine. As a doctor, he parallels both Freud and Lermolieff/Morelli, the Italian physician and detective of forgeries in painting whom Freud discusses in "The Moses of Michelangelo," comparing Morelli's methods to those of psychoanalysis. General parallels of this sort, however, are perhaps less striking than other features of Winckelmann's life that directly relate to Freud's ambivalences about Rome. As his career developed, Winckelmann actually converted to Catholicism and moved to Rome, where he became librarian of the Vatican. There he wrote his epochal history of Greek art—but never visited Greece. Despite repeated invitations, he never made the journey, which he feared as dangerous. If the parallel to Freud's deferred longing to visit Rome were not clear enough, the end of Winckelmann's life truly provides a cautionary tale. After some years' residence in Rome, he finally made a trip home to Dresden and then to Vienna. On his way back from Vienna to Rome, he was murdered, by a man he had befriended en route and with whom he appears to have become romantically involved.[3]

This last aspect of Winckelmann's life may remind us of the footnote at the end of the *Traumdeutung* in which Freud tells us that he has refrained from discussing the sexual aspect of his dreams, as this "would involve me deeply in the still unsolved problems of perversion and bisexuality" (*S.E.* 5:606–7). Carl Schorske, who devotes a long footnote to Winckelmann, notes that by his elision of Winckelmann in favor of Hannibal, "Freud conceals an important truth from us, if not from himself, concerning his problems of political guilt as scientist and son. The Rome of his mature dreams and longings is clearly a love-object. That is not Hannibal's Rome but Johann Joachim Winckelmann's" (338). Perhaps it can best be said that Freud's Rome is *both* Hannibal's and Winckelmann's, an object both of aggressive and of romantic interest.

The erotics of touristic conquest can be clearly seen in a parallel episode from 1904, which Freud recounted in 1936 in a birthday letter to Romain Rolland, published as "A Disturbance of Memory on the Acropolis." In September of 1904 Freud was visiting Corfu, when an unexpected opportunity arose to visit Athens, which Freud had never seen. He found himself strangely reluctant to make the journey, and oddly incredulous once he had arrived; in 1936 he analyzed this reluctance as stemming from guilt at exceeding his father's more limited intellectual and financial horizons. As he says, "I had long seen clearly that a great part of the pleasure of travel . . . is rooted, that is, in dissatisfaction with home and family. When first one catches sight of the sea, crosses the ocean and experiences as realities cities and lands which for so long had been distant, unattainable things of desire—one feels oneself like a hero who has performed deeds of improbable greatness" (*S.E.* 22:247). Here Freud is a Hannibalesque hero, but a few pages earlier, he develops the romantic aspect of his desire, comparing himself to a shy young woman: "It is an example of the incredulity that arises so often . . . when a girl learns that the man whom she has secretly loved has asked her parents for leave to pay his addresses to her" (242).

Political ambition and romantic desire are intertwined in Freud's thoughts about Rome and Athens. We should not conclude, as has often been done, that the childhood identifications with Hannibal, Caesar/Brutus, Napoleon, Cromwell, and Alexander the Great have all persisted almost unchanged in the adult Freud, with the tacit conclusion that Freud must be enormously self-deluding in claiming to have outgrown his childhood ambitiousness. In fact he has outgrown it, and has displaced it onto much more realistic adult role models. Displacement is not abandonment, but an overlaying of resonances: Cromwell as Darwin, Hannibal as Winckelmann.

Rome, Egypt, Israel: Aeneas as Moses

Where Freud *is* prepared to delude himself is in the belief that his adult ambition to develop an archaeology of the psyche can dispense with mysticism. He often makes this claim, as in a passage at the beginning of the *Traumdeutung,* which clearly shows that science is the heir to his earliest wish to be a military man: "We may leave on one side pietistic and mystical writers, who, indeed, are perfectly justified in occupation of what is left of the once wide domain of the supernatural so long as that field is not conquered by scientific explanation" (*S.E.* 4:4).

Freud clearly wishes his archaeology to be a comparatively straightforward matter of uncovering the pagan roots of Rome, but the matter is not so simple. The roots he traces reach a stratum where they become entangled with the roots stretching down from the ancient Near East as well, just as, for Dante, the descent beneath Italy leads to the axis of Jerusalem and the mountain of Purgatory. For in Rome Freud finds his Jewish roots, as we see in no fewer than three Rome dreams among the half dozen reported. After he tells us of his inability to visit Rome for reasons of health, he briefly mentions two dreams in which he sees Rome from a distance. The second of these is explicitly biblical: "Another time someone led me to the top of a hill and showed me Rome half-shrouded in mist; it was so far away that I was surprised at my view of it being so clear. There was more in the content of this dream than I feel prepared to detail; but the theme of 'the promised land seen from afar' was obvious in it" (*S.E.* 4:194).

This brief reference sets the context for the next dream, which develops the theme of the Pisgah view: "I had at last got to Rome, as the dream itself informed me; but I was disappointed to find that the scenery was far from being of an urban character. *There was a narrow stream of dark water; on one side of it were black cliffs and on the other meadows with big white flowers.* . . . I was clearly making a vain attempt to see in my dream a city which I had never seen in my waking life" (194). The fact that Freud had never actually seen Rome hardly accounts for the country landscape that appears in his dream, particularly as he had been studying Rome's topography and monuments for some years previously. It would appear that this vision of the unattainable city brings it closer to Moses' view of the Promised Land, here represented for Freud by elements from various vacation spots, notably at Ravenna (that pseudo-Rome) and at his customary country retreat, "our own Aussee" (194). In analyzing the dream, Freud retells an anecdote of an impecunious Jew who is trying to reach the spa at Karlsbad but is not sure he can hold out long enough to get there.

A more troubled connection between the journeys to Rome and to the Promised Land is explicitly made in a later Rome dream:

> On account of certain events which had occurred in the city of Rome, it had become necessary to remove the children to safety, and this was done. The scene was then in front of a gateway, double doors in the ancient style (the "Porta Romana" at Siena, as I was aware during the dream itself). I was sitting on the edge of a fountain and was greatly depressed and almost in tears. A female figure—an attendant or nun—brought two boys out and handed them over to their father, who was not myself. The elder of the two was clearly my eldest son. . . . The boy refused to kiss her, but, holding out his hand in farewell, said, *"Auf Geseres"* to her, and then *"Auf Ungeseres"* to the two of us (or to one of us). I had a notion that this last phrase denoted a preference.
>
> (*S.E.* 5:441–42)

Here the denied wish to visit Rome surfaces as a need to flee the city. Freud links this flight from Rome not only with the Exodus from Egypt but also—in classic biblical fashion—with the Babylonian captivity. His comment on the detail of the fountain is: " '*By the waters of Babylon we sat down and wept.*' Siena, like Rome, is famous for its beautiful fountains" (*S.E.* 5:442). The association to the Exodus is made by more indirect means. Freud determines that *Geseres* is a Hebrew word, meaning "weeping and wailing," and he then associates it and the neologism *ungeseres* with the German pair *gesalzen/ungesalzen*, "salted/unsalted." This in turn he associates with *gesäuert/ungesäuert*, "leavened/unleavened." If anyone other than Freud had constructed this chain of association, it would surely have seemed far-fetched, particularly as closer verbal parallels could be cited,[4] but Freud seems to seek out the parallel between his children in the dream and the Children of Israel fleeing Egypt, who "had not time to allow their dough to rise and, in memory of this, they eat unleavened bread to this day at Easter" (443).

The strange thing in this explanation, if we suppose that Rome continues to symbolize the resistance of Judaism to Catholicism, is Freud's substitution of "Easter" for "Passover." The substitution is motivated by a recollection that follows, of an incident the previous Easter when Freud had been unable to give directions to a lost child in a strange city. Further, though, Freud is already identifying Moses with Jesus, as he will do openly in *Moses and Monotheism,* where he sees Jesus as a pale repetition of Moses. Here the situation is almost reversed, as "Easter" crowds out "Passover." Freud goes on to say that after meeting the lost child, he spotted the office of a doctor named Herodes, and jokingly remarked to his companion (Fliess) that he hoped Herodes wasn't a children's doctor—a reference to the extermination of Jewish children at the time of Jesus' birth. The association to Moses is particularly apt here, as it is Herod's slaying of Hebrew children that causes Joseph and Mary to flee into Egypt with the baby Jesus (Matthew 2:13 ff.). Here Freud, protecting his sons, is once again identifying himself with a Joseph. Rome is simultaneously the Egypt from which Moses flees and the Egypt *to* which Joseph flees with Mary and Jesus.

In this dream, as in Freud's images of dreams as battles, the struggle is tinged with defeat despite its surface success. Freud has brought his sons to safety—but he sinks down in tears, and the boys are given to another father. His son's preferential *Ungeseres* remains a negative formulation and does not change his being taken away from Freud, by a nun no less, who must represent Christian culture in its least desirable aspects for Freud. We may recall that Freud's definition of a hero in *Moses and Monotheism* is "someone who has had the courage to rebel against his father and has in the end victoriously overcome him"(*S.E.* 23:12). To play Jesus' father is scarcely the happiest role Freud could choose for himself.

As with the Caesar/Brutus analogy, furthermore, Freud may variously link himself with both terms of the comparison. Here we may recall the first Rome dream, in which someone leads Freud to the top of a hill and shows him Rome. The analogy Freud himself makes to Moses is certainly appropriate but not exact, as it should be Moses who is the leader. As told, the dream could equally suggest the devil leading Jesus to the hilltop from which he is shown the kingdoms of the earth and is tempted with earthly political power—which he can only receive, like Freud's hero, by rebelling against his Father's will.

The further we proceed in examining Freud's ethics, the more thoroughly intertwined appear the terms that he often so distinctly contrasts: Jewish and Christian, pagan and religious, scientific and mystical, ancient and modern. Freud exposes the pagan roots of Rome, and the Egyptian roots of biblical religion, but at bottom Rome and Egypt are themselves closely linked in Freud's thought. Even the extended Roman archaeological metaphor in *Civilization and Its Discontents,* quoted earlier, is a direct reworking of an Egyptian original, a comparison in the "Wolf Man" case fifteen years before:

> So it was that his mental life impressed one in much the same way as the religion of Ancient Egypt, which is so unintelligible to us because it preserves the earliest stages of its development side by side with the end-products, retains the most ancient gods and their attributes along with the

most modern ones, and thus, as it were, spreads out upon a two-dimensional surface what other instances of evolution show us in the solid.

(*S.E.* 17:119)

Uncovering the roots of Rome, Freud uncovers roots that are as Jewish as they are pagan. This concern underlies Freud's rather fanciful folk etymology of "Jove" in *Moses and Monotheism,* an etymology that he wisely advances with care: "I am certainly not the first person to be struck by the resemblance of the sound of the name 'Yahweh' to the root of the other divine name 'Jupiter (Jove)'. . . . bringing to light a resemblance which may possibly mean nothing or possibly a very great deal. At this point, extensive but very uncertain prospects open up before us" (*S.E.* 23:45–46 n.2). In keeping with this intermingling, the *Traumdeutung's* opposed metaphoric trains, the Hebraic mountain journey and the Roman archaeological excavation, also turn out to be inseparable. Not only are the Titans buried beneath the mountain; in one dream Freud actually transposes an Etruscan grave onto the upper slopes of a mountain. In the dream, he is making a journey "through a changing landscape with an Alpine guide" (*S.E.* 5:453), and comes to a hut, over a chasm, in which two men are lying stretched out. This, Freud says, reproduces his one experience of entering a grave, "an excavated Etruscan grave near Orvieto. . . . The inside of the wooden house in the dream looked exactly like it" (454).

Freud strengthens the linkage of the mountain climb with an underworld descent by recalling a conversation the day before the dream about two of Rider Haggard's novels:

In both novels the guide is a woman; both are concerned with perilous journeys; while *She* describes an adventurous road that had scarcely ever been trodden before, leading into an undiscovered region. . . . The end of the adventure in *She* is that the guide, instead of finding immortality for herself and the others, perishes in the mysterious subterranean fire. A fear of that kind was unmistakeably in the dream-thoughts.

(*S.E.* 5:454)

Freud invites us to consider a classical precedent: Odysseus's visit to the underworld in Book 11 of the *Odyssey.* Freud twice alludes to this episode, referring to our repressed wishes as behaving like the ghosts that Odysseus must make speak by a gift of blood (*S.E.* 4:249, *S.E.* 5:553). Similarly, the book's epigraph recalls Aeneas, and indeed the book seems written in the spirit of the *Aeneid,* with the journey from the ruined Troy toward a Rome that Aeneas will make possible but never himself see, in the closest classical parallel to Moses' Pisgah sight of Israel. If Freud is the archaeologist of Rome, he is also, as he wrote to Fliess, a new Schliemann excavating Troy.

The fullest vision Aeneas ever receives of the future Rome is granted him precisely in the underworld, where the ghost of his father tells him of the future of his race: a future of constant battles, and of the need to master the world, and to subordinate libidinal impulses to the overriding task of rulership:

> Others will forge more supply the breathing bronze,
> will draw, I know, the living features from the marble;
> they will plead causes better, their rods will trace out
> the paths of the heavens and tell the stars' rising;
> you, Roman, remember to rule the peoples with your power—
> these will be your arts—to establish peace with law,
> deal gently with those subdued, and fight down the proud.
>   (*Aeneid* 6.847–53)

It should be noted that if Freud sees the dreamworld as a kind of Virgilian underworld, he is only building on Virgil's vision of the underworld as a kind of dreamworld. Aeneas tries to embrace his father, but the image eludes his grasp, *volucrique simillima somno,* "most like a winged dream" (6.702)—truly a Pisgah sight of his own father. Further, Aeneas exits from the underworld by the famous gate of ivory, through which false dreams enter the world of the living.

In the underworld, Aeneas meets his father's ghost and discovers his destiny, the future history of Rome. In the underworld of dreams, Freud pursues "a portion of my own self-analysis, my reaction to my father's death" (*S.E.* 4:xxvi), and explores his Roman past. The longing for Rome, proleptically fulfilled in dreams (and literally fulfilled a year after the publication of the book), is a return to Freud's roots in more ways than one might suppose. In his *Autobiographical Study* we learn that Freud's family had come originally from Cologne, moving out of Germany in the fourteenth century (*S.E.* 20:8). In *Moses and Monotheism,* Cologne reappears as an example of longstanding Jewish settlements in regions where Jews are still thought to be newcomers: "The reproach of being aliens is perhaps the weakest [anti-Semitic argument], since in many places dominated by anti-semitism to-day the Jews were among the oldest portions of the population or had even been there before the present inhabitants. This applies, for instance, to the city of Cologne, to which the Jews came with the Romans, before it was occupied by the Germans" (*S.E.* 23:90). One can only conclude that Freud actually believed that his ancestors had come to Germany from Rome itself, and thus in his very ancestry the distinction between Jewish and classical culture is blurred. Without stressing the personal aspect of this far-from-random example of Jewish migration, Freud goes on to make just this general point: the Jews "are not Asiatics of a foreign race, as their enemies maintain, but [are] composed for the most part of remnants of the Mediterranean peoples and heirs of the Mediterranean civilization" (91).

As Aeneas, as Moses, Freud constructs an ethics in which classical concepts like Destiny and Retribution perform biblical functions. Thus in the first major dream in the book, that of Irma's injection, Freud discovers the principle of substitution: "It had never occurred to me before, but it struck me now almost like an act of retribution on the part of destiny [*eine Schicksalsvergeltung*]. It was as though the replacement of one person by another was to be continued in another sense: this Mathilde for that Mathilde, an eye for an eye and a tooth for a tooth" (*S.E.* 4:112).

The *via reggia* of the interpretation of dreams leads to a highly Near Eastern Rome. In Freud's mystically tinged political ethics, the simple political/religious allegories of his childhood dreams of Hannibal have refined and extended themselves: backward to mythic exiles like Aeneas and Moses, forward to the founder of scientific archaeology, himself murdered on the mountain road to Rome.

Such images, then, shape the context of Freud's ethics. While he emphasizes a classicizing, political ethics as against a Judaically moral ethics, the grounds of this distinction are not separate territories after all. The world of dreams is the Virgilian underworld, yet it is also our access to a biblical, Edenic memory: "When we look back at this unashamed period of childhood it seems to us a Paradise; and Paradise itself is no more than a group phantasy of the childhood of the individual. . . . But we can regain this Paradise every night in our dreams" (*S.E.* 4:245). The dreamer, Freud tells us, is "the exile" from this Edenic childhood (247).

Though he closes his volume with a typically sardonic aside about "our antiquated morality," Freud knows that the dreamer molds his vision of the future "by his indestructible wish into a perfect likeness of the past" (*S.E.* 5:621). This is in fact precisely the fate with which Juno threatens Aeneas, at the close of the speech from which Freud takes his epigraph. Aeneas, like an emblematic Freudian dreamer, is fleeing the destruction of his past, hoping to recreate the pre-Fall Troy of his childhood in a new land, in place of the beseiged Troy of his adolescence and the fallen Troy of his adulthood.[5] Juno's promise, her threat, is that one cannot bring one's past along selectively: in order to recreate Troy, Aeneas must relive its fall. The struggle to mold the future into the perfect image of the past will indeed leave a bloody battlefield:

> To their people's cost do son and father-in-law unite.
> . . . .
> for Venus's child will be another Paris,
> another funeral torch for a reborn Troy.
>
> $\qquad\qquad\qquad\qquad\qquad\qquad\qquad$ (*Aeneid* 7.317–22)

Notes

1. In *Freud: The Mind of the Moralist,* Philip Rieff insists that religion and Freudian psychoanalysis have no genuine common ground. While avoiding the polemical edge that enters Rieff's prose in considering religion, Steven Marcus, in *Freud and the Culture of Psychoanalysis,* similarly stresses the secular, scientific basis to Freud's ethics, and gives only occasional references to Judaic roots to Freud's enterprise. Instead, he sees Freud, for example, as "completing work that had, historically, begun with the Greeks" (20). Against such Hellenic readings, Susan Handelman, in *The Slayers of Moses,* claims that "psychoanalysis was the Jewish science in a far deeper way than has been recognized. Its founder . . . created what might be called a secular version of Talmud, and an interpretive science whose methodology was in its finest details deeply Rabbinic" (132). In a related argument, David Bakan, in *Sigmund Freud and the Jewish Mystical Tradition,* sees Freud's rebellion against orthodox Judaism as still a highly Jewish maneuver, ranking him with the radical Jewish mystics in the Sabbatian tradition.

2. Among others already mentioned, while Freud openly admits to a childhood identification with Napoleon's general Masséna, the Corsican Emperor (and lawgiver) must be a covert role model as well. In this connection, it is rather charming that though nothing is openly said about such an identification, we are twice told that Napoleon "was an extremely sound sleeper" (*S.E.* 4:233; *S.E.* 5: 554)—like Freud himself. Freud directly compares himself to Napoleon in "A Disturbance of Memory on the Acropolis," going so far as to mistakenly place Napoleon, in the anecdote recounted, in Notre Dame de Paris, Freud's favorite church, in place of the proper locale, Milan.

3. See Butler, *The Tyranny of Greece over Germany,* chap. 2, "The Discoverer: Winckelmann," and Hatfield, *Winckelmann and His German Critics, 1755–1781.*

4. Any second-guessing of a dreamer's associations is, as Freud says, pure speculation, but still it must be said that there could be alternatives to the rather convoluted chain linking *Geseres* and *gesäuert.* For example, *Geseres* could more nearly suggest *besseres,* by which the son would be saying in farewell that it was better for him to be in a new father's safekeeping. This issue is at any rate one that is clearly present in the dream, and one that Freud does not discuss at all.

5. In *Moses and Monotheism*, Freud explicitly identifies the quest for one's childhood as the origin of epic. In making this comparison, Freud is at his most Stoic, indeed his most Virgilian, in noting the difficulty of achieving any epic re-creation of the past:

> Surprise has been felt that the epic as an art-form has become extinct in later times. The explanation may be that its determining cause no longer exists. The old material was used up and for all later events historical writing took the place of tradition. The greatest heroic deeds of our days have not been able to inspire an epic, and even Alexander the Great had a right to complain that he would find no Homer.
>
> Long-past ages have a great and often puzzling attraction for men's imagination. Whenever they are dissatisfied with their present surroundings—and this happens often enough—they turn back to the past and hope that they will now be able to prove the truth of the unextinguishable dream of a golden age. They are probably still under the spell of their childhood, which is presented to them by their not impartial memory as a time of uninterrupted bliss. (*S.E.* 23:71)

Freud adds an interesting footnote to this: "This was the situation on which Macaulay based his *Lays of Ancient Rome*. He put himself in the place of a minstrel who, depressed by the confused party strife of his own day, presented his hearers with the self-sacrifice, the unity and the patriotism of their ancestors" (*S.E.* 23:71 n.1). Freud himself is doing just what he describes Macaulay as doing, but with a modernist's ironic reversals. Amid the confused strife of Austria in the late 1930s, so eloquently alluded to a few pages earlier (see especially *S.E.* 23:54–55), Freud recreates "ancient Rome"—substituting self-interest, disunity, and civil unrest for the Edenic dreams of a Winckelmann or of Macaulay's minstrel. The many assertions of incompleteness in all of Freud's work, from the *Traumdeutung* to *Moses and Monotheism*, place Freud in the line of modernist writers who create epics about the loss of epic.

For illuminating discussions of Freud's narrative techniques in his case histories, see Marcus (1984, chaps. 3 and 4, on Dora and the Rat Man), and Brooks ("Fictions of the Wolfman: Freud and Narrative Understanding").

References

Aristotle. *Ethics*. Book 1, chap. 2. Translated by J.A.K. Thomson. New York: Penguin, 1953.

Bakan, David. *Sigmund Freud and the Jewish Mystical Tradition*. Boston: Beacon Press, 1975.

Brooks, Peter. "Fictions of the Wolfman: Freud and Narrative Understanding." In Brooks, *Reading for the Plot*. New York: Vintage, 1984.

Butler, E. M. *The Tyranny of Greece over Germany*. Boston: Beacon Press, 1958.

Freud, Sigmund. *The Standard Edition of the Complete Psychological Works of Sigmund Freud*. Edited and translated by James Strachey. 24 vols. London: Hogarth, 1953–74.

The Interpretation of Dreams (1900–1901), vols. 4, 5.

"The Moses of Michelangelo" (1914), vol. 13.

From the History of an Infantile Neurosis (1918), vol. 17.

An Autobiographical Study (1925), vol. 20.

Civilization and Its Discontents (1930), vol. 21.

"A Disturbance of Memory on the Acropolis" (1936), vol. 22.

Moses and Monotheism (1939), vol. 23.

Handelman, Susan. *The Slayers of Moses: The Emergence of Rabbinic Interpretation in Modern Literary Theory.* Albany: State University of New York Press, 1982.

Hatfield, Henry. *Winckelmann and His German Critics, 1755–81.* New York: King's Crown Press, 1943.

Marcus, Steven. *Freud and the Culture of Psychoanalysis.* Boston: Allen & Unwin, 1984.

Rieff, Philip. *Freud: The Mind of the Moralist.* Chicago: University of Chicago Press, 1979.

Schorske, Carl. "Politics and Patricide in Freud's *Interpretation of Dreams.*" *American Historical Review* 78 (1973): 328–47. Reprinted in *Fin-de-Siècle Vienna.* New York: Alfred A. Knopf, 1980.

Virgil. *The Aeneid.* In *Virgil,* edited by H. R. Fairclough. 2d ed. Cambridge, Mass.: Heinemann, 1934.

Winckelmann, Johann. *Gedanken über die Nachahmung der griechischen Werke in der Malerei und Bildkunst* (1755). Heilbronn: Henninger Verlag, 1885.

———. *Geschichte der Kunst des Altertums* (1764). Vienna: Phaidon-Verlag, 1934. English version: *History of Ancient Art.* Translated by G. H. Lodge. New York: Ungar, 1969.

7   Love and Fame:
The Petrarchan Career

Gordon Braden

The most striking distinction between the erotic life of antiquity and our own,'' Freud ventures in a late footnote to his *Three Essays on the Theory of Sexuality,* ''no doubt lies in the fact that the ancients laid the stress upon the instinct itself, whereas we emphasize its object. The ancients glorified the instinct and were prepared on its account to honour even an inferior object; while we despise the instinctual activity in itself, and find excuses for it only in the merits of the object'' (*S.E.* 7: 149). Those are not equal options; psychoanalysis aligns itself with the ancient wisdom: ''Anyone who looks down with contempt upon psycho-analysis from a superior vantage-point should remember how closely the enlarged sexuality of psycho-analysis coincides with the Eros of the divine Plato'' (134). Understanding such Eros means undoing a major disposition of our culture: ''We have been in the habit of regarding the connection between the sexual instinct and the sexual object as more intimate than it in fact is. . . . It seems probable that the sexual instinct is in the first instance independent of its object; nor is its origin likely to be due to its object's attractions'' (147–48). The immediate context here is the question of unconventional object choices, homosexual and other; but the real point is that any successful settlement of our sexual attention is going to be something of an effort, the result of a complicated process that has more to do with us than with the others who satisfy us or let us down—and that it is possible to be more lucid about this than Western culture since the end of antiquity has tended to be.

This chapter argues on behalf of Freud's historical generalization, which I think will take more weight than he asks it to carry; his graph of the course of Western moral thought tracks more than superficial

126

standards of sexual behavior and taste. I end by corroborating, in a widened sense, Freud's alignment of psychoanalysis with the classical emphasis on the instinct over the object. But I also want to argue that the psychoanalytic critique of romantic love has important historical roots in the world that intervenes between the two paganisms, in a Christian moral tradition that is deeply involved in the very literature that I assume is on Freud's mind and that certainly does the most to legitimate the contrast he makes. There is nothing in classical literature comparable to the exaltation of woman that arises with the Troubadours of the Pays d'Oc in the twelfth century and is transmitted from them to the rest of Europe: to northern France and the Trouvères, to Germany and the Minnesänger, and to Italy and the *stilnovisti.* These poets sing, time and again, of the woman who is the decisive event in a man's life, whose arrival divides that life in two ("Incipit uita noua . . ."), who makes all other concerns trivial in comparison. Among the classical poets, Catullus adumbrates such an enthrallment, but he has other things—and other kinds of love—to write about, too. Freud is right to see the elevation of the feminine object into the alpha and omega of masculine desire as in some ways the special mark of postclassical Western culture. Yet the very origins of that hypostatization are also perceptibly troubled about just what is being so rapturously affirmed; some of the founding works of Western European lyric poetry testify to a distressed awareness that Freud might be right about the nature of love as well.

The significant figure, historically and otherwise, is Petrarch (1304–74), the inheritor of Provençal and stilnovist lyric who gives it the shape in which it becomes the dominant form for serious love poetry for the next three centuries. During the general European Renaissance of the fifteenth and sixteenth centuries, it is Petrarchan imitation that trains the lyric poets of the developing vernaculars: imitation Petrarchan in form—the sonnet, which owes its prominence among the wide repertoire of Italian verse forms to Petrarch's example—but also, and more surprisingly, Petrarchan in content. Italian, French, Spanish, English, German poets, and others, will recount, as though on their own experience, a love that in its general outlines and often in specific details mimics that presented in Petrarch's own *Canzoniere,* the sequence of lyrics about his love for the blond woman with black eyes (and eyebrows) whom he calls Laura. He saw her first during morning services in the Church of St. Claire in Avignon, April 6, 1327, and she took over his life:

I' vidi Amor che' begli occhi volgea
soave sì ch' ogni altra vista oscura
da indi in qua m'incominciò apparere. . . .

[I saw Love moving her lovely eyes so gently that every other
sight from then on began to seem dark to me. . . .]

(Canzoniere 144.9–11, 1976)

His devotion remained constant and all-consuming; even her death
from the plague twenty-one years later—at exactly the same hour and
day of the year at which he first saw her—did not loosen her hold on
him. Petrarch's inability to think of anything else ramifies through
the Renaissance and beyond.

Yet if that becomes the great love story of its time, literary history
has some explaining to do as to why it should have become so central.
For it is a peculiar story, peculiarly told: a story, for one thing, in which
virtually nothing happens. The preceding paraphrase includes almost
all the clearly recoverable events, and some of those can be specified
only from information available outside the poems. The surviving
evidence of Petrarch's intense interest in the order of his 366 poems—
there were several states of the collection, with much meticulous
rearranging—sorts oddly with the modern impression that the poems
could be read in almost any order (as they usually are: even scholars
seldom read them straight through). The very point of the sequence's
main event—Laura's death, announced in poem 267—is that it
changes almost nothing. The situation Petrarch writes about is largely
a static one, and at least ostensibly for a simple but important reason:
Laura responds with implacable indifference, if not active hostility, to
her lover's attention. In the face of this, he can muster few resources;
what he most famously expresses is his despair. The *fin amor* cele-
brated by Petrarch's predecessors was itself characteristically uncon-
summated: "the concept of true love was not framed to include success" (Valency 1982, 160). Petrarch's extraordinary elongation of that
frustration is echoed in almost all of the *Canzoniere's* Renaissance
descendants, a run of masculine bad luck so insistent that it becomes
almost a joke, a sign of Petrarchism's monotonous conventionality.
But jokes have their reasons; and one may meditate on why the
European lyric celebration of the feminine object of desire should
begin with several centuries fixated on the unavailability of that
object.

Petrarch himself for the most part attributes Laura's unresponsive-
ness to her virtuousness; tradition assumes (as in Provençal lyric) a
husband (perhaps ambiguously referred to in 219), so that she is
simply doing what Petrarch himself can admit is the correct thing:
"veggio ch' ella / per lo migliore al mio desir contese," "I see it was
for the best that she resisted my desire" (1976, 289.5–6). Later
Petrarchists will be more willing to attack the woman's behavior as, in

the usual accusation, cruelty: "Cruell fayre Love, I justly do complaine, / Of too much rigour, and thy heart unkind" (Giles Fletcher
the Elder 1964, *Licia* 44.1–2). The claim draws on Renaissance lore
about female nature, in which cruelty was often listed as a characteristic flaw. Subtler thoughts on the matter, however, take us into an
important area of psychoanalytic theory about erotic development;
Freud's own delineation of "the type of female most frequently met
with, which is probably the purest and truest one" (*S.E.* 14: 88), is a
credible portrait of the Petrarchan mistress: "Women, especially if
they grow up with good looks, develop a certain self-contentment
which compensates them for the social restrictions that are imposed
upon them in their choice of object. Strictly speaking, it is only
themselves that such women love with an intensity comparable to that
of the man's love for them. Nor does their need lie in the direction of
loving, but of being loved" (88–89). What is happening makes sense
because it is in fact a reversion to the original disposition of the libido,
which in its first stages is invested not in any external presence, male
or female, but in the self; and the spectacle of that reversion can be
riveting: "The importance of this type of woman for the erotic life of
mankind is to be rated very high. Such women have the greatest
fascination for men" (89). It is indeed the allure of their selfishness
that may be said to exact the spectacular selflessness of their lovers'
devotion, and the man's despair in the Petrarchan story overlays a
profound congruence: he and his mistress both adore the same thing.
Extreme object love is symbiotic with an extreme self-love that is if
anything the more powerful force; the anaclitic lover is trained by the
narcissistic beloved.

Which is in fact to use Petrarch's own language from one of the few
significant reproaches he ever brings himself to make against Laura:

> Il mio adversario in cui veder solete
> gli occhi vostri ch' Amore e 'l Ciel onora
> colle non sue bellezze v'innamora
> più che 'n guisa mortal soavi et liete.

> Per consiglio di lui, Donna, m'avete
> scacciato del mio dolce albergo fora:
> miserio esilio! avegna ch' i' non fora
> d'abitar degno ove voi sola siete.

> Ma s' io v'era con saldi chiovi fisso,
> non dovea specchio farvi per mio danno
> a voi stessa piacendo aspra et superba.

Certo, se vi rimembra di Narcisso,
questo et quel corso ad un termino vanno—
ben che di sì bel fior sia indegna l'erba.

[My adversary in whom you are wont to see your eyes, which Love and
Heaven honor, enamors you with beauties not his but sweet and happy
beyond mortal guise. By his counsel, Lady, you have driven me out of my
sweet dwelling: miserable exile! even though I may not be worthy to
dwell where you alone are. But if I had been nailed there firmly, a mirror
should not have made you, because you pleased yourself, harsh and
proud to my harm. Certainly, if you remember Narcissus, this and that
course lead to one goal—although the grass is unworthy of so lovely a
flower.]

(*Canzoniere* 1976, 45)

The flower is of course the narcissus, into which, according to Ovid's
Metamorphoses, the Greek youth is transformed at his death. The
flower's appearance gives a grace to Narcissus's end, but his dying
itself is a punishment inflicted by Nemesis for spurning the nymph
Echo, who in rejection fades into the phenomenon that carries her
name. In Ovid, Narcissus has an early disposition toward his fate—
"in tenera tam dura superbia forma," "such harsh pride in that
tender form" (1916, 3.354)—but he does not actually look into the
fatal pool, does not become a narcissist, until after he has refused to
love another. A minor adjustment of cause and effect allows Petrarch
to make the myth into a telling version of his own relation to Laura:
hypnotized self-absorption paired with tragic anaclisis. And in so
doing he indeed gives the classical myth a remarkable approximation
of what has become its modern meaning, to sound a sophisticated
warning. Laura's indifference is hardly virtue, and worse than mere
cruelty to him; it is a self-destructive perversion of her own capacity
for love.

Putting it that way only slightly overstates the polemical force of
psychoanalysis: "A strong egoism is a protection against falling ill,
but in the last resort we must begin to love in order not to fall ill"
(Freud *S.E.* 14: 85). Secure object love is an important achievement of
psychic health, likely for all its difficulties to be the most fortunate
outcome for the individual, while secondary narcissism is a frequent—
increasingly frequent—and proper target for therapeutic correction.
Rorty, in chapter 1 in this volume, reminds us of Freud's larger sense,
stated on several occasions, that the mission of psychoanalysis was to
attack "the universal narcissism of men, their self-love" (Freud, *S.E.*
17:139). If, as Rorty argues, Freud has not entirely thought through
his point here, that is in great part because of the august heritage

behind such a stand: at least as much a moral as a scientific heritage, and one that in this regard Freud shares with Petrarch. Petrarch's own accusatory diagnosis of Laura's state draws on the late medieval mythography in which Narcissus's pride, *superbia,* became a matter of special interest: for pride is, in Christian thinking, not a mere character flaw but the most insidious of human sins.[1]

Of all sins, pride is perhaps the cleverest in its disguises; Petrarch's philosophical writings brood on its capacity for, indeed, passing itself off as virtue (e.g., *De remediis utriusque fortunae,* book 1, chap. 10, in Petrarch 1554, 1:14–15). Instructing such wariness is the spirit of Augustine, who identified pride as the primal sin of the fall: " 'Pride is the start of every kind of sin' [Ecclesiasticus 10.15]. And what is pride except a longing for a perverse kind of exaltation? For it is a perverse kind of exaltation to abandon the basis on which the mind should be firmly fixed, and to become, as it were, based on oneself, and so remain. This happens when a man is too pleased with himself" (*City of God* 1984, 14.13; see also Green 1949). In its original context, much of Augustine's polemic was aimed at the heroic values of classical pagan culture, a culture that, for all its sensitivity to the dangers of overreaching, was much less severe on self-regard and had no trouble praising *autarceia* as a goal. But the Empire had provided ample evidence of the civic and other dangers of such values, and Augustine spoke for a new ethical dispensation from which classical narcissism was to be uprooted: "The earthly city was created by self-love reaching the point of contempt for God, the Heavenly City by the love of God carried as far as contempt of self" (*City of God* 1984, 14.28). Humility becomes a central standard, and the self's comfort must be understood as depending on something beyond its own borders; under Christian influence, the contrast between self-love and the love of others, Eros and agapê, becomes newly visible as a contrast of profoundly moral urgency.

Petrarch's application of that urgency to the matter of courtship accordingly informs some of the most compelling arguments in the tradition to follow:

> Ach, Freundin, scheu der Götter Rache,
> dass du dir nicht zu sehr gefällst,
> dass Amor nicht einst deiner lache,
> den du itzt höhnst und spöttlich hältst.
> Dass, weil du nichts von mir wilst wissen,
> ich nicht mit Echo lasse mich,
> und du denn müssest mit Narzissen
> selbst lieben und doch hassen dich.

[Ah, darling, avoid the gods' wrath; do not be too pleased with yourself, do not let Love, whom you now disdain and treat mockingly, some day laugh at you. Do not make me lose myself, like Echo, because you take no notice of me, and so make yourself, like Narcissus, love yourself and yet hate yourself.]

(*Oden* 5.38.25–32, in Fleming 1965)

Addressing the threat of corrosive pride in the woman's resistance is not merely a seducer's ploy; it is nowhere more eloquently rendered than in the tradition's most adroitly Christian sequence:

Ne none so rich or wise, so strong or fayre,
   but fayleth trusting on his owne assurance:
   and he that standeth on the hyghest stayre
   fals lowest: for on earth nought hath enduraunce.
Why then doe ye proud fayre, misdeeme so farre,
   that to your selfe ye most assured arre.

(Spenser, *Amoretti* 1926, 58.9–14)

At least as embodied in poetry, however, the moral stand here comes with an acknowledgment of narcissism's indelibility; and what is, at best, in the offing is not a mere humbling of the woman. Other moral issues are still in play; even contaminated with pride, resistance to lust is a virtue, and the most sophisticated Petrarchan sequences trace a complicated response to the strength behind that resistance. The sonnet of Spenser's just quoted is immediately followed by a twin that praises something very close to what the first poem seems to attack:

   Thrise happie she, that is so well assured
     Unto her selfe and setled so in hart:
     that nether will for better be allured,
     ne feard with worse to any chaunce to start

(*Amoretti* 1926, 59.1–4)

And Spenser's sequence is in fact moving toward a happy ending in marriage that allows us to say just what the telos of the Petrarchan love story actually is. Petrarch briefly adumbrates that telos in offering himself as the replacement for Laura's mirror; Spenser expands the hint:

   Leave lady in your glasse of christall clene,
     Your goodly selfe for evermore to vew:
     and in my selfe, my inward selfe I meane,
     most lively lyke behold your semblant trew.

Within my hart, though hardly it can shew
  thing so divine to vew of earthly eye,
  the fayre Idea of your celestiall hew,
  and every part remaines immortally:
And were it not that through your cruelty,
  with sorrow dimmed and deformd it were:
  the goodly ymage of your visnomy,
  clearer then christall would therein appere.
But if your selfe in me ye playne will see,
  remove the cause by which your fayre beames darkned be.

(Amoretti 1926, 45)

The traditional reproach is there, yet the alternative being imagined is not a fundamental alteration of the woman's narcissism, but rather its incorporation into a cooperative endeavor. The lover's bid to replace the mirror in the lady's affections involves a promise to perform the function that his old adversary performs: she can continue to admire herself in the mirror of his admiration. This possibility is itself no more than the fundamental congruence of their situation; the chance for happiness lies in her capacity to acknowledge it and to trust her lover to live up to his role in it. That trust can, as it were, reconcile pride and dependence, and provide a basis for communion within which her self-absorption nevertheless has a privileged place. Milton's Eve follows a similar path. The Petrarchan drama of selfless devotion, in one of its dimensions, is actually a testing of the possible arrangements between narcissistic selfhood and the world around it.

The real truth of that proposition, however, takes us into darker territory, beyond the prospect of any familiar romantic success. If Spenser presents his lady as a narcissist, he offers Narcissus himself as a figure for the poet who loves her:

My hungry eyes through greedy covetize,
  still to behold the object of their paine,
  with no contentment can themselves suffize:
  but having pine and having not complaine.
For lacking it they cannot lyfe sustayne,
  and having it they gaze on it the more:
  in their amazement lyke Narcissus vaine
  whose eyes him starv'd: so plenty makes me poore.

(Amoretti 1926, 35.1–8; also Amoretti 83)

And the tradition of such references is a rich one, extending back beyond Petrarch:

Come Narcissi, in sua spera mirando,
s'inamorao, per ombra, a la fontana,

veggendo se medesimo pensando
ferissi il core e la sua mente vana,

gittovisi entro, per l'ombria pilgliando,
di quello amore lo prese morte strana;
ed io, vostra bieltate rimembrando,
l'ora ch'io vidi voi, donna sovrana,

inamorato sono sì feramente,
che, poi ch'io volglia non poria partire,
sì m'ha l'amor compreso strettamente.

Tormentami lo giorno e fa languire,
com'a Narcissi parami piagente,
veggendo voi, la morte sofferire.

[As Narcissus, gazing in his mirror, came to love through the shadow in
the fountain, and, seeing himself in the midst of regretting—his heart
and vain mind smitten—plunged in, to catch the shadow, and then
strange death embraced him with that love, so I, remembering how beautiful you were when I saw you, sovereign lady, fall in love so wildly I could
not, though I might want to, part from you, love holds me in its grip so
tightly. Day torments me, draws off my strength, and, like Narcissus, to
me it looks like pleasure, as I gaze on you, to suffer death.]
                    (Chiaro Davanzati, *Sonetti* 26, in Goldin 1973, 276–77[2])

In particular instances one may be less sure than with the poems about
the lady's mirror just how far the mythic reference is meant to reach;
but cumulatively the examples make too much sense to ignore within
a tradition where the beloved, for all one actually gets to see of her,
might as well not exist.

An ongoing topos in discussion of Petrarchan poets has been to
wonder if the lady in question was, actually, *real;* the questioning
began in fact in Petrarch's own time, with his defensive insistence to
Giacomo Colonna that Laura was not merely a literary character (*Epistolae familiares,* trans. Bernardo 1975–85, 2.9). Enlightened criticism
has come to insist that the question is irrelevant to an appreciation of
the poems themselves, but it is still impressive how systematically
Petrarchan love poems, and especially the *Canzoniere,* veer away from
direct encounter with a substantial presence. As a character, Laura is
not called upon to do much work. Most of the poems in which she
actually speaks to Petrarch come after her death, in dreams or visions;
what few exchanges we have before that are ambiguous in their status:

Chinava a terra il bel guardo gentile
et tacendo dicea, come a me parve:
"Chi m'allontana il mio fedele amico?"

[She bent to earth her lovely noble glance and in her silence said,
  as it seemed to me: "Who sends away from me my faithful friend?"]

$\qquad\qquad\qquad\qquad\qquad\qquad$ (1976, 123.12–14)

The impression of comparative eventlessness in the *Canzoniere* is generated in great part by this overlay of interpretive subjectivity. Apparent events are seldom followed up; it is possible that this particular poem is answered not much later when the detection of Laura's goodwill turns out to be presumptuous:

Quella ch' amare et sofferir ne 'nsegna
e vol che 'l gran desio, l'accesa spene
ragion, vergogna, et reverenza affrene,
di nostro ardir fra se stessa si sdegna.

Onde Amor paventoso fugge al core,
lasciando ogni sua impresa, et piange et trema;
ivi s'asconde et non appar più fore.

[She who teaches us to love and to be patient, and wishes my great desire,
my kindled hope, to be reined in by reason, shame, and reverence, at our
boldness is angry within herself. Wherefore Love flees terrified to my
heart, abandoning his every enterprise, and weeps and trembles; there he
hides and no more appears outside.]

$\qquad\qquad\qquad\qquad\qquad\qquad$ (140.5–11)

Yet the rebuke is of a piece with the encouragement: Laura's anger "fra se stessa" is enough to send the lover fleeing (inward) in terror. Indeed, we are not sure his own aggression was anything more than a nuanced look; elsewhere we hear of his virtual inability to speak in Laura's presence:

Ben, si i' non erro, di pietate un raggio
scorgo fra 'l nubiloso altero ciglio,
che 'n parte rasserena il cor doglioso;

allor raccolgo l'alma, et poi ch' i' aggio
di scovrirle il mio mal preso consiglio,
tanto gli ò a dir che 'ncominciar non oso.

[If I do not err, I do perceive a gleam of pity on her cloudy, proud brow,
which partly clears my sorrowing heart: then I collect my soul, and, when
I have decided to discover my ills to her, I have so much to say to her that
I dare not begin.]

$\qquad\qquad\qquad\qquad\qquad\qquad$ (169.9–14)

The reality of that gleam of pity remains untested, and it should not surprise us to be told in the last poem in the sequence that Laura actually knew nothing of Petrarch's torment; his conviction that she would have refused him out of virtue is entangled with the likelihood that she was not even clearly challenged to do so:

> tale è terra et posto à in doglia
> lo mio cor, che vivendo in pianto il tenne
> et de mille miei mali un non sapea;
> et per saperlo pur quel che n'avenne
> fora avvenuto, ch' ogni altra sua voglia
> era a me morte et a lei fama rea.

[one is now dust and makes my soul grieve who kept it, while alive, in weeping and of my thousand sufferings did not know one; and though she had known them, what happened would still have happened, for any other desire in her would have been death to me and dishonor to her.]

$$(366.92\text{--}97^3)$$

It seems a fair guess that the lover's frustration is actually self-censorship, and that anything he has to say about his beloved's own state of mind is effectively preempted by his own actions and imaginings.

The general run of poems in the *Canzoniere* do not essay direct presentation of Laura at all. She shows up obliquely, sometimes through a fetishized object such as a veil or—a particularly influential detail—a glove (Mirollo 1984, 99–159). Most famously, she appears in the abstracted symbols for parts of her body that become the conventional decor by which later Petrarchan verse is most quickly recognized: "La testa or fino, et calda neve il volto, / ebeno i cigli, et gli occhi eran due stelle," "Her head was fine gold, her face warm snow, ebony her eyebrows, and her eyes two stars" (1976, 157.9–10). What is here spelled out is often the merest shorthand, as such metaphors take on a life of their own that can make Petrarch's poetry surreal and baffling at first encounter:

> L'oro et le perle e i fior vermigli e i bianchi
> che 'l verno devria far languidi et secchi
> son per me acerbi et velenosi stecchi
> ch' io provo per lo petto et per li fianchi.

[The gold and the pearls, and the red and white flowers that the winter should have made languid and dry, are for me sharp and poisonous thorns that I feel along my breast and my sides.]

$$(46.1\text{--}4)$$

A famous seventeenth-century portrait literalizing such conventions—the woman's eyes *are* suns, her teeth *are* pearls, her breasts *are* globes, with the lines of longitude visible on them—makes blatant, after long impatience, a grotesquerie implicit from the start (see the reproduction in Booth 1977, 453). The motifs do not converge but scatter into incongruent areas of metaphorical reference, and do as much to conceal or replace the woman as to present her. They are verbal fetishes, displacements of erotic intent away from its normal object; what they communicate is not the woman's beauty but the fierceness of the energy that fixes on it. They are only the appropriate mode of description for a poetry whose principal business is the hyperbolic dramatizing of the lover's reaction to his condition: "O passi sparsi, o pensier vaghi et pronti, / o tenace memoria, o fero ardore . . . ," "O scattered steps, O yearning, ready thoughts, O tenacious memory, O savage ardor . . ." (161.1–2). The most important reason for Petrarch's ongoing haziness as to what, if anything, is actually happening is that his real interest is in a private intensity of response most memorable exactly for being able to swamp the lineaments of its particular occasion. This is not the least of the reasons for speaking of him as the first modern lyric poet.

Petrarch's response is, of course, primarily one of distress, yoked to strong feelings of helplessness; yet the distress has its rewards: "in tale stato / è dolce il pianto più ch' altri non crede," "in such a state weeping is sweeter than anyone knows" (1976, 130.7–8). And the most convincing and substantial passages of relief the *Canzoniere* provides the lover are not the brief moments when a favorable response is (probably) hallucinated from Laura herself, but come rather with a deeper plunge into alienation. The poet of incurable love is also the poet of actively sought solitude:

> In una valle chiusa d'ogn' intorno,
> ch' è refrigerio de' sospir miei lassi,
> giunsi sol con Amor, pensoso et tardo;
>
> ivi non donne ma fontane et sassi
> et l'imagine trovo di quel giorno
> che 'l pensier mio figura ovunque io sguardo.

> [In a valley closed on all sides, which cools my weary sighs, I arrived alone with Love, full of care, and late; there I find not ladies but fountains and rocks and the image of that day which my thoughts image forth wherever I may glance.]
>
> (116.9–14)

The cooling of the sighs afforded by such retreat from the object of desire is not a lessening of desire but quite the contrary: away from all human interference, that desire can exercise itself with a new freedom and ease, in the image that the mind can project onto the passive landscape. It is in just this mode that Petrarch can become his most rapturous:

> I' l'ò più volte (or chi fia che mi 'l creda?)
> ne l'acqua chiara et sopra l'erba verde
> veduto viva, et nel troncon d'un faggio
>   e 'n bianca nube, sì fatta che Leda
> avria ben detto che sua figlia perde
> come stella che 'l sol copre col raggio;
>   et quanto in più selvaggio
> loco mi trovo e 'n più deserto lido,
> tanto più bella il mio pensier l'adombra.

> [I have many times (now who will believe me?) seen her alive in the clear water and on the green grass and in the trunk of a beech tree and in a white cloud, so beautiful that Leda would have said that her daughter faded like a star covered by the sun's ray; and in whatever wildest place and most deserted shore I find myself, so much the more beautiful does my thought shadow her forth.]

>   (129.40–48)

The woman's very distance (*lontonanza*) enables a heady sense of power on the lover's part, of the capacity of his own mind to transform or displace external reality. At its most cogently celebratory, Petrarchan love poetry can seem an exaltation less of the woman herself—"Whose presence, absence, absence presence is" (Sidney, *Astrophil and Stella* 60.13)—than of the poet's own imagination.

An awareness of the deep connection between love and the imagination is one of Petrarch's most important legacies to the Renaissance. "Love lookes not with the eye, but with the minde" (Shakespeare, *Midsummer Night's Dream* 1968, 1.1.234); the lover's eye learns to see what he wants it to see:

>   if it see the rud'st or gentlest sight,
> The most sweet-favor or deformedst creature,
> The mountaine, or the sea, the day, or night:
> The Croe, or Dove, it shapes them to your feature.
>   Incapable of more, repleat with you,
>   My most true minde thus maketh m'eyne untrue.
> (Shakespeare, *Sonnets* 113.9–14, Q1 emended, see Booth 1977, 374–75)

A major interpretation of Petrarchism is that its experience of frustrated enamorment is, properly handled, the first step into an autonomous mental reality. Erotic enlightenment begins when the absence of the presumed object of desire prompts the lover to replace it with a more secure one of his own making: "To escape the torment of this absence and to enjoy beauty without suffering, the Courtier, aided by reason, must turn his desire entirely away from the body and to beauty alone . . . and in his imagination give it a shape distinct from all matter; and thus make it loving and dear to his soul, and there enjoy it; and let him keep it with him day and night, in every time and place, without fear of ever losing it" (Castiglione 1959, 351). Loving the woman's image is better than loving the woman herself, on both practical and ontological grounds; and the effort of intellectual abstraction so provoked can lead the lover to the wisdom of a desire wholly independent of worldly objects, leaving his original beloved far behind: "Among such blessings the lover will find another much greater still, if he will make use of this love as a step by which to mount to a love far more sublime . . . he will no longer contemplate the particular beauty of one woman, but that universal beauty which adorns all bodies; and so, dazzled by this greater light, he will not concern himself with the lesser, and burning with a better flame, he will feel little esteem for what at first he so greatly prized" (352). Petrarchism, in such theorizing, intersects the arc of Neoplatonic philosophy, that great Renaissance recovery of "the Eros of the divine Plato" that nurtures so much of the period's glorification of artistic creativity.

Much of the power of that philosophy lies in its ability to guarantee that a withdrawal from external reality—"instead of going outside himself in thought . . . let him turn within himself, in order to contemplate that beauty which is seen by the eyes of the mind" (Castiglione 1959, 353)—can in fact give access to the true ground of that reality: "Just as from the particular beauty of one body [love] guides the soul to the universal beauty of all bodies, so in the highest stage of perfection beauty guides it from the particular intellect to the universal intellect" (354). What may be mistaken for self-absorption is in fact the truest route beyond the self. Extrapolated to those levels, however, Neoplatonism—to which Petrarch himself had no direct recourse—does not really give us the *Canzoniere*. Petrarch's own faith in his visions is never more than poignant:

> Ma mentre tener fiso
> posso al primo pensier la mente vaga,
> et mirar lei et obliar me stesso,

sento Amor sì da presso
che del suo proprio error l'alma s'appaga;
in tante parti et sì bella la veggio
che se l'error durasse, altro non cheggio.

[But as long as I can hold my yearning mind fixed on the first thought,
and look at her and forget myself, I feel Love so close by that my soul is
satisfied by its own deception; in so many places and so beautiful I see
her, that, if the deception should last, I ask for no more.]

(1976, 129.33–39)

What the mind holds to is still, in the final analysis, an error; it can be
argued that the true focus of the *Canzoniere* is not the erotic vision
but its dispersal, when a less exalted but more realistic version of the
poet's work than Neoplatonism tends to propagate makes its appearance:

Poi quando il vero sgombra
quel dolce error, pur lì medesmo assido
me freddo, pietra morta in pietra viva,
in guisa d'uom che pensi et pianga et scriva.

[Then, when the truth dispels that sweet deception, right there in the
same place I sit down, cold, a dead stone on the living rock, like a man
who thinks and weeps and writes.]

(129.49–52)

A pun used elsewhere as well encrypts a signature—"me freddo,
pietra": I, Francesco Petrarca—and the residue of the vision is a
return to self in a toughened, newly frightening form, whose climactic
activity is writing. And for all the torment that Laura seems to impose
on him, Petrarch's most telling anguish comes with his consideration
of what is involved in a poetic career of the sort he has set for himself.
    That anguish is keyed to an even more momentous pun:

Giovene donna sotto un verde lauro
vidi più bianca et più fredda che neve
non percossa dal sol molti et molt'anni;
e 'l suo parlare e 'l bel viso et le chiome
mi piacquen sì ch' i' l' ò dinanzi agli occhi
ed avrò sempre ov' io sia in poggio o 'n riva.

[A youthful lady under a green laurel I saw, whiter and colder than snow
not touched by the sun many and many years, and her speech and her
lovely face and her locks pleased me so that I have her before my eyes and
shall always have wherever I am, on slope or shore.]

(1976, 30.1–6)

Laura the woman is never wholly separable from *lauro,* the laurel, the crown of poetic fame; and Petrarch's desire for the woman in Avignon grades into the desire for literary immortality. The mythic version of that transformation gives the *Canzoniere*—indeed, perhaps the whole of Petrarch's oeuvre—its master trope:

> Apollo, s' ancor vive il bel desio
> che t'infiammava a le tesaliche onde,
> et se non ài l'amate chiome bionde,
> volgendo gli anni, già poste in oblio,
>
> dal pigro gelo et dal tempo aspro et rio
> che dura quanto 'l tuo viso s'asconde
> difendi or l'onorata et sacra fronde
> ove tu prima et poi fu' invescato io.

[Apollo, if the sweet desire is still alive that inflamed you beside the Thessalian waves, and if you have not forgotten, with the turning of the years, those beloved blond locks; against the slow frost and the harsh and cruel time that lasts as long as your face in hidden, now defend the honored and holy leaves where you first and then I were limed.]

(34.1–8[4])

Among the first of the famous stories in the *Metamorphoses* is that of Apollo's desire for the nymph Daphne, who by Cupid's design flees from him: "auctaque forma fuga est," writes Ovid (1916, 1.530), "her beauty was enhanced by her flight." On appeal to her father, the river-god Peneus, she is transformed into a laurel tree, and Apollo finds recompense for his sexual frustration in appropriating her leaves as his special insigne:

> "at, quoniam coniunx mea non potes esse,
> arbor eris certe" dixit "mea! semper habebunt
> te coma, te citharae, te nostrae, laure, pharetrae."

["Since you cannot be my wife, you will certainly be my tree," he said. "Forever will my hair, my lyres, my quivers carry you, laurel."]

(557–59)

Ovid goes on to rehearse the classical role of the laurel as the honor given to victorious Caesars, but the detail that interests Petrarch is the cithara. For him, Apollo is preeminently the god of poetry, and the laurel crown is most important as the one that certifies poetry as a potential source of public recognition at least as great as that accorded princes and generals: "Since both Caesars and poets move toward the same goal, though by different paths, it is fitting that one and the same reward be prepared for both, namely, a wreath from a fragrant tree, symbolizing the fragrance of good fame and of glory" (Wilkins 1955, 309). So Petrarch on the most momentous public occasion of his life: his own receipt of the laurel crown in 1341, on the Capitoline Hill in Rome, in a ceremony that he himself had done much to reestablish, after a millennial lapse ("non percossa dal sol molti et molt' anni"), as the centerpiece of the program that came to be known as humanism, the revival of classical literary culture as a field both of study and of new endeavor. Fueling that program is the promise of a classical style of heroic recognition—*bona fama et gloria*—achievable in the process, now by the exercise not merely of physical and political prowess but of intellectual capability as well. Opening onto that possibility, the pun in Laura's name is perhaps the strongest connection between the dazed obsessiveness of the *Canzoniere* and the agora of normal human business. Frustrated desire and professional success somehow belong together.

Even though (aside from one Mistress Bays in the mid-sixteenth century [Rollins 1966, 1:251–53]) the different names of later Petrarchan ladies cannot supply the same pun, the connection sustains itself throughout the tradition. Adoration of the woman is seldom far from an assertion of the immortalizing powers of the poetry written about her: "Then would I decke her head with glorious bayes, / and fill the world with her victorious prayse" (Spenser, *Amoretti* 1926, 29.13–14). The topos comes with many valences to fit local situations. The most straightforward rationalization for its persistence is that the loved one's resistance shows her worthy of praise (the mythographers take the myth of Daphne primarily as a celebration of virginity), and in this connection the lover's own posture can reach a special purity of selflessness: "No publike Glorie vainely I pursue, / All that I seeke, is to eternize you" (Drayton, *Idea* 1931–41, 47.13–14).

Yet the injection of this theme into the tradition also does more than perhaps anything else to queer such protestations; it is on just this point that the shifty politics of the situation declare themselves most obviously. The beloved ostensibly being immortalized is, in simple historical fact, almost invariably unknown, and even when known is not actually being made famous. Elizabeth Boyle (who?) is not famous; Edmund Spenser is. The author of the last lines quoted is also capable of being, to my mind, more honest:

> though in youth, my Youth untimely perish,
> To keepe Thee from Oblivion and the Grave,
> Ensuing Ages yet my Rimes shall cherish,
> Where I intomb'd, my better part shall save;

And though this Earthly Body fade and die,
My Name shall mount upon Eternitie.

(Idea 44.9–14)

This is in a sense only fair, indeed an act of psychic health in making the best of a bad situation: the fulfillment sacrificed to the woman's indifference is recuperated in artistic achievement. One may even cheer the hint of revenge (in some writers more than that) in such a maneuver. But the most challenging intimation is the more duplicitous one that Petrarch reports was put to him by Colonna: "That I invented the splendid name of Laura so that it might be not only something for me to speak about but occasion to have others speak of me; that indeed there was no Laura on my mind except perhaps the poetic one for which I have aspired as is attested by my long and untiring studies" (*Epistolae familiares*, trans. Bernardo 1975–85, 2.9). The arrangement here posited in its crudest form fits in subtler ways as well with the poetry before us—"deh, ristate a veder quale è 'l mio male," "ah, stay to see what my suffering is" (*Canzoniere* 1976, 161.14)—and there are good reasons for thinking professional calculation not merely a compensatory response to erotic failure but its partner and even master from the first. The story of the ego's apparent impoverishment may itself be a strategy for its extraordinary enrichment. ·

It is accordingly not only or even primarily the Petrarchan mistress who lies open to the charge of superbia. Petrarch's Christian heritage is skillfully accusatory toward love such as his, and especially toward the involuted dynamics of the male imagination. An important tradition of late medieval moral thought makes much of the lover's *immoderata cogitatio*, in a way that can be related to deployment of the Narcissus myth in the age's love poetry. Erotic fascination is actually self-fascination, a sophisticated sin of idolatry that threatens to substitute the lover's own fantasizing for proper devotion to the true creator (Robertson 1962, 65–113; Freccero 1975). Petrarch assents to such language—"l'idolo mio scolpito in vivo lauro," "my idol carved in living laurel" (*Canzoniere* 1976, 30.27, on which see Durling 1971)—and adding the cult of literary fame (previously only hinted at; see Valency 1982, 95–96) to the thematics of courtly love gears with the accusation and gives it new power, a condemnatory force that outlasts many more transient aspects of Christian morality. Freud himself, as Kerrigan shows in chapter 8 in this volume, felt that force in a quite personal way; unpagan anxiousness over a classical style of personal ambition pushes what little Freud has to say about fame, for all its obvious relevance to the theory of narcissism, into virtually the last of his writings. One may both confirm and extend that theory by listening to Petrarch's articulate fear for the state of his soul, a fear in which the sin of sexual desire is characteristically entangled with the sin of pride.

In his most directly personal work, the Latin prose dialogue *De secreto conflictu curarum mearum,* Petrarch invokes the very spirit of Augustine ("that other fiction of mine," as he puts it in the letter to Colonna) to interrogate and accuse him, in a scenario of scathing introspection about "the causes that inflate your mind with pride [*superbis flatibus*]" (1911, 55). The brief opens with superbia in some of its most obvious forms: "Will you perchance be taken in by your own good-looking face, and when you behold in the glass your smooth complexion and comely features are you minded to be smitten, entranced, charmed?" (54–55). Petrarch parries such attacks—"I will not deny that in the days of my youth I took some care to trim my head and to adorn my face; but the taste for that kind of thing has gone with my early years" (57)[5]—only to confront subtler diagnoses: "I cannot disguise from you one word in your discourse which to you may seem very humble, but to me seems full of pride and arrogance. . . . To depreciate others is a kind of pride more intolerable than to exalt oneself above one's due measure" (59). And the final chicane, of course, is from Laura to *lauro:* "As for your boasting that it is she who has made you thirst for glory, I pity your delusion, for I will prove to you that of all the burdens of your soul there is none more fatal than this" (124). A lengthy penultimate denunciation of Petrarch's lust leads to a final assault on his other desire: "Ambition still has too much hold on you. You seek too eagerly the praise of men, and to leave behind you an undying name. . . . I greatly fear lest this pursuit of a false immortality of fame may shut for you the way that leads to the true immortality of life" (165–66). "I freely confess it," says Petrarch (166), but the admission gains no purchase on the passion itself: "I am not ignorant that . . . it would be much safer for me to attend only to the care of my soul, to relinquish altogether every bypath and follow the straight path of the way to salvation. But I have not strength to resist that old bent for study altogether" (192). And there the dialogue ends, with a parting shot from Augustine: "uoluntatem impotentiam uocas," "what you call lack of strength is in fact your own doing." In Petrarch's own divided understanding, the greatest impediment to his salvation is an insidiously complacent selfishness: "The story of Narcissus has no warning for you" (55).

The point rewards further meditation. Augustine's trajectory of accusation passes through what has, since the nineteenth century, seemed unexpectedly "modern" territory: "You are the victim of a

terrible plague of the soul . . . which the moderns call *accidie"*
(Petrarch 1911, 84; on the term, see Wenzel 1961). The *uoluptas
dolendi* that in the *Canzoniere* is mainly focused on Laura is here
abstracted and generalized:

> While other passions attack me only in bouts . . . this one usually has
> invested me so closely that it clings to and tortures me for whole days and
> nights together. In such times I take no pleasure in the light of day, I see
> nothing, I am as one plunged in the darkness of hell itself, and seem to
> endure death in its most cruel form. But what one may call the climax of
> the misery is, that I so feed upon my tears and sufferings with a morbid
> attraction [*atra quadam cum uoluptate*] that I can only be rescued from it
> by main force and in despite of myself. (84–85).

The cryptic pleasurability of such suffering is one of the marks that for
Freud distinguishes melancholia from grief; the nearest thing to an
explanation that Petrarch himself can muster is his inability to mourn:
"In my case there is no wound old enough for it to have been effaced
and forgotten: my sufferings are all quite fresh, and if anything by
chance were made better through time, Fortune has so soon redou-
bled her strokes that the open wound has never been perfectly healed
over" (86–87). It is well within the spirit of the *Secretum* to adduce
Freud's thesis that what is at work here is a narcissistic regression of an
especially powerful sort, the active withdrawal of libido from an
object-choice that was itself probably narcissistically based (Freud *S.E.*
14:249–50). Introjected disaffection with reality is a not altogether
paradoxical strategy for denying transience and loss: "By taking flight
into the ego love escapes extinction" (257). Petrarch's misery has its
links to his drive for self-bestowed immortality.

One may accordingly expect the assertiveness that stirs even as
Petrarch catalogues his unhappiness. The blame shifts perceptibly
outward from himself to malicious fortune, and *accidia*—which
Dante and Chaucer both linked with the sin of wrath[6]—passes into
the resentment of unacknowledged virtue: "In the pushing and
shameless manners of my time, what place is left for modesty, which
men now call slackness or sloth?" (Petrarch 1911, 91). Augustine
reminds Petrarch of his frequently professed scorn for popular opin-
ion, and has it reaffirmed: "I care as much for what the crowd thinks
of me as I care what I am thought of by the beasts of the field."
"Well, then?" "What raises my spleen is that having, of all my
contemporaries whom I know, the least exalted ambitions, not one of
them has encountered so many difficulties as I have in the accomplishment of my desires" (91). Anyone exercising the second part of the

Platonic soul should be on guard against claiming humility as his motivation (Braden 1985, 10 ff.). Augustine responds with some sensible remarks about realistic expectations and the control of anger ("first calm down the tumult of your imagination"—104), but we may well consider the topic open until the subject of reputation comes up again and Petrarch is brought to acknowledge the actual reach of his ambition: "Now see what perversity is this! You let yourself be charmed with the applause of those whose conduct you abominate" (167–68). That is one of Augustine's most skillful thrusts: in dealing with his audience, the writer can find himself in a posture uncannily similar to that of the Petrarchan mistress toward her admirers.

Had Freud had more to say about fame, he might well have dwelt on the narcissistic convolutions of an artist's involvement with his public. It is certainly not hard to recognize Petrarch's case in psychoanalytically inspired critiques of the modern cult of celebrity: "Studies of personality disorders that occupy the border line between neurosis and psychosis . . . depict a type of personality that ought to be immediately recognizable . . . to observers of the contemporary cultural scene: facile at managing the impressions he gives to others, ravenous for admiration but contemptuous of those he manipulates into providing it; unappeasably hungry for emotional experiences with which to fill an inner void; terrified of aging and death" (Lasch 1978, 38). The connection is not merely anachronistic; Petrarch was arguably the first major example of a seductively treacherous kind of literary celebrity. In his later years especially, his fame served him in a very immediate way as his ticket to prestigious but unstable accommodations in a series of northern Italian city-states; and his inner disequilibrium legitimately anticipates fuller experiences of the cost of life lived through a negotiable self-image. (Petrarch left his own polemics against the literary marketplace; their mixture of detachment and involvement is well discussed by Trinkaus 1979, 71–89.) Yet more august problematics loom as well. The isolation within which Petrarch locates himself with his scorn for those on whom he makes his impression manifests something inescapably narcissistic in the career of writing itself: an intersection, if you will, of the myth of Apollo and Daphne with that of Narcissus and Echo.[7] Petrarch's own life and work invite us to reflect on the ways in which the literary enterprise, in particular, works to elide its real audience into one that is in some important dimension a figment of the writer's imagination.

Consider this. A writer, sitting alone, facing a blank sheet of paper, puts on that paper words that are the words of speech but are not being spoken, and translates into silence the gestures of speaking to someone who in all but the most peculiar circumstances is not there, but whose presence the writer nevertheless tries in some form to imagine. Similarly, when that writing is read, the writer ostensibly speaking is, in all but very special situations, not there—though one tends to say writers succeed to the extent that they can nevertheless make us feel their presence. Cutting in two the face-to-face encounter that speech (one assumes) originally developed to serve, the skill of writing traffics at both ends in absent presences; a simulacrum of speech, it diverts language from literal to fictive others whose existence depends on the operations of a solitary's fantasy. Most of the important human connections of Petrarch's life seem to have been so mediated, in an immense epistolary corpus that was itself carefully organized and revised with an eye on eventual publication. Within that corpus Petrarch made no firm distinction between actual and imagined recipients, almost filling one book with Herzog-like letters to Cicero, Seneca, Homer, and the like ("do give my greetings to Orpheus and Linus, Euripides and the others"—*Epistolae familiares,* trans. Bernardo 1975–85, 24.12); a prose autobiographical fragment is in the form of a letter to Posterity. Petrarch was quite attuned to writing as "an unyielding passion" of strange self-sufficiency, indifferent to any external reference: "Incredible as it may seem, I desire to write but I know not about what or to whom to write" (13.7). And on this level we may seek some of the most cogent reasons that Petrarch and his avatars should choose as their great literary theme the otherwise perplexing story of the tongue-tied lover devoted for years to a distant woman to whom he can barely bring himself to speak, and who scarcely deigns to answer him when he does. It is a story in which utterance fails systematically of its ostensible external goal, to double back on its originator.

Such a course is most overtly dramatized in one of Petrarch's most compelling but difficult poems—the longest of the *Canzoniere,* and at least in appearance the sequence's fullest piece of autobiographical narrative:

> canterò com' io vissi in libertade
> mentre Amor nel mio albergo a sdegno s'ebbe;
>   poi seguirò sì come a lui ne 'ncrebbe
> troppo altamente e che di ciò m'avenne,
> di ch' io son fatto a molta gente esempio.

> [I shall sing how then I lived in liberty while Love was scorned in my abode; then I shall pursue how that chagrined him too deeply, and what happened to me for that, by which I have become an example for many people.]

(1976, 23.5–9)

It is also the poem that presents the fullest narrative unfolding of the Laura-laurel pun, in a personalized retelling of Ovid. Yet it is a retelling with a strange twist:

> sentendo il crudel di ch' io ragiono
> infin allor percossa di suo strale
> non essermi passato oltra la gonna,
> prese in sua scorta una possente Donna
> ver cui poco giamai mi valse o vale
> ingegno o forza o dimandar perdono;
> ei duo mi trasformaro in quel ch' i' sono,
> facendomi d'uom vivo un lauro verde
> che per fredda stagion foglia non perde.

[that cruel one of whom I speak [Love], seeing that as yet no blow of his arrows had gone beyond my garment, took as his patroness a powerful Lady, against whom wit or force or asking pardon has helped or helps me little: those two transformed me into what I am, making me of a living man a green laurel that loses no leaf for all the cold season.]

(32–40)

The lover himself becomes the laurel. His own previous refusal to love mythically identifies him with Daphne to some extent, but Laura does not become identified with Apollo in the process; rather, the lover becomes both pursuer and pursued:

> Qual mi fec' io quando primier m'accorsi
> de la trasfigurata mia persona,
> e i capei vidi far di quella fronde
> di che sperato avea già lor corona. . . .

[What I became, when I first grew aware of my person being transformed and saw my hairs turning into those leaves which I had formerly hoped would be my crown. . . .]

(41–44)

The frightening unexpectedness of the result produces neither the satisfaction nor the resignation that Ovid's Daphne and Apollo respectively feel. Part of what makes Petrarch's poem so difficult is that, however catastrophic, the event is not decisive; the lover is merely beginning a series of wrenching metamorphoses, adapted with similar dark compression from Ovid. Having undergone the fate of Daphne, he swerves into the fate of Cygnus:

Né meno ancor m'agghiaccia
l'esser coverto poi di bianche piume
allor che folminato et morto giacque
il mio sperar che tropp' alto montava
. . . .
et giamai poi la mia lingua non tacque
mentre poteo del suo cader maligno,
ond' io presi col suon color d'un cigno.

[Nor do I fear less for having been later covered with white feathers, when
thunderstruck and dead lay my hope that was mounting too high . . . and
from then on my tongue was never silent about its evil fall, as long as it
had power; and I took on with the sound of a swan its color.]

(1976, 50–53, 58–60)

Presumably this myth figures some subsequent act of erotic aggression, obscure in the usual Petrarchan manner. The narrative event is less clear and less important than its role in intensifying the lover's poetic vocation: the failure of his presumption has loosed his tongue, given him his voice. Yet true to its origins, it is a special kind of voice:

Così lungo l'amate rive andai,
che volendo parlar, cantava sempre,
mercé chiamando con estrania voce;
né mai in sì dolci o in sì soavi tempre
risonar seppi gli amorosi guai
che 'l cor s'umiliasse aspro et feroce.

[Thus I went along the beloved shores, and, wishing to speak, I sang
always, calling for mercy with a strange voice; nor was I ever able to make
my amorous woes resound in so sweet or soft a temper that her harsh and
ferocious heart was humbled.]

(Translation changed, 61–66)

Speech, which aims to persuade its addressee, is diverted into song, a use of language that may ravish with its beauty but makes nothing happen. In the events that follow, what one can recover most clearly is the woman's insistence on denying speech its usual purpose:

Questa che col mirar gli animi fura
m'aperse il petto el' cor prese con mano,
dicendo a me: "Di ciò non far parola."
Poi la rividi in altro abito sola,
tal ch' i' non la conobbi, o senso umano!
anzi le dissi 'l ver pien di paura;

ed ella ne l'usata sua figura
tosto tornando fecemi, oimè lasso!
d'un quasi vivo et sbigottito sasso.

[She, who with her glance steals souls, opened my breast and took my
heart with her hand, saying to me: "Make no word of this." Later I saw
her alone in another garment such that I did not know her, oh human
sense! rather I told her the truth, full of fear, and she to her accustomed
form quickly returning made me, alas, an almost living and terrified
stone.]

(72–80)

Following the logic of this suppression, the poetic career becomes
literary:

le vive voci m'erano interditte,
ond' io gridai con carta et con incostro:
"Non son mio, no; s' io moro il danno è vostro."

[Words spoken aloud were forbidden me; so I cried out with paper and
ink: "I am not my own, no; if I die, yours is the loss."]

(98–100)

"Interditte" and, in the previous line, "afflitte," take their rhyme,
after a long postponement, from line 92: "scritte."

The agenda of that last word's appearance itself bears further
thought. To speak in paper and ink is to speak *con estrania voce,* with
an estranged voice that the speaker almost does not recognize as his
own; the process of estrangement moves toward a complete split of
speech and speaker:

ancor poi ripregando i nervi et l'ossa
mi volse in dura selce, et così scossa
voce rimasi de l'antiche some,
chiamando Morte et lei sola per nome.

[when I prayed again, she turned my sinews and bones into hard flint,
and thus I remained a voice shaken from my former burden, calling
Death and only her by name.]

(1976, 137–40)

The voice of his love is simultaneously the voice of death, the inverse
of the interdicted *vive voci.* Again, there is an Ovidian text in the
background, and perhaps the most readily Petrarchan of Ovid's stories: "tamen haeret amor crescitque dolore repulsae," "though

rejected, her love sticks and grows with her grief" (*Metamorphoses* 1916, 3.395). The character in question—about to separate into petrified body and abstracted voice—is Echo; and her appearance points us toward the myth that is conspicuously not used in Petrarch's poem but that, as Durling has shown, is almost there in the recurring motifs of the myths that are: "With the exception of the Battus myth they take place near a body of water into which at least one of the characters gazes. With the exception of the Daphne myth they involve characters who are punished for something they have seen. All of them concern frustrated—or even disastrous—speech or writing, and in each case the speech involves deception or confusion or some question about the identity of one of the protagonists" (Petrarch 1976, 28). There are reasons (31–32) for suspecting that the story of Narcissus is about to come up around line 90, when, after some documentable trouble in the composition, Petrarch changes the subject, so: "più cose ne la mente scritte / vo trapassando," "I pass over many things written in my mind" (92–93). The absent presence written in the mind is credibly the myth that hovers over the whole poem like a guilty secret.

Remembering Narcissus at any rate allows us to track the movement between the poem's opening event and its impendingly violent end:

> I' segui' tanto avanti il mio desire
> ch' un dì, cacciando sì com' io solea,
> mi mossi, e quella fera bella et cruda
> in una fonte ignuda
> si stava, quando 'l sol più forte ardea.
> Io perché d'altra vista non m'appago
> stetti a mirarla, ond' ella ebbe vergogna
> et per farne vendetta o per celarse
> l'acqua nel viso co le man mi sparse.
> Vero dirò; forse e' parrà menzogna:
> ch' i' senti' trarmi de la propria imago
> et in un cervo solitario et vago
> di selva in selva ratto mi trasformo,
> et ancor de' miei can fuggo lo stormo.

[I followed so far my desire that one day, hunting as I was wont, I went forth, and that lovely cruel wild creature was in a spring naked when the sun burned most strongly. I, who am not appeased by any other sight, stood to gaze on her, whence she felt shame and, to take revenge or to hide herself, sprinkled water in my face with her hand. I shall speak the truth, perhaps it will appear a lie, for I felt myself drawn from my own image and into a solitary wandering stag from wood to wood quickly I am transformed and still I flee the belling of my hounds.]

(1976, 147–60)

The myth—from the same book of the *Metamorphoses* as that of Narcissus—is the story of the hunter Actaeon, who saw the goddess Diana bathing, and in punishment was turned into a stag, to be hunted and torn apart by his own dogs, whom he could not call off:

> clamare libebat:
> "Actaeon ego sum: dominum cognoscite uestrum!"
> uerba animo desunt; resonat latratibus aether.

> [He wanted to cry, "I am Actaeon! Know your master!" His words failed his spirit; the air resounded with barking.]

> (3.229–31)

Durling attributes the story's appearance here to Petrarch's perception of it as "an inversion of the myth of Daphne. In one, it is the beloved who flees, in the other, the lover. In one, the end result is speech: poetry and fame; in the other, silence. In one, there is evergreen eternizing; in the other, dismemberment. Daphne, as she runs, looks into the water and becomes a tree, takes root; Actaeon, who is standing still, branches into a stag, grows hooves, flees, sees his reflection and flees the more" (Petrarch 1976, 28–29).

But the linkage is not only one of contrast. The story of Actaeon also parallels that of Daphne in Petrarch's alteration of the latter: at the end of the poem as at the beginning, the lover suddenly, catastrophically, becomes the object of his own pursuit. And if the concluding episode allows Laura to take uniquely unguarded, direct action, her motives are intentionally made uncertain—"per farne vendetta o per celarse"—while the verbs describing the metamorphosis become reflexive—"i' senti' trarmi"—as they move from the narrative past to the definitive present: "mi trasformo." The myth becomes a popular one in the tradition to come (Barkan 1980), where it is often moralized as a cautionary fable about the self-destructiveness of lust: "J'ay pour mes chiens l'ardeur & le jeune âge," "For my dogs I have passion and youth" (Ronsard 1966–70, *Amours* 1.120.7). Within Petrarch's own context, however, it intimates subtler but deeper terrors as a paradigm for the reflexive aggression of narcissistic melancholy; and the roaring that rises toward him at the end—"fuggo lo stormo"—supplies the climax to the trajectory of his estranged new voice. The barking of his hounds, I would argue, is the plaintive song whose development the *canzone* has narrated, returning to its now speechless creator.[8] The terror on the other side of narcissistic beguilement—Freud locates it as the point at which melancholia becomes suicidal (*S.E.* 14:252)—is the experience of one's own self as the other, the outsider. The lover in Petrarch's poem flees from the sound of his own poetic voice, echoing murderously inside the bell jar.

That horrific climax is one of the reaches of Petrarch's moral self-arraignment, its mythic subtlety—I have tried to show—answerable to a coincidence of Christianity and psychoanalysis in their understanding of what the self is up to in its dealings with the world, and of the dangerousness of its way. Yet a final turn still awaits us; Petrarch's poem itself is not over, and what follows is not entirely the obvious conclusion:

> né per nova figura il primo alloro
> seppi lassar, ché pur la sua dolce ombra
> ogni men bel piacer del cor mi sgombra.

> [nor for any new shape could I leave the first laurel, for still its sweet shade turns away from my heart any less beautiful pleasure.]

(1976, 167–69)

The allure of the deadly object is suavely reaffirmed, almost as if the lover had learned nothing at all; we might almost wonder if Petrarch is tacking on a *commiato* written for another, less relentless poem. There is, nevertheless, a continuity of action if not of tone in the sustaining of the present tense, as if to insist on the tenacity of the state to which the lover has come. No mere terror is going to change things. And a further twist to Petrarch's moral thought unfurls in his poem's final disjunction, which has its own meaning within the context of his life and work as a whole. We are led back once more to the standoff at the end of the *Secretum*.

The irresolution there is felt with particular acuteness because of the counterexample provided by Augustine himself: "A deep meditation at last showed me the root of all my misery and made it plain before my eyes. And then my will after that became fully changed, and my weakness also was changed in that same moment to power, and by a marvellous and most blessed alteration I was transformed instantly and made another man, another Augustine altogether" (1911, 19–20). By the standard set in Augustine's *Confessions* (which, he goes on to say, I'm sure you've read) Petrarch's self-scrutiny ought to be leading to a summary transformation of the personality, whereby self-love is replaced by the love of God with a definitiveness answerable to that first, profane enamorment. The *Canzoniere* eventually seeks to give appropriate form to such expectations with a renunciation of Laura and a hymn to the Virgin Mary: at last the suitable object, love for which will not be a screen for something base. Such a prospect lodges in the tradition as in some ways the proper end to the story ("Leave me ô Love, which reachest but to dust . . ."—Sidney 1962, *Certain Sonnets* 32.1), and the biographical tradition on Petrarch has sought for a major change of life around the time of the *Secretum*. There are those who claim to have found it (Tatham 1925–26, 2:277ff.). Yet the evidence is inevitably shifty and a bit wishful, subject to varying interpretation; and among the least uncertain facts is that, whatever Petrarch did or did not purge from his soul, the *desiderium gloriae* stayed with him (Baron 1971). In the specifically literary terms with which the *Secretum* finally hardens its conflict, Petrarch's indecisiveness endured almost to the very end; one of the last letters puts by Boccaccio's plea that Petrarch ease up on his studies: "I do hope that death may find me reading or writing, or, if it should so please Christ, in tearful prayer" (*Epistolae seniles,* book 17, epistle 2, in Wilkins 1959, 248). Scholars now find it credible to read Petrarch's story as a "lifelong wait" for a repeatedly deferred Augustinian conversion, colored by "his growing fear, his growing realization that the miracle of will and grace was not to be vouchsafed him" (Greene 1968, 247).

Learning to live with that realization brings hints of a shift in ethical standards. Greene senses a reaching back behind the Christian dispensation: "Insofar as [Petrarch's] psychology came to focus on the soul's instability without any opening to the divine, he recalls not so much Augustine as those pagan moralists who had earlier recognized the volatility of passion" (1968, 247)—who had, in other words, recognized that desire is intractably prior to its object (Greene is thinking specifically of Horace, *Epistolae* 1.1.90ff.). And one may, to at least some extent, place Petrarch as a moralist within what Freud, as described in the opening lines of this chapter, delineated as the pre-Christian dimension of psychoanalysis. We are certainly at the point where the intersection of Freud and Augustine ends; for the psychoanalyst as for the virtuous pagan, the ultimate external object of desire that would unclasp us from our specific individuality does not exist, except in our own imagination. This is not to say that such imagining will not be good for us, even essential; but the narcissistic roots of love are never simply extirpated, and the real comfort and obligation toward which we strive is not transcendence but clearheadedness as to what we are doing. The *Secretum* has occasionally been likened in passing to a series of psychoanalytic sessions, and the analogy can be made fairly specific. Petrarch's positive act is as it were to accept Augustine's diagnosis while avoiding its transcendental imperative, and with that the apparent indecisiveness becomes more clearly a therapeutic achievement. *Voluntatem impotentiam uocas:* as the speakers find their way to the topic of Petrarch's literary career, they move toward a disclosure of the calculation within what had presented itself as mere helplessness, the psychic purpose behind consequences previously disowned. From such a point we would now extrapolate not successful or failed conversion, but a lifelong conversation with the secret logic of an intimate stranger.

Notes

1. See Petrarch's own austere formulation: "Placere sibi superbire est," "to be pleased with oneself is to be prideful" (*De remediis utriusque fortunae,* book 1, chap. 13, in Petrarch 1554, 1:17). The fullest source on the mythography of Narcissus is Vinge 1967; I have tried to respect her caution about overconflating the mythological character and the psychoanalytic concept, but want to argue here for serious continuity of meaning between the two, at least as mediated by Christian moral interpretation. My general perspective in this regard is close to that of Zweig 1980. Zweig also has some acute things to say on the not quite mastered complexities of the Christian position: in being linked to the promise of individual immortality, the ideal of selfless love is really inseparable from its proclaimed opposite, and keeps nourishing its own heresy. For my own purposes, I take Christianity pretty much at its word, but the deconstructive force of its critique of Petrarchan love potentially rebounds against the religion itself.

2. I choose an Italian sonnet for effect, but the trope is already well established (and just as startling) among the Troubadours. See Vinge 1967, 66–72; Zweig 1980, 85–99; and, at great length, Goldin 1967.

3. An alternative conclusion is, to be sure, imagined in Petrarch's *Trionfi,* his other major work in vernacular poetry, where the spirit of Laura informs him that she not only knew of his love but fully returned it, keeping quiet for the good of both their souls (*Triumphus mortis* 2.76 ff., see Bernardo 1974, 123–27). The dream-vision frame keeps the status of this revelation, at least by the standards of the *Canzoniere,* uncertain.

4. This particular poem originally stood first in the collection. On Petrarch's developing involvement with the story, the fullest discussion is still Calcaterra (1942); see especially 35–87. On Daphne's general mythographic history (and the innovative character of Petrarch's role in it), see Stechow (1965) and Giraud (1968).

5. Those early years are more fully described in a letter to Petrarch's brother Gherardo: "What should I say about the curling irons and the care we took of our hair? How often did the resulting pain interrupt our sleep" (*Epistolae familiares,* trans. Bernardo 1975–85, 10.3). The claim in the *Secretum* to have outgrown such things has on inspection an odd spin. Petrarch twice identifies himself in this connection with the psychopathic, prematurely gray emperor Domitian (57, 154), and insists that his own fading hair color provides him moral instruction as a *memento mori.* There is good reason to credit Petrarch's obsession with that change, which is a recurring topic in the *Canzoniere*—"Dentro pur foco et for candida neve, / sol con questi pensier, con altre chiome," "Inwardly fire, though

outwardly white snow, alone with these thoughts, with changed locks" (30.31–
32)—but of course you only stay aware of your hair color if you check the mirror
regularly.

6. Dante, *Inferno* 7.100–26 (on which see Wenzel 1967, 200–2); Chaucer, *The
Parson's Tale*: "Envye and Ire maken bitternesse in herte, which bitternesse is
mooder of Accidie" (1957, 249).

7. There are visible if not fully articulated signs of contamination between the
two stories in late medieval mythography. Several commentators—including
Petrarch's friend Boccaccio—allegorize Echo as *bona fama* (Vinge 1967, 73–76,
102–04); and a twelfth-century French *Narcisse* replaces Echo by "Dané," that is,
Daphne (Thiry-Stassin 1978).

8. Kilmer's translation is felicitous: "I can hear the dogs while I write this"
(Petrarch 1981).

References

Augustine. *Concerning the City of God against the Pagans*. Translated by Henry
    Bettenson. Harmondsworth: Penguin, 1984.
Barkan, Leonard. "Diana and Actaeon: The Myth as Synthesis." *English Literary
    Renaissance* 10 (1980): 317–59.
Baron, Hans. "Petrarch: His Inner Struggles and the Humanistic Discovery of
    Man's Nature." In *Florilegium Historiale: Essays Presented to Wallace K.
    Ferguson,* edited by J. G. Rowe and W. H. Stockdale. Toronto: University of
    Toronto Press, 1971.
Bernardo, Aldo S. *Petrarch, Laura, and the Triumphs*. Albany: State University
    of New York Press, 1974.
Booth, Stephen, ed. *Shakespeare's Sonnets*. New Haven: Yale University Press,
    1977.
Braden, Gordon. *Renaissance Tragedy and the Senecan Tradition: Anger's Privi-
    lege*. New Haven: Yale University Press, 1985.
Calcaterra, Carlo. *Nella selva del Petrarca*. Bologna: Cappelli, 1942.
Castiglione, Baldesar. *The Book of the Courtier*. Translated by Charles S. Single-
    ton. Garden City, N.Y.: Doubleday Anchor, 1959.
Chaucer, Geoffrey. *Works*. Edited by F. N. Robinson. 2d ed. Boston: Houghton
    Mifflin, 1957.
Drayton, Michael. *Works*. Edited by J. William Hebel, Kathleen Tillotson, and
    Bernard H. Newdigate. 5 vols. Oxford: Shakespeare Head, 1931–41.
Durling, Robert M. "Petrarch's 'Giovene donna sotto un verde lauro.' " *Modern
    Language Notes* 86 (1971): 1–20.
Fleming, Paul. *Deutsche Gedichte*. Edited by J. M. Lappenberg. 1865. Reprint.
    Darmstadt: Wissenschaftliche Buchgesellschaft, 1965.
Fletcher, Giles, the Elder. *English Works*. Edited by Lloyd E. Berry. Madison:
    University of Wisconsin Press, 1964.
Freccero, John. "The Fig Tree and the Laurel: Petrarch's Poetics." *Diacritics* 5
    (1975): 34–40.
Freud, Sigmund. *The Standard Edition of the Complete Psychological Works of
    Sigmund Freud*. Edited and translated by James Strachey. 24 vols. London:

Hogarth, 1953–74:

Three Essays on the Theory of Sexuality (1905), vol. 7.

"On Narcissism: An Introduction" (1914), vol. 14.

"Mourning and Melancholia" (1917a), vol. 14.

"A Difficulty in the Path of Psycho-analysis" (1917b), vol. 17.

Giraud, Yves F.-A. *La fable de Daphné*. Geneva: Droz, 1968.

Goldin, Frederick. *The Mirror of Narcissus in the Courtly Love Lyric*. Ithaca: Cornell University Press, 1967.

———, ed. *German and Italian Lyrics of the Middle Ages*. Garden City, N.Y.: Anchor, 1973.

Green, William M. "Initium Omnis Peccati Superbia: Augustine on Pride as the First Sin." *University of California Studies in Classical Philology* 13 (1949): 407–32.

Greene, Thomas M. "The Flexibility of the Self in Renaissance Literature." In *The Disciplines of Criticism: Essays in Literary Theory, Interpretation, and History,* edited by Peter Demetz, Thomas M. Greene, and Lowry Nelson, Jr. New Haven: Yale University Press, 1968.

Lasch, Christopher. *The Culture of Narcissism: American Life in an Age of Diminishing Expectations*. New York: W. W. Norton, 1978.

Mirollo, James V. *Mannerism and Renaissance Poetry: Concept, Mode, Inner Design*. New Haven: Yale University Press, 1984.

Ovid. *Metamorphoses*. Edited by Frank Justus Miller. 2 vols. Loeb Classical Library. London: Heinemann, 1916.

Petrarch. *Petrarch's Secret*. Translated by William H. Draper. London: Chatto & Windus, 1911.

———. *Opera quae extant omnia*. 4 vols. Basel, 1554. Reprinted as 3 vols., Ridgewood, N.J.: Gregg, 1965.

———. *Letters on Familiar Matters*. Translated by Aldo S. Bernardo. 3 vols. Baltimore: Johns Hopkins University Press, 1975–85.

———. *Petrarch's Lyric Poems*. Edited and translated by Robert M. Durling. Cambridge, Mass: Harvard University Press, 1976.

———. *Songs and Sonnets from Laura's Lifetime*. Translated by Nicholas Kilmer. San Francisco: North Point Press, 1981.

Robertson, D. W. *A Preface to Chaucer: Studies in Medieval Perspectives*. Princeton, N.J.: Princeton University Press, 1962.

Rollins, Hyder Edward, ed. *Tottel's Miscellany (1557–1587)*. 2d ed. 2 vols. Cambridge, Mass.: Harvard University Press, 1966.

Ronsard, Pierre de. *Oeuvres*. Edited by Isidore Silver. 8 vols. Chicago: University of Chicago Press, 1966–70.

Shakespeare, William. *The First Folio*. Edited by Charlton Hinman. New York: W. W. Norton, 1968.

Sidney, Philip. *Poems*. Edited by William A. Ringler, Jr. Oxford: Clarendon Press, 1962.

Spenser, Edmund. *Poetical Works*. Edited by J. C. Smith and E. de Selincourt. London: Oxford University Press, 1926.

Stechow, Wolfgang. *Apollo und Daphne*. 2d ed. Darmstadt: Wissenschaftliche Buchgesellschaft, 1965.

Tatham, Edward H. R. *Francesco Petrarca: The First Modern Man of Letters, His Life and Correspondence.* 2 vols. London: Sheldon, 1925–26.

Thiry-Stassin, Martine. "Une autre source ovidienne de *Narcisse?*" *Moyen Age* 84 (1978): 211–26.

Trinkaus, Charles A. *The Poet as Philosopher: Petrarch and the Formation of Renaissance Consciousness.* New Haven: Yale University Press, 1979.

Valency, Maurice. *In Praise of Love: An Introduction to the Love-Poetry of the Renaissance.* 2d ed. New York: Schocken Books, 1982.

Vinge, Louise. *The Narcissus Theme in Western European Literature up to the Early 19th Century.* Lund, Sweden: Gleerups, 1967.

Wenzel, Siegfried. "Petrarch's *Accidia.*" *Studies in the Renaissance* 8 (1961): 36–48.

———. *The Sin of Sloth: Acedia in Medieval Thought and Literature.* Chapel Hill: University of North Carolina Press, 1967.

Wilkins, Ernest Hatch. *Studies in the Life and Works of Petrarch.* Cambridge, Mass.: Medieval Academy of America, 1955.

———. *Petrarch's Later Years.* Cambridge, Mass.: Medieval Academy of America, 1959.

Zweig, Paul. *The Heresy of Self-Love.* 2d ed. Princeton: Princeton University Press, 1980.

8   What Freud Forgot:
A Parable for Intellectuals

William Kerrigan

Sigmund Freud's "A Disturbance of Memory on the Acropolis" (1936) normally gets dismissed as a late trifle. Pleasant and precise, to be sure, and more than that in spots, Freud being Freud, this delayed afterthought can hardly be classed with major cultural papers like "The Theme of the Three Caskets," "Mourning and Melancholia," and "The Uncanny." To the contrary, I want to argue, this is a moment of great radiance in Freud's work. Of the day in Athens that inspired the piece, Jones recorded the charming detail that Freud wore his best shirt (1955, 2:24). Dressed for success, the tourist was not disappointed: "More than twenty years later he said that the amber-colored columns of the Acropolis were the most beautiful things he had ever seen in his life" (2:24). When I think back on my experience with the texts of Freud, this essay stands in my memory much as the day itself stood in his. The ancient breaks into the modern. No other paper gives itself so fully and beautifully—I am tempted to say, so allegorically—to the historical rhythms of Western culture. Nowhere else does Freud seem closer in spirit to the tribe of intellectuals destined to treasure his work and extend its cultural projects. The strategic boundaries that Freud elsewhere tried to erect between literature and psychoanalysis, even when conceding their affinity, seem here to dissolve without much ado, as if the master, assured at last of the survival of his new discipline, could finally relax with us. "Well now," he seems to be saying to longstanding readers, "I just remembered a few obvious things I have been forgetting to tell you. It all goes back to another forgetting, long ago on the Acropolis." Then Freud guides us through many involutions to the theme of his own intellectual ambition.

What Freud forgot may prove useful to intellectuals now, as we are asked by thinkers like Rorty to adjust downwards the tables of theoretical happiness inherited from the Enlightenment, making do without truth as the discovery of the right representation, morality as the application of the right principle, and personhood as contingencies added to the given soul of reason. Major shifts in intellectual paradigm always enlarge our perception of the roles played by motive and cause in the history of thought. Since the old positions were not really necessary, what made them seem so? But this latest one, which does not seek to replace an illusory necessity with a new and reliable necessity, highlights the function of political, historical, and psychological factors in its renovated thinking. If people are, as Rorty suggests in chapter 1 of this volume (following Davidson), lists of beliefs and desires wrapped in performing lumps of atoms, and these beliefs cannot aspire to the old correspondential merger with reality—which rendered invisible the operations of desire—but are governed solely by a tendency toward mutual consistency, then desire would appear to be a strengthened element in the equation of thought. Where the Enlightenment intellectual would ask "Is it certainly true?" the Rortean pragmatist will ask "What's it for?" By the end of the conversation, I expect, everyone will be talking about what they believe inseparably from what they want.

What do intellectuals want? Authority—which is to say, beliefs relatively uncontaminated by desires, beliefs that do not cry out for psychoanalysis. Intellectuals often become uneasy over the question of character and vocation. Granted, this is an area prone to shallow illumination. But the idea that philosophers or anthropologists fall into typical characterological patterns, which is not on the face of it absurd, raises the threat of radical perspectivism: the top sinks into the bottom; if we think X because we are the kind of people predisposed to think X, our disciplines, or so it looks, collapse into psychology or politics. To guard the authority of a field, a certain group of beliefs and desires (I call them "character") must be kept separate from the intellectual product. Character and vocation often coincide in the rhetoric of authority, except that the bottom rises to the top. Thus, when summarizing their wisdom, intellectuals commonly fall into locutions like "Speaking as a philosopher . . ." or "As a long-time student of African ritual. . . ." But can we really believe that vocation absorbs character so neatly, that someone ceases to pull the strings self-interestedly when this authoritative "as . . ." introduces itself? To what extent is a familiar response to this rhetoric—come off it!—justly aimed?

Investigating Freud's ambitions will not bring us to the touchiest issues here, which are specific to particular disciplines. But "A Disturbance of Memory" can open up an ecumenical discussion of the wishes, defenses, and calculations known to intellectuals who write, or are expected to write, and usually to write about what others have written.

Freud, too, was uneasy about certain connections between his character and his vocation. His repeated puzzlement over sublimation can be traced to a reluctance to examine in full his own case—the creation of his brainchild, psychoanalysis. How should sublimation be described? How can it occur? How rare a phenomenon is it? These questions still trouble psychoanalysts, and part of this difficulty in the path of psychoanalysis stems from the fact that when Freud thought about sublimation he generally *was* thinking about a rare phenomenon, some conspicuous psychic liberation that one must go to a Leonardo or a Goethe to observe. As Freud developed it, or rather did not develop it, sublimation preserves in his theory the romantic cult of genius. It is a sport by definition, dooming analysts to theoretical self-defeat, since genius ceases to be genius whenever you can adduce its explanation. The incorporation into his theory of the romantic cult of genius discouraged Freud from making dangerous explorations into himself. Analytic scrutiny might have disturbed the steady hum of his efficient intellect. More dangerous still, this scrutiny might have compromised the scientific self-image that psychoanalysis required in Freud's mind to establish itself as an ongoing discipline independent of the vagaries of his own spiritual autobiography. Sublimation was for Freud the authority that intellectuals crave, the guarantee that his theory would not loop back anarchically to seize its own discourse— but, for whatever reasons, Freud could not get this guarantee in order. Does the conjunction in his work of a rarefied notion of sublimation with a failure to examine his own indicate modesty, or on the other hand an intellectual vanity too embarrassing to be broached in public?

But, as I think Freud remembered in his eightieth year, his reluctance on this score almost left psychoanalysis deficient in a main region of human behavior—one that the Periclean Athenians, for whom the Acropolis was a civic center rather than a monument, understood very well. The two supreme motives for action in the culture of antiquity were passion (anger, primarily) and reputation. Of the first, in its theories of aggression, frustration, and loss, psychoanalysis has much to say. Of the second it has a little to say, but nothing, or almost nothing, about the form of reputation peculiar to vocations that importantly involve writing. I mean fame, that classical pursuit repatriated into the European imagination with such fervor and near-delirium during the Renaissance. Summarizing "Creative

Writers and Day-Dreaming" (1908) in his *Introductory Lectures on Psycho-Analysis*, Freud spoke of the male artist's desire for "honour, power, wealth, fame and the love of women" (*S.E.* 16:376), and concluded that a successful artist achieves "*through* his phantasy what originally he had achieved only *in* his phantasy—honour, power and the love of women" (376–77). Wealth disappears from the reiterated catalogue of motives, which may be telling, but the suppression of fame is perfectly typical. The subject keeps sliding away.

The careful, thorough index in the final volume of *The Standard Edition* does not even contain an entry on fame. Freud wrote volumes about the immortal wish, but drew a blank, or very nearly so, on the wish for immortality. This is certainly an odd lacuna in a body of work that has influenced literature and literary study as profoundly as psychoanalysis has. For what is the sweetest dream of wordsmiths? I will let Milton, who knew in his panting heart and beating pulse that "Fame is the spur," speak for the entire tribe of publishing intellectuals:

> And shall I ignore a satisfaction to which no parallel can be found? To be the oracle of many peoples, to have one's home become a shrine, to be the object of invitations from kings and commonwealths and of visits from neighbors and distant foreigners, and of pride for still others who will boast it an honorable distinction merely to have had a single glimpse of one. These are the rewards of study and the profits that learning can and often does bring to those who cultivate her in private life. (1957, 625)

This you may strive for during your lifetime. Envisioning aftertimes, you can savor the thought of legions of visitors to your tomb and text, some of whom will count it fulfillment if they glimpse what you meant by your mysterious "two-handed engine," and will call themselves "Miltonists." People do not become intellectuals for money. The modern university, with its clientele of respectful notetakers and its faculty ranks of ascending sanctity, is in psychological terms a vast supply system for narcissistic gratification. Fame is the intellectual's chief compensation. Renaissance humanists, precursors to the modern faculty, metaphorically equated the praise that passed between themselves with money, and to this day intellectuals become disturbed over "inflation" in the language of praise.

That fame in its modern guise should have pervaded Western civilization during the Renaissance supports Jacob Burckhardt's controversial dictum about Renaissance man: "Medieval man was conscious of himself only as a member of a race, people, party, family, or corporation—only through some general category. In Italy this veil first melted into air. . . . Man became a spiritual individual, and recognized himself as such" (1958, 1:143). Fame typically comes to intellectuals in two phases. In the first, one becomes famous as . . . an art historian, an analytic philosopher, a physicist, a defender of socialism. "Fame-as" subordinates a person to his or her authority within "some general category." There are rules and proprieties comparable to those observed by everyone in our economy who provides services. People famous-as are doing something for others, answering to a preexistent demand. The art historian one turns to for an informed assessment of Delacroix cannot say, anymore than an interior decorator can, "I am doing this for myself, not for you." Fame-as is dutiful, serviceable, and in psychoanalytic terms, obsessional, a reward dispensed under the aegis of the superego.

But as we gather from Milton, fame-as does not exhaust the human appetite for renown. People want to be not famous-as, but famous-for-being. We have an archaic desire to bask in unbroken regard, with our every twitch of character and sensibility, our brief feelings and throwaway opinions, returned to us amplified in the fascination of our beholders. Fame-for-being is clearly infantile in its appeal, permitting one to resume on adult grounds the role played early in life that Freud liked to call "His Majesty the Baby." Indeed, it is probably a fair generalization that intellectuals who were not allowed to inhabit that first role with an appropriate balance of indulgence and correction become the most anxious seekers for fame-as (see Freud, *S.E.* 5:398, 17:156), which they convert in their minds, with no license from their beholders, to fame-for-being. I have seen them at faculty meetings, these chaired babies, demanding everyone's time to straighten out confusions that could only have arisen from an unimaginable inattentiveness inseparable from narcissistic enclosure. Although no academic community lacks occasions to ridicule its pretense, fame-for-being belongs to the motivational structure of the intellectual life. One may find workable substitutes—with students, for example. But coming to maturity for most intellectuals means making peace with their failure to win fame-for-being, and this narcissistic injury takes its toll in bitterness, depression, envy, denial, reaction formation, and the like.

Fame in this perfected form presupposes individualism—or is, it might be better to say, a main cultural expression of individualism. During the Renaissance man not only became "a spiritual individual, and recognized himself as such," but wished as well to be recognized as such. In fame-as, something—a subject, an art, an artist, an argument—is already interesting, and interest in the famous person derives wholly from this prior curiosity. In fame-for-being, however, the famous person is already interesting, and whatever he or she does or says or writes becomes interesting simply because he or she is its author. Such a person has a "following": fame-for-being as the cultural projection of individualism might be described as leadership without real political power. "True genius," Emerson wrote, mocking the idolatry of fame-for-being, "seeks to defend us from itself" (1983, 623). Yet the reason why few true geniuses, Emerson included, have been able to fend off fame-for-being lies not in the character of their statement, but in the character of this fame. It presents us with a captivating image of regressive satisfaction. Great men and women have nonpragmatic uses.

How is one to achieve fame-for-being? The transition from the lesser fame to the grander is a familiar crisis in the successful intellectual career. These must be delicate calculations. If those who are famous-as declare their deeper wish for fame-for-being they threaten the fame they have already achieved, their foothold on public attention. For their authority as spokespersons for a "general category" depends, once again, on serving their audience, on objectivity and unbiased judgment, on the subordination of personal glory to the impersonal truth, and on similar kinds of expected self-discipline. Once they admit a wish to be famous-for-being, they reveal that the desired situation is the opposite of providing a service for their audience; the audience should provide a service for them. The safest course is for them to remain authorities in the hope that, if they are good enough, fame-for-being will gradually come their way. When and if it does, their work will take a personal turn. The anecdotes will pile up; the media will do interviews; publishers will request memoirs. At last their biographers will appear, and when they do, the intellectuals will be ready with journals and correspondence, the treasures of a selfhood denied exposure by fame-as. Wallace Stevens actually revised his private journals (Richardson 1985, 93–94).

This is the slow way. One may risk the bad taste of public confession, as in the films of Warhol, where self-revelation is tied intimately to the greed for fame. Norman Mailer declared as a young man that he wished to change the consciousness of his times. This turned out to mean that he would trumpet his urge to be famous (*Advertisements for Myself*), win fame for such outrageous displays, then place himself so that we might view important historical events like presidential elections and moon launches through his presence. It is instructive to realize, as Braden reminds us in the previous chapter in this volume, that Petrarch, the prototype of the modern intellectual, took this more audacious route to individualist fame. Publishing his letters and arranging his own coronation, Petrarch sought to be famous for seeking to be famous. Put another way, fame goes all the way down into the self, infecting every privacy. The individual offered for public recognition by Petrarch was already deeply marked by moral and psychological conflicts pertaining to that very recognition. Thus the theme of fame surfaces in his most personal works, the *Canzoniere* and the *Secretum,* where love and religious salvation seem displacements of, or variations on, the search for personal fame. It is as if Petrarch were saying to his successors: "This is what being a threshold-of-publishing humanist is all about."

Petrarch's Renaissance testimony is still to the point, as the first psychoanalyst, the man who invented his own vocation, invented what he would write as when writing authoritatively, does in fact concede. The eclipse of the subject of fame in Freud is not quite total. An arresting footnote in *The Standard Edition*'s text of *The Psychopathology of Everyday Life* (*S.E.* 6:260) informs us that Freud made some notations in the 1904 edition of this work. After underscoring the role of anger in superstition, he proceeded to write a sentence that opens up the possibility of a new beginning on this business of writerly sublimation.

Elsewhere the model for sublimation is purely sexual. Freud supposes that libidinal energy directed at an object becomes transformed into a narcissistic cathexis of the ego, which then makes it possible for the ego to redirect the aim of an instinctual impulse. But here, in a fragile self-annotation that might have been lost to us in any number of ways, Freud starts all over again, and the key issue is death, not sex: "My own superstition has its roots in suppressed ambition (immortality) and in my case takes the place of that anxiety about death which springs from the normal uncertainty of life" (*S.E.* 6:260 n.3). *In my case:* in Freud's case of ambition, the case that is always covertly at issue in his discussions of sublimation, anxiety about death has been siphoned off into a superstitious, sign-interpreting concern with immortality, the authorial and laureate ambition. The mark of the tribe is on Freud, and cut deep, to where "that anxiety about death" lives in nonintellectuals.

"A Disturbance of Memory" is Freud's keenest inspection of the ambition confessed in the margins of *The Psychopathology of Everyday Life.* Aware that his career draws to a close, Freud at eighty commemorates the seventieth birthday of Romain Rolland with a brief meditation on a day thirty-two years earlier, when he visited the Acropolis with his younger brother (like Rolland, ten years his junior) and suffered a lapse of memory. I have been suggesting that this local disturbance is emblematic of a memory failure throughout the creation and development of psychoanalysis. Other metaphors envelop this essay on a journey, which concludes with reflections on the very

metaphor of the journey. It could hardly be otherwise, since its destination is so resonant with the history of our culture.

The Acropolis, by God: Western civilization is virtually its graffiti.
What better setting for this layered psychodrama? In education and
intellectual style, Freud was in striking ways the heir of Renaissance
humanism (Kerrigan 1984, 101–2). Like an imaginative citizen of that
period, the Freud of "A Disturbance of Memory." comes before the
hard evidence of the classical world, of seminal and unforgotten
fathers. In their stubborn endurance the monuments would have
tended to activate immortal longings in this tourist, for Freud's mate-
rialism had as its complement an awed respect for the fine arts of
antiquity, the persistence of stone and clay; he gathered a fair collection of Roman artifacts, death masks in particular. The Renaissance,
standing before the classical, knew in this image its own aspirations.
Freud also, through the interpretation of his unconscious, will learn of
his ambition in the presence of antiquity.

Freud and his brother had been intending to journey to Corfu,
when an acquaintance in Trieste suggested Athens instead. Freud
found himself oddly depressed at this prospect. Then, taking the
advice, he entered a strange state of mind on the Acropolis, which
could be summarized like so: "Ah ha, so it's real after all!" The
response assumes that in the past he had felt that the Acropolis was
not real, but if memory serves him well, Freud had never entertained
such a presumption. What is the meaning of this involuntary, distinctly non-Cartesian form of doubt? Why such incredulity over the
existence of the Acropolis? On the day in question Freud kept his
silence, refusing to share his interpretations with his brother. Now he
opens himself in a public letter to Rolland, a substitute brother.

The first clue is the depression at Trieste, for that was when the
sense of unreality began, the feeling that a piece of real event had to
be rejected or found counterfeit. "And now," Freud writes, "we
know where we are. It is one of those cases of 'too good to be true'
that we come across so often" (*S.E.* 22:242). But as so often, the
familiar turns mysterious under Freud's gaze. One can understand
why the mind would seek to repudiate unpleasurable chunks of reality; this is so "natural" as not to require a theory. But why does the
psyche, like a rigorous stoic, insist on repudiating the good chunks as
well? What sort of strategy is the familiar "too good to be true"? A
guilty one, Freud answers: "too good to be true" stems from the
conviction that one is undeserving, or that, if one does enjoy this good
fortune, own it, seize it, let it be real and really enjoyed, then one will
be punished by Fate, the external mirror of the punitive superego.
Exhilarated pleasure and the apprehensive fear of commensurate pun-

ishment combined on the Acropolis, where the torque of Fortune's wheel twisted Freud's memory.

At this point one is treated to a brief but intense display of the old man's intellectual powers, and one sees immediately why this mind would be revered by structuralists to come. Quickly and decisively, Freud places his incredulity on the Acropolis in a differential set of such disturbances. Stemming from primitive repression, which does not distinguish between internal and external realities, there are two fundamental defenses against the emergence of distressing events— derealization, the disavowal of a piece of external reality, and depersonalization, the disavowal of a piece of one's own self. Another set of phenomena "may be regarded as their positive counterparts" (*S.E.* 22:245), bestowing rather than repudiating reality. On the Acropolis ("Ah ha, so it is real after all!") the present was suddenly real, as if in the past it had not been real. In *déjà vu* one finds "Ah ha, I have been here before," and the present is suddenly doubly real, as if in the past it had already been real. In *fausse reconnaissance* or *déjà raconté* one finds distortions like "I don't have to mail the letter, for I already have," or "I don't have to tell you that, for I already have," and an event need not become real in the present because it is assumed to have already been real in the past. The relationships among the elements of this typology of memory disturbances are complex and admittedly "little mastered scientifically" (245). Thus, in the case at hand, Freud's lapse appears to be a derealization, denying past reality to the Acropolis. It is in fact a depersonalization, repudiating the ego's pleasure at having come so far as to behold the Acropolis.

One must not, however, get lost in these woods, as in a way Freud himself does. It is the usual expectation in psychoanalysis that symptoms born of conflict will be multivalent, expressing desires even as they cancel them. Freud emphasizes the negating aspects of his memory disturbance, and forgets, if you will, the hyperbolic aspirations of his ego; to a degree his interpretation of the disturbance repeats the disturbance, deflecting the personal onto the external. There he was, a Renaissance pilgrim standing before the supreme monument of the classical world, the touchstone of achieved ambition and the representative in external reality of his own drive for greatness. And what did he think? "It's real after all!" Tremendous ambition can be read in this lapse, for if one implication is that the Acropolis had not been real in the past, another, at heart, is this: "The Acropolis was not real until I, Sigmund Freud, visited it!" The very same symptom that declares "I am not up to the Acropolis" simultaneously proclaims "The Acropolis depends on me." Something of the imperial egoism here surfaces in Freud's treatment of the parable of King Boabdil

(*S.E.* 22:246), who kills the messengers and burns the letters that bring him news of his demise. In Freud, as in the Renaissance, the idealization of antiquity will be tolerated only insofar as it serves the sovereignty of living ambitions.

Freud goes on to muse about the psychology of travel. Traveling has profound connections with ambition, our early desire to leave home and "go farther than" our parents:

> It is not true that in my schooldays I ever doubted the real existence of Athens. I only doubted whether I should ever see Athens. It seemed to me beyond the realms of possibility that I should travel so far—that I should "go such a long way". This was linked up with the limitations and poverty of our conditions of life in my youth. My longing to travel was no doubt also the expression of a wish to escape from that pressure, like the force which drives so many adolescent children to run away from home. I had long seen clearly that a great part of the pleasure of travel lies in the fulfillment of these early wishes—that it is rooted, that is, in dissatisfaction with home and family. When first one catches sight of the sea, crosses the ocean and experiences as realities cities and lands which for so long had been distant, unattainable things of desire—one feels oneself like a hero who has performed deeds of improbable greatness. I might that day on the Acropolis have said to my brother: "Do you still remember how, when we were young, we used day after day to walk along the same streets on our way to school, and how every Sunday we used to go to the Prater or on some excursion we knew so well? And now, here we are in Athens, and standing on the Acropolis! We really *have* gone a long way!" So too, if I may compare such a small event with a greater one, Napoleon, during his coronation as Emperor in Notre Dame, turned to one of his brothers—it must no doubt have been the eldest one, Joseph—and remarked: "What would *Monsieur notre Père* have said to this, if he could have been here to-day?" (1936, 246–47)

Comparing small things with great, Freud repeats a Vergilian topos: "Thus I was wont to compare small things with great" (*Eclogues* 1.23). It is, as Freud has demonstrated in this essay, the key trope of ambition, built into the unconscious behavior of the psyche. The small would be great. An ego makes this kind of comparison as a child, and again when visiting the Acropolis, and now again when interpreting itself. Freud at last acknowledges his triumph on the Athenian hill. Napoleon in victory replaces Boabdil in defeat, and the echoes sweep back through the centuries—Napoleon, romantic successor to the would-be emperors of the Renaissance, themselves successors to the emperors of antiquity. A footnote informs us that the anecdote is usually situated in Milan (*S.E.* 22:247 n.1). Why does Freud choose a less popular variant? Is this another memory disturbance? If so, the tracks of association are not far to seek. Freud's Napoleon, the figure of the ego, enjoys his triumph over *notre Père* when receiving a crown in Notre Dame, thus recalling what is, for Freud, the summary instance of a son's desire to outgo his father: empire over and in the mother.

Freud feels that the mystery has at last been solved. His essay closes with a tone of resolution that in the final sentence movingly transforms into the stillness of a dying man:

> But here we come upon the solution of the little problem of why it was that already at Trieste we interfered with our enjoyment of the voyage to Athens. It must be that a sense of guilt was attached to the satisfaction in having gone such a long way: there was something about it that was wrong, that from earliest times had been forbidden. It was something to do with a child's criticism of his father, with the undervaluation which took the place of the overvaluation of earlier childhood. It seems as though the essence of success was to have got further than one's father, and as though to excel one's father was still something forbidden.
>
> As an addition to this generally valid motive there was a special factor present in our particular case. The very theme of Athens and the Acropolis in itself contained evidence of the son's superiority. Our father had been in business, he had had no secondary education, and Athens could not have meant much to him. Thus what interfered with our enjoyment of the journey to Athens was a feeling of *filial piety*. And now you will no longer wonder that the recollection of this incident on the Acropolis should have troubled me so often since I myself have grown old and stand in need of forbearance and can travel no more. (*S.E.* 22:247–48)

It may help to know at this point that one of the fellow travelers on the journey to Athens was a certain Professor Dörpfeld (Jones 1955, 2:23), an assistant to Schliemann, excavator of Troy. For as the Acropolis becomes the emblem of antiquity, and antiquity the emblem of knowledge, of every ambitious intellectual son's journey beyond the ken of his father, Freud's own language flexes to an epic scope. The "little problem" again requests greatness in this essay so full of *déjà vu*, return, and renaissance. *Filial piety* is the undeniable theme of Freud's physical and intellectual journeying, and as a contribution to the imagery and style of filial piety, "A Disturbance of Memory" memorably reanimates the famous conclusion to Book 2 of the *Aeneid*, where the hero bears his father Anchises on his shoulders as he leaves the ruins of Troy. "I myself," Freud has been telling us, "like all heroic men, bear with me the burden of my father as I journey into lands that my father under his own power could never reach." The submission of filial piety and the triumph of filial impi-

ety turn out to be entwined strands of the same destiny. And so they
are, to compare small things with great, in the history of our culture.
Freud's deferential/ambitious journey to the beginnings of Western
civilization retraces the Roman, and later the Renaissance, and later
the Romantic journeys back to, yet away from and beyond, those
origins.

Freud knows that the double trip back and beyond must be perpet-
ually renewed. "I myself have grown old and stand in need of forbearance and can travel no more." "Forbearance" translates the German
Nachsicht—"indulgence," "pity," "excuse," literally "looking
after." Aging is cruel to ambition. There comes the inevitable con-
finement, the destination, where one can in truth "travel no more."
Who looks after former travelers, meeting their needs for forbearance?
Who carries them or shoulders them, continuing the journey beyond
the point where the dying heroes can no longer travel under their own
power? As Freud has told us a few pages back, "An investigation is at
this moment being carried on close at hand which is devoted to the
study of these methods of defence: my daughter, the child analyst, is
writing a book upon them" (*S.E.* 22:245). Anna, of course, was the
Aeneas to this Anchises, looking after her dying father and continuing
the intellectual journey begun in this very essay. The same year this
piece appeared, 1936, Anna Freud published her masterwork, *The
Ego and the Mechanisms of Defense*. In some imaginative way this old
father, Freud Père, knows that he travels on the shoulders of Anna—
that he is now, as he waits at his destination, *somebody else's classic*.
We keep on journeying. Aeneas eventually must become Anchises.
Freud was Anna's classic, and Anna is now ours. From the book she
published in 1936 Harold Bloom (1973, 1975, 1976) drew the fundamental mechanisms for a psychology of immortal yearnings tailored to
the vocation of writing.

As they appear before their fellows, scientists are people who,
because they believe in things like progress, utilitarianism, and collab-
orative effort, cannot afford to be indulgent toward the classical urge
for complete and unending fame. This is the official stance in Freud's
work. His findings are provisional; he participates in a communal
process; he writes in the expectation of being refuted, foreseeing his
own obsolescence. Fame-as will have to do for a psychoanalyst. Freud
considered science the maturest form of thought, thought least in the
service of our wishes, and this disciplined maturity must extend
beyond the methods and results of scientists to their public self-
presentation: scientists above all are the providers of a good-for-the-
moment service, content as a matter of ideology with the instrumen-
tality of fame-as. But as we have seen, there are distinct traces in

Freud of a wish to be famous-for-being, a gratification he associated with the artist as opposed to the scientist. An attitude of filial piety toward the famous sublime geniuses of art (before such mysteries, as we know, psychoanalysis must lay down its arms) exists in his work alongside the filial impiety of wanting to be remembered whole and complete, his text an enduring monument like the Acropolis, achieved once and for all time, irrefutable, the goal of future pilgrimages, in whose image the young heroes and heroines of coming generations will conceive their tasks and desires. This conflict in its various guises led him to forget, or almost forget, the psychology of fame.

One should recall in this context the work of Jacques Derrida, since he has demonstrated for our age that the writer's effort to quell normal anxieties about death through the fantasy of an immortal work is, as the tradition itself was not above admitting, a dream and folly of expectation. Derridean notions such as "iterability" (Derrida 1977) strike against both the old authorial wish and those scholar-rememberers who believe themselves to be realizing it in their devotion to "intentional meaning," the author as ratified by the author. Once there is a text, the author is as dead. Writing will be read and misread, fragmented through citation and translation, dispersed like crumbling atoms into the realm of chance Derrida terms "intertextuality." Nevertheless, to return to my initial discussion, there is widespread suspicion that the new paradigm championed by writers like Derrida and Rorty will remove desirable constraints on intellectual vainglory.

Consider the postmodern canon as laid out in Rorty's tradition of edifying philosophers. "These writers," he maintains, "have kept alive the suggestion that, even when we have justified true belief about everything we want to know, we may have no more than conformity to the norms of the day" (1979, 367), a suggestion that would seem to chasten the desire for infinite fame. Since edifying writers do not believe it is possible to have "all of Truth" (377), they discourage "the institutionalization of their own vocabulary" (369). Their work tends to adopt conventionally literary forms such as "satires, parodies, aphorisms" (369). But literature does not die out with the norms of the day. It is to be noted that edifying figures like Kierkegaard, Wittgenstein, and Heidegger, forswearing fame-as-philosophers, have achieved a great deal of fame-for-being, and their literary, counterinstitutional jargons have in fact become thoroughly institutionalized, so much so that philosophical literacy is to some degree the ability to speak them. To this list we must add Derrida, probably the most widely and slavishly imitated intellectual alive today. Edifying philosophy stands out. It does not retreat into the background of the dominant philosophical traditions. Its calculation with respect to fame is all or nothing: either it will be forgotten as an eccentricity, or, achieving fame, will achieve it to the hilt. I think the apparent anomaly of a conception of truth that stresses historical finitude and a canon of writers so self-regardingly obscure that they could scarcely be deciphered without granting them the gift of fame-for-being accounts for some of the resistance to the new paradigm. Fame-as goes out with authority-as, and the result is, or can be, an unchecked expansion of the authorial ego, whatever may be said up front about the fates of published texts. A neighboring phenomenon is the narcissism of some contemporary attacks on narcissism—e.g., the grandiose Lacan, indulging everything he purports to deplore. Postmodernism has the bad habit of gaining back impoverishing concessions about truth in the currency of vain stylistic extravagance.

In this light Freud appears to me exemplary. "A Disturbance of Memory" belongs in some way to the line of Petrarch, seeking fame for the desire to be famous. But Freud exhibits himself as an analytic specimen. His archaic wish for fame is permitted expression only as checked by the gaze of his psychoanalytic authority. The wish acknowledged is simultaneously controlled and belittled—a small thing made great in order to be shrunk once more. The two great banes of the intellectual life are the linked vices of vanity and self-loathing, which oftentimes revolve about the unacknowledged centrality of fame to intellectual vocations. It was Freud's peculiar sublimation to acknowledge both but avoid either. Putting this in the language of Rorty's Davidson, we might say that two quasi persons took over on the Acropolis—a boy terrified of paternal retribution and a boy savoring oedipal victory, a shunner of fame and a lover of fame. Their antipathy produced a symptom. Their cooperation produces "A Disturbance of Memory." Sublimation occurs when an assembly of these quasi people can agree with the mature ego to do the same thing for different reasons. The wary boy can agree with the scientist, disavowing fame-for-being. The triumphant boy can agree to write it all down, showing the world how rich that fleeting moment on the Acropolis really was. The mature ego, facilitating this cooperation, can forgive the boys. Psychoanalysis is a scrupulous, arduous, deeply moral route to the sublimation of self-forgiveness.

Like all tribes, intellectuals bear their ancestral gods. Texts and their vicissitudes include the classic, which has its own characteristic genre, invented by Renaissance humanists at the dawn of modern fame: the annotated edition. From the beginning its overriding purpose has been to restrain the play of chance in the transmission of the classic text. As early as 1904 Freud probably believed that he would be remembered in this relatively undisturbed way—that he could write in the second edition of his book on superstition, "My own superstition has its roots in suppressed ambition (immortality) and in my case takes the place of that anxiety about death which springs from the normal uncertainty of life" (*S.E.* 6:260 n.3) and feel pretty certain, given the omens, that the sentence itself would not be allowed to die a normal death, but would instead achieve, when gathered into the memory bank of an editorial apparatus, immortality, its suppressed ambition, waiting there in the record for any pilgrim who would wonder why this master of psychological truths said so little about fame. The vocation of psychoanalysis will probably turn out to be mortal, but the man is a classic, famous for having been. If he can teach us honest self-forgiveness about our motives as intellectuals, the classic will have served its purposes.

We are a superstitious tribe. The best omen for the achievement of fame is, having inspected the wish, to try to forget about it and go on with our work.

References

Bloom, Harold. *The Anxiety of Influence.* New York: Oxford University Press, 1973
———. *A Map of Misreading.* New York: Oxford University Press, 1975.
———. *Poetry and Repression.* New Haven: Yale University Press, 1976.
Burckhardt, Jacob. *The Civilization of the Renaissance in Italy.* Translated by S. Middlemore. 2 vols. New York: Harper, 1958.
Derrida, Jacques. "Limited Inc." Supplement to *Glyph* 2 (1977).
Emerson, Ralph. *Essays and Lectures.* New York: Library of America, 1983.
Freud, Sigmund. *The Standard Edition of the Complete Psychological Works of Sigmund Freud.* Edited and translated by James Strachey. 24 vols. London: Hogarth, 1953–74.
The Interpretation of Dreams (1900–1901), vol. 5.
The Psychopathology of Everyday Life (1901), vol. 6.
"Creative Writers and Day-Dreaming" (1908), vol. 9.
Introductory Lectures on Psycho-Analysis (1916–17), vol. 16.
"A Childhood Recollection from *Dichtung und Wahrheit*" (1917), vol. 17.
"A Disturbance of Memory on the Acropolis" (1936), vol. 22.
Jones, Ernest. *The Life and Work of Sigmund Freud.* 3 vols. New York: Basic Books, 1953–57.
Kerrigan, William. "Atoms Again: On the Deaths of Individualism." In *Taking Chances: Derrida, Psychoanalysis, and Literature,* edited by Joseph H. Smith and William Kerrigan, Vol. 7 of *Psychiatry and the Humanities.* Baltimore: Johns Hopkins University Press, 1984.
Milton, John. *Complete Poems and Major Prose.* Edited by Merritt Hughes. New York: Odyssey Press, 1957.
Richardson, Joan. "Stevens: Toward a Biography." *Raritan* 4 (1985): 42–65.
Rorty, Richard. *Philosophy and the Mirror of Nature.* Princeton: Princeton University Press, 1979.

Index

175